UNFREEDOM

Early American Places is a collaborative project of the University of Georgia Press, New York University Press, Northern Illinois University Press, and the University of Nebraska Press. The series is supported by the Andrew W. Mellon Foundation. For more information, please visit www.earlyamericanplaces.org.

UNFREEDOM

Slavery and Dependence
in Eighteenth-Century Boston

JARED ROSS HARDESTY

New York University Press

NEW YORK AND LONDON

NEW YORK UNIVERSITY PRESS
New York and London
www.nyupress.org

First published in paperback in 2018

Library of Congress Cataloging-in-Publication Data

Names: Hardesty, Jared Ross, author.
Title: Unfreedom : slavery and dependence in eighteenth-century Boston / Jared Ross
    Hardesty.
Description: New York : New York University Press, 2016. | Series: Early American places
    | Includes bibliographical references and index.
Identifiers: LCCN 2015043166 | ISBN 9781479816149 (cl : alk. paper)
ISBN 978-1-4798-0184-8 (pb : alk. paper)
Subjects: LCSH: Slavery—Massachusetts—Boston—History—18th century. | Slaves—
    Massachusetts—Boston—History—18th century. | Indentured servants—
    Massachusetts—Boston—History—18th century. | Boston (Mass.)—History—
    Colonial period, ca. 1600–1775. | Boston (Mass.)—Social conditions—18th century.
Classification: LCC F73.4.H37 2016 | DDC 306.3/620974461—dc23
LC record available at http://lccn.loc.gov/2015043166

References to Internet Web sites (URLs) were accurate at the time of writing. Neither the
author nor New York University Press is responsible for URLs that may have expired or
changed since the manuscript was prepared.

New York University Press books are printed on acid-free paper, and their binding
materials are chosen for strength and durability. We strive to use environmentally
responsible suppliers and materials to the greatest extent possible in publishing our
books.

Manufactured in the United States of America

10 9 8 7 6 5 4 3 2 1

Also available as an ebook

For Dana, with love

Contents

CONTENTS

Figures and Tables

Figures

Tables

Acknowledgments

This book would not have been possible without the assistance and patient guidance of many people and institutions. The project began as a dissertation at Boston College supervised by Lynn Lyerly, an amazing mentor and teacher. She helped shepherd the project from vague ideas about slavery and cultural appropriation to a work that makes a contribution to our understanding of freedom and slavery in early America and the Atlantic world. When I describe my book, I cannot help but engage in my own form of appropriation, still borrowing language from our many conversations about the project. Although Lynn's advising responsibilities ended after I defended my dissertation, her support and advice about transitioning from a graduate student to a faculty member has proven invaluable. Alan Rogers, whom I had the privilege to work with from my first day at Boston College, proved instrumental to this project. It was with his encouragement that I began looking through the judicial archives in Massachusetts to better understand slavery in New England and was able to craft a project out of such underutilized sources. His vast knowledge of the law and legal history was also advantageous when navigating sometimes-tricky legal records. Alan continues to be a good friend and mentor. Owen Stanwood, whom I worked with from his first day at Boston College, provided an incredible amount of support. From our casual conversations about early American history to his intense questioning and challenging of the intents and assertions of this project, his guidance proved—and continues to prove—invaluable.

I also need to thank Joanne Pope Melish, the outside reader of my dissertation. I had the privilege of being a fellow at the Massachusetts Historical Society with Joanne. Our long conversations about the nature of freedom, slavery, race, labor, and the economy of early America have profoundly shaped this book, especially its argument. Joanne is one of the most gracious and generous people I know and continued to offer valuable advice and suggestions for revision after I completed the dissertation. For her support of this project, I owe a debt that I fear can never be repaid.

In addition to my committee, there are numerous librarians, archivists, research coordinators, and institutions that need to be thanked for their help with this project. I spent nearly five hundred hours at the Massachusetts State Archives reading legal and probate records. Despite my numerous inquiries and often confusing requests, Jennifer Fauxsmith and her staff were wonderful. Likewise, Elizabeth Bouvier, the judicial archivist for the Commonwealth of Massachusetts, proved helpful in my quest for ever more legal records. The New England Regional Fellowship Consortium provided much-needed research time and funding for the 2012–2013 academic year. The fellowship permitted me to spend time at the Massachusetts Historical Society, Boston Athenaeum, Houghton Library at Harvard University, and the Baker Library at the Harvard Business School. Conrad Wright and Kate Viens at the MHS deserve special thanks for their continued research support.

There are innumerable colleagues and friends at Boston College, Western Washington University, and further afield that also deserve to be acknowledged, although I am sure I will forget a few people. Jeff Dyer, Janet Kay, John Morton, Chris Staysniak, Jim O'Toole, Sarah Ross, Lynn Johnson, Zach Morgan, Andrea Wenz, and Chris Riedel at BC were all supportive colleagues. Alex Noonan and Craig Gallagher both read significant portions of this dissertation, provided helpful commentary, continue to be good friends, and deserve special mention. Outside of BC, I had the opportunity of being on a panel with Gloria Whiting and Richard Boles in the summer of 2011 that resulted in not only extensive cross-collaboration, but also two great friendships. Likewise, Ted Andrews, Linda Rupert, Travis Glasson, and Lin Fisher have commented on various conference papers and chapters that I have presented from this project. In addition, I have to thank Andrea Mosterman, Wim Klooster, Sean Condon, Hannah

Farber, Brendan McConville, and Rob Murray for their support and interest in the project.

Since arriving in the Pacific Northwest, I have found a great community of scholars. I count myself fortunate to have landed at Western Washington University. As a junior faculty member, I have found the university community supportive and helpful, especially the dean of the College of Humanities and Social Sciences, LeaAnn Martin. The History Department has likewise been a wonderful place to start my career. My colleagues, especially Kevin Leonard, Steven Garfinkle, Amanda Eurich, and Chris Friday, have all been supportive of this project and a sometimes-naïve junior colleague. Hunter Price read significant portions of the book and has been a sounding board as it underwent final revisions. Finally, Richard R. Johnson deserves recognition for organizing a wonderful seminar for early Americanists in the PNW.

I would be remiss not to thank Robert Waters, my undergraduate adviser. If there is one person who has helped me understand this sometimes-crazy profession, it is him—even if that meant learning from his mistakes. I sometimes wonder how different my career trajectory would have been without someone with such erudite observations and a sharp, quick-witted mind as an ally, and for that I am happy to call him not only my mentor but also a friend.

NYU Press has been a great publisher for a first-time author. My editor, Clara Platter, has been supportive of the project and enthusiastic about its argument since reading my book proposal. Constance Grady has provided helpful administrative support. Tim Roberts, the managing editor at the Early American Places Initiative, has helped shepherd the book through its final stages and quickly answered my many inquiries. Likewise, the two anonymous readers deserve special thanks for their thoughtful, thorough, judicious, and encouraging reviews.

Parts of this book have appeared elsewhere, and I would like to take this opportunity to thank both MIT Press for allowing me to republish a version my essay "'The Negro at the Gate': Enslaved Labor in Colonial Boston" from the *New England Quarterly* (March 2014) and Taylor and Francis (www.tandfonline.com) for permission to republish a version of "An Angry God in the Hands of Sinners: Enslaved Africans and the Uses of Protestant Christianity in Colonial Boston" from *Slavery & Abolition* (March 2014).

On a more personal note, I would like to thank my family for their love and support throughout my academic career. This book is dedicated to my wife, Dana. At the risk of sounding cliché, she has been my rock throughout this whole process. I could use a number of platitudes describing how lucky I am to have found such a wonderful partner in life, but I hope she knows how I feel and how much I appreciate her affection and support.

Unfreedom

Introduction: A World of Unfreedom

In the spring of 1709, authorities in Boston accused Jack, a black inden-tured servant, of stealing a "considerable Sum in Money and Gold" from David Gwin, a wealthy merchant. When brought before the court, Jack stated that before arriving in Boston, he was a "Bondslave" belonging to Benjamin Hale, a merchant residing in Barbados. A few years prior to the alleged crime, Hale hired Jack out to serve onboard the *Dragon*, a London ship that traded around the Caribbean. For this trip, Jack was to serve on a crew carrying timber from Tobago to Bar-bados, but French privateers seized the vessel. They carried Jack to Martinique, where he labored on a sugar plantation for the next four years. One night, Jack and four other slaves stole a canoe and rowed to Montserrat and from there to Antigua. In the latter colony, Jack joined an English privateering venture and, after capturing a French ship, ended up on St. Christopher. There, Jack encountered Thomas Diamond, a captain of a "New England Sloop," and being familiar with the region, Jack joined Diamond's crew. He arrived in Boston sometime in the fall of 1708 and immediately indented himself to the farmer Edward Clap of Dorchester for four years in exchange for a new set of clothes every year and a cash payout. In the spring of 1709, Jack's master allowed him to travel to Boston to find employment.

Jack's story raises an important question for understanding slav-ery and freedom in the eighteenth-century American colonies. Why, after escaping from Martinique and effectively winning his freedom, did Jack sacrifice that freedom in order to enter into a dependent relationship soon after his arrival in Boston? Jack's actions suggest he understood the society he inhabited. A free black stranger would have made people suspicious and had no place in the local community. The indentured servant of a local farmer, however, would have immediately found a place in the social order. Clap also seems to have given Jack considerable autonomy, allowing him to go to Boston to find work. Throughout his life, Jack had many different statuses—slave, free black, and indentured servant—but ultimately opted to remain in a state of dependence, although one certainly not as degrading as slavery, and live in Boston rather than have a tenuous freedom in the Caribbean.[1] *Unfreedom* peers into the lives of slaves and other bound laborers like Jack to better understand the lived experience of enslaved Africans in eighteenth-century Boston, British North America, and the early modern Atlantic world.

Unfreedom uses an early modern, transnational lens to examine slavery in eighteenth-century Boston. Rather than the traditional dichotomous conception of slavery and freedom, colonial-era slavery should be understood as part of a continuum of unfreedom. In Boston, African slavery existed alongside many other forms of oppression, including indentured servitude, apprenticeship, pauper apprenticeship, and Indian slavery. In this hierarchical, inherently unfree society, slavery must be put in the context of a larger Atlantic world characterized by a culture of dependence. Unfreedom for enslaved Bostonians, emanating from both their African heritage and New World slavery, shaped their behavior, making them more concerned with their everyday treatment and honor than they were with emancipation. By understanding slavery within this context, this study demonstrates not only how African slaves were able to decode their new homeland and shape the terms of their enslavement but also how marginalized people ingrained themselves in the very fabric of colonial American society.

This book is a cultural history of slavery that uses a new conceptual framework for understanding slave life in colonial America and the Atlantic world—the continuum of unfreedom.[2] Examining slavery in Boston using this concept allows us to develop a deeper understanding of early modern slavery and the world slaves inhabited. In this sense, racial and class boundaries collapsed due to the labor needs of Boston's economy, leaving a large bound laboring class that interacted and intermarried on society's margins.[3] While other scholars have certainly looked at the intersection of race and class in early America, slavery often stands outside the class system.[4] In a world of unfreedom, however, slavery was an integral part of a divinely ordained hierarchy that structured society and everyday relations. Although early modern Britons began deploying a language of individual freedom during the tumultuous seventeenth century, it had a specific meaning. Essentially, independent individuals had full possession of a set of customary rights, controlled their own property and labor, and commanded the labor of their dependents. Such a narrow definition placed the unfree at the service of the free, enabling the latter to gain from the work of the former, thus accumulating more property, rights, and freedom. This scenario played out across any society where slavery and other forms of bound labor existed in the Americas.[5]

Individual rights in a world built on dependence meant that notions of those rights still penetrated colonial society, only in a specific way. Instead of believing in universal human rights, both the free and unfree in eighteenth-century Boston believed that everyone had a set of customary and defensible rights dependent on his or her class and status. Men had more rights than women, while artisans had different rights than laborers. In such a rights-based system, enslaved Africans came to appropriate their own set of liberties, were able to enjoy the fruits of their labor, and were able to make the best of an admittedly poor situation.[6] Slavery in this context was not a totalizing system of oppression but a structure that slaves learned to navigate and manipulate to their advantage.

For the majority of slaves in Boston, the alternatives to slavery were often nonstarters. Open defiance was ultimately futile. Because they were heavily outnumbered, rebellion would end in slaughter. Running away to the frontier was uncertain and fraught with danger. Even if a slave won his or her legal freedom, liberty was always amorphous in an unfree world that steadfastly refused to recognize black freedom. Free blacks in Boston, such as the Humphreys family, actually saw their material circumstances decline after manumission and became dependent on public and private aid. Week after week, Betty Humphreys had to beg for alms from Christ Church. Even then, she and her husband could not support their two sons, James and Thomas, whom the Boston Overseers of the Poor removed from their household and apprenticed to a wealthy sail maker. The Humphreys did not have "freedom" in any meaningful sense—even their family was not protected—and still lived in a state of dependency.

Rather than face such uncertainty, slave action took on a subtler form. When compared to unfree whites, this trend becomes clear.

Benjamin Franklin serves as a good example. Franklin's experience as an apprentice during his teenage years in Boston was both similar and dissimilar to that of slaves. His life story—running away to Philadelphia while still an apprentice to find remarkable success as first a printer and later a scientist and politician—speaks to the exceptional nature of Franklin's experience. It likewise tells us that race did sometimes matter in this world. Franklin's white skin allowed him to escape without raising the same suspicions that a runaway African slave would. The same can be said of Franklin's many accomplishments, which it is doubtful any runaway slave could have achieved in eighteenth-century America. That said, the printer's experience of unfreedom bore much resemblance to that of many enslaved Bostonians. Franklin faced "harsh & tyrannical Treatment" from his master—his own brother—including the many "Blows his Passion too often urg'd him to bestow upon [Benjamin]." It was this treatment that Franklin believed instilled in him an "Aversion to arbitrary Power that . . . stuck to [him] thro' [his] whole Life."[7] Abuse and tyranny not only taught Franklin to resent his master's authority but also encouraged him to take flight and find opportunity elsewhere. Enslaved Bostonians also inhabited a space where the former was true but the latter exceptionally difficult. Instead, they created new and clever ways to resist the arbitrary authority of their masters and find autonomy in their personal lives, such as being able to use the legal system to their advantage or developing a skill set that allowed them to work independently.

The story of the Humphreys and Franklin suggests that there was an inherent tension between class and race in eighteenth-century Boston. Simply put, race mattered in eighteenth-century Boston, but class and status mattered *more*.[8] We can clearly see this in the numerous references regarding slaves, free blacks, Native Americans, and poor whites as people of "mean and vile condition."[9] Other laws grouped blacks, free and slave, and Indians in one monolithic underclass. What this strongly suggests is a world where there was a clear hierarchy, and race determined place in that social order. On the one hand, it meant slaves were at the bottom of the social hierarchy, but on the other, the bottom was still a place, meaning slaves were ingrained in the societies in which they lived and had communal ties. This factor explains why free blacks like the Humphreys proved so vexing to colonial authorities as they stood outside the social order. There were certainly pejorative notions of cultural difference and fears of miscegenation, but these only bubbled to the surface periodically until coming to full fruition during the revolutionary era. What we see in eighteenth-century Boston, then, is a society in flux, shaped by early modern notions of social order but also actively creating race and defining racial difference. Enslaved Bostonians took advantage of this ambiguity, using it to their advantage, fighting to reshape the boundaries of their enslavement, seeking greater autonomy from the master class, and forcing their way into Euro-American society to demand a place within it.

Because of this tension, Boston is an important site in which to study slavery and unfreedom. It had many distinctive features yet was a typical port town in a seaborne network that fostered the circulation of goods, ideas, and people. By the middle of the eighteenth century, over sixteen hundred slaves lived in Boston, comprising between 10 and 15 percent of the total population, filling vital positions in the labor force—so vital, in fact, that if they suddenly disappeared from the historical landscape, Boston's economy would have collapsed. The study of slavery in New England has been a thriving area of scholarship in recent years, and this study contributes to this dynamism but also offers a new interpretation by arguing that Boston was different from the rest of New England.[10] The town had a larger slave population than almost every part of New England, and unlike rural New England towns and smaller seaports where slaves provided only supplemental labor, slavery was central to Boston's economy.

To better understand the exceptionality, I mostly disaggregate slavery in Boston from the historiography of slavery in New England. While the scholarship on slavery in New England provides important context for this study, it is important to remember that during the eighteenth century, Boston had transformed itself from a Puritan city on a hill to an Atlantic port reliant on unfree labor to keep its economic engine running. The town was an urban center with deep ties to the Atlantic economy and reliant on slave labor like other cities in the Americas, such as New Orleans, Havana, and Charleston, South Carolina. In this sense, Boston was one of many Atlantic entrepôts where slavery intermixed with other forms of bound labor, and slaves worked within the unfree, hierarchical society to carve out a space for themselves.[11]

As such, my study contributes to an ongoing conversation concerning slavery and freedom in early America and the Atlantic world. By reading the lives of enslaved Bostonians through legal and ecclesiastical records, I reveal them as being full of complexity and contradiction. Enslaved Bostonians were part of a particular eighteenth-century world, which was quite different, especially in regard to liberty and rights, than the modern one. In this context, we have to redefine and rethink central themes in the history of slavery, most importantly resistance and agency. These are problematic terms to begin with, but historians subscribe—consciously or not—to a "liberal-republican ideology" that emerged during the American Revolution, where slave resistance, especially violence, ultimately undermined slavery as an institution and made slaves worthy of freedom.[12] More importantly, this line of reasoning inextricably links resistance and agency to a desire for individual freedom and an end of slavery as an institution. Although resistance was sometimes a path to freedom, this ideological lens precludes and obfuscates other aims and desires of resistance. Moreover, to use this context when examining slavery in Boston between 1700 and 1775 would be imposing a revolutionary ideology on a prerevolutionary world.[13] Indeed, a better way of understanding slave resistance in eighteenth-century Boston is as a form of early modern popular protest. Deeply conservative in nature, these struggles did not look to upend the social order but rather to defend long-standing customs and traditions. Usually provoked by changes in labor arrangements, food shortages, or increased taxation, these actions were locally focused, were untethered from larger ideologies, and sought to reestablish a mythical status quo in which violated rights would be restored and grievances addressed.[14] Much like angry artisans writing letters of grievance to London newspapers or hungry peasants rioting over the price of flour, slaves in Boston utilized weapons of the weak. Work stoppages, running away, and even joining large crowd actions such as the Impressment Riot of 1747 allowed slaves to increase their autonomy, ameliorate their condition, or actively reshape the terms of their enslavement, all without necessarily advocating for their freedom.[15] Engaging in these types of protest allowed enslaved Bostonians to find effective ways of bettering their lives and participating in colonial life, all without challenging the social order.[16]

Until the American Revolution, resistance to slavery in Boston focused on the fight for autonomy more than legal freedom. Autonomy in this sense meant the possession of a certain degree of independence from the master class. In finding that autonomy through workplace arrangements, the formation of communities and families, the articulation and defense of rights and privileges, and religious affiliation, slaves were largely successful and had a degree of de facto freedom—within slavery, of course—that was largely unknown in other parts of the Americas where slavery existed. That is not to say that this work follows the old trope that slavery was more benign in New England than elsewhere.[17] As this work attempts to demonstrate, slavery in Boston was one part of a larger system of African slavery, one that had many similarities and differences with other parts of that system but was still an exploitative institution designed to extract labor from legally unfree people. Benevolence and autonomy, this line of thinking goes, was only sometimes a gift of the master but was more often demanded and won by the slave.

To better understand how slavery in Boston was part of this larger system of slavery, this study engages with the ever-burgeoning literature on the Atlantic world. In doing so, it joins a chorus of voices proclaiming, "We are all Atlanticists now."[18] Using transnational methodology allows us to understand how American (especially Caribbean), African, and European notions of slavery, freedom, and dependence combined in Boston to create its unique cultural landscape.[19] While examining how unfree and marginal people interacted is relatively rare in early American historiography, an Atlantic approach allows us to examine the Latin American tradition, in which these studies are much more common.[20]

In order to reconstruct slavery and the lives of enslaved Bostonians, this study draws heavily from legal records, including trial papers, wills, probate inventories, decision books, and justice of the peace record books. While these sources have allowed me to reveal the "otherwise invisible or opaque realms" of the lives of enslaved people and have a better understanding of their "social and cultural worlds," the records are problematic. Most of the trial records come from criminal proceedings in which slaves were accused of and often perpetrated heinous crimes. Because of this fact, these sources are inherently biased. First and foremost, not all slaves were criminals, making it difficult to extrapolate the experiences of all slaves on the basis of the transgressions of a few. Likewise, depositions and testimonies often offer conflicting narratives, and those who were being interrogated lied. All of these voices must be respected, especially since it is nearly impossible to discern guilt and innocence nearly three centuries after many of these trials took place. Also, any reader must recognize the power dynamics at play. Judges and magistrates gathering evidence and conducting these trials were powerful men in Boston and the colony of Massachusetts, while slaves were at the bottom of the hierarchy. Certainly slaves would have been deferential—even if only pretending—and their answers tailored to better assuage the men questioning them.

A final, and perhaps the most important, concern when using legal records is that it is often too easy to read thought into action. To truly understand the subjects of this book, however, is to accept that, in this case, actions speak much louder than thoughts. It is completely possible that slaves dreamed of being free, but they were also keen enough to understand that they lived in a world that found black freedom troublesome and oxymoronic. They had to look no further than free black men being forced to labor or the children of free black families being removed from their households to understand that liberty for blacks was often fraught and rendered meaningless by the state. Rather than vocalize their thoughts about freedom, slaves operated within the institution of slavery to carve out a considerable degree of autonomy and find ways to better their condition materially. This approach was much more practical—thus the use (perhaps overuse) of the word *abstract* throughout this study to contrast pragmatic action with ultimately unknowable thought.

Nevertheless, despite the limitations of legal records, they demonstrate that alternative interpretations of the social order existed and uncover a hidden world, one where enslaved Bostonians attempted to exercise control over their own lives and function in an oppressive society.[21]

To uncover the diverse origins of black Boston, the study begins in chapter 1 by reconstructing the Atlantic origins of Boston's black population. While there was a small native-born population descended from those who arrived in the seventeenth century, most slaves came from the Caribbean or Africa in the eighteenth century, usually through Boston's connection to the transatlantic slave trade. Most important, these people were slaves from slave societies. Slaves from Africa, for example, would have understood slavery as a customary institution in which enslaved people were accorded more customary rights. Unlike New World slavery, then, the objective of African slaves was not to overthrow the entire slave system in the name of universal emancipation but to become part of their master's society and obtain the rights that came with such affiliation.

Chapter 2 examines slaves once they arrived in Boston, where many would have encountered a society both familiar and alien. The town, like the rest of British North America, was in the midst of an ongoing cultural transformation. Residents of white Boston were moving away from their Puritan roots, becoming closer with their cousins across the sea by appropriating their attitudes, norms, and monarchical notions of societal organization. This hierarchy emphasized deference to social superiors and living within networks of dependence. Most Bostonians, whether European, Native American, or African, were legal dependents: women, children, servants, and slaves. Such a society was a perfect match for the newly evolving social order. Despite the inherent unfreedom, life in colonial Boston ensured that everyone from the lowliest pauper to the wealthiest merchant had a set of customary and defensible rights and privileges. Slaves, fighting for a place in this order, adapted and laid claim to a set of rights of their own.

Buttressing their position, Afro-Bostonians built strong and resilient social worlds (chapter 3). They made friends and acquaintances with similarly unfree people of all races and fought vociferously to protect their marriages and families. They built cross-class, cross-racial, and cross-gender networks both within their masters' households and in Boston at large. Although marriage between whites and blacks was expressly forbidden, slaves intermarried with each other, free blacks, and Native Americans. Avoiding classifying black communities as racially exclusive, chapter 3 argues that the social reality was much more fluid and dynamic.

Although many slaves' personal interactions could be violent and unstable, most proved especially resilient in the town's labor market (chapter 4). They were a highly versatile workforce and could be found in almost every industry, working in artisanal trades and making important contributions to the town's economic growth. Any visitor to Boston would have encountered slaves like Cato, Nero, Quaco, and Scipio, skilled tanners who absconded from their master's tannery in Boston to work under much less onerous—and more sanitary conditions—for a Cambridge farmer. They would have been fed, clothed, and waited on by bondswomen who served as cooks, seamstresses, and washerwomen for many of Boston's families and were important to domestic production. If guests were observant, they might even catch a glimpse of Boston's many enslaved sailors, like Briton Hammon, who made a thirteen-year journey around the Atlantic as a slave, prisoner of the Spanish governor of Cuba, and mariner in the merchant fleets of two different nations before returning to Boston. All these contributions were not lost on Boston's elite, who recognized the economic importance of slavery and gave their bondsmen and bonds-women considerable autonomy in their working lives, autonomy that empowered enslaved Bostonians to reshape and redefine the terms of their enslavement. It also freed enslaved laborers to form an occupational identity, one created by proactive workers to protect their workplace rights.

Likewise, enslaved Bostonians appropriated white institutions and discourse to better their everyday lives (chapter 5). They channeled much of their energy into learning and using local institutions, namely, the law and Boston's many Protestant churches, to obtain valuable skills like the ability to read and write and acquire a basic understanding of Anglo-American jurisprudence. White Bostonians never created specialized mechanisms of control, such as slave courts, to govern slavery, and slaves actively worked to ingrain themselves in local institutions. On any given Sunday, the pews of Boston's churches were full of black faces learning not only the gospel but how to read and write, while slaves knew to approach local justices if their masters were being cruel or abusive and would almost always receive a fair hearing. Comprehending their larger society and understanding its basic contours enabled enslaved Bostonians to navigate their enslavement and fight for concessions from the master class.

The afterword examines how enslaved Bostonians came to use natural rights language to fight for personal liberty and emancipation during the 1760s and 1770s. This struggle coincided with white Bostonians' parallel efforts to free themselves from British imperial rule. While the slaves appropriated natural rights discourse from their masters and used it against them, the stakes for the slaves were much higher. Throughout the imperial crisis and the early years of the Revolution, the world of dependence unraveled, hierarchy collapsed, and the house of unfreedom fell. Sons defied their fathers, women disobeyed their husbands, and slaves challenged their masters' authority. Prerevolutionary society with its strict, patriarchal social order began to come undone at the seams, presenting opportunities to defy that order and, for Afro-Bostonians, an opportunity to make a claim for freedom. For the first time, personal liberty was a real option, and this became the goal for black Bostonians, who saw it as the ultimate safeguard for property and families and an avenue to becoming full members of American society. To do this, slaves and free blacks in Boston employed a petition campaign to end slavery once and for all in Massachusetts, culminating in a 1783 legal victory that dealt a serious blow to the institution of slavery. Even after the 1783 decision, however, freedom was not ensured. Their courtroom victory was by no means decisive, and its consequences were ambiguous. Moreover, the legacy of unfreedom did not disappear after the American Revolution. In this new world of freedom, old obligations and duties fell to the wayside, leaving newly freed slaves out in the cold, without a safety net, and unprepared to confront the racial structures formed around emancipation. The book ends with a reexamination of the petition of Belinda, an impoverished, recently freed slave, allowing us to see how the language of dependence survived revolutionary upheaval.

The records left behind by enslaved Bostonians reveal a different narrative than historians of slavery are used to telling, one that complicates freedom as a category of analysis. Although such an interpretation can be troubling for readers with modern conceptions of liberty, these slaves inhabited a world where those ideas and ideologies were neither transcendent nor a universal desire. Instead of producing despair, however, I contend that the ability to adapt to— and often succeed in—an inherently unfree world with such skill and tenacity demonstrates the flexibility and dynamism of Boston's slave population. Assumptions about the diametrical opposition of freedom and slavery in colonial America denies this adaptability and transforms the enslaved into mere caricatures of who they actually were. These were people who had families and friends, who loved and, most importantly, lived life to the fullest given their circumstances. Ultimately, then, *Unfreedom* not only reconsiders assumptions about slave life but also demonstrates how enslaved Bostonians were able to fully and richly inhabit their humanity.

Note on Terminology: Throughout the text, I use "slave," "black," and "African" interchangeably despite recognizing the existence of free and indentured blacks. I do this to avoid being too repetitious. When discussing nonslave Africans, I explicitly note it, but otherwise, I use the terms interchangeably.

1 / Origins

Boston, a slave who belonged to James Gardner and who was on his deathbed in 1761, accused Quaco, another slave, of poisoning him a month earlier. Although Boston later died, William Stoddard, the justice assigned to investigate the matter, believed Boston's allegation alone was not enough to convict Quaco. The judge decided to dig deeper into Quaco's past, and upon further investigation, he learned Quaco was from the Dutch colony of Suriname on the northern coast of South America. A plantation colony specializing in sugar, coffee, cocoa, and cotton production and heavily dependent on slave labor, Suriname was a regular trading partner with the New England colonies. Boston merchants sold dried fish, agricultural products, and manufactured goods for molasses and other commodities. Occasionally, as the case of Quaco demonstrates, merchants purchased a few slaves in the Dutch colony and brought them back to Boston to sell. Stoddard, aware of this trade, approached a ship captain, Duncan Ingraham, who knew Quaco's Surinamese master. According to Ingraham, Quaco's former master, a Mr. Felix, sold the slave to Captain John Fraiser of Boston, and Ingraham "never heard that said Quaco was confined for poisoning or any other crime at Suriname to Occasion his being sent off." Quaco was a good slave, according to Ingraham, but another witness did not share Ingraham's optimistic conclusion.[1]

On 19 September 1761, shortly after Boston's death, Stoddard summoned Arnold Wells's slave named Boar, whose name was possibly a corruption of the Dutch *boer*, meaning "farmer." Like Quaco,

Boar was from Suriname; he remembered Quaco from his time there and even had a family connection. According to Boar, he knew the accused poisoner because his mother and Quaco were imprisoned together "on account of poison." While Boar's mother was executed for the crime, once Boar arrived in Boston, he often heard Quaco say he was only "sent away" for the crime. Unfortunately, we do not know the outcome of Stoddard's investigation or if Boar's testimony was important in convicting Quaco. More importantly, however, Quaco had a past, one deeply embedded in Atlantic slavery that did not disappear when he arrived in Boston.

While Quaco's past came back to haunt him in a deeply personal way, all of Boston's slaves carried both their own experiences and larger cultural values with them when they arrived in New England. To better understand the world of Boston's slaves, we need to analyze these origins, especially their relationship with slavery. Eighteenth-century slaves in Boston were the descendants of a small native-born black population that had been in New England since the 1630s; American-born creoles or Africans who had resided in the Americas for a long period of time; or native Africans mostly, but not exclusively, from West Africa, including the Senegambia region and the Gold Coast. Slavery was deeply entrenched in each of these places, meaning that all Afro-Bostonians had encountered and had experience with slavery as an institution. Although the slave system they came from could be very different from the one they entered, they nevertheless had experience with commodification and unfreedom, allowing them to find more effective ways to adapt to their new homeland.[2]

Black Bostonians also had prior experiences with other institutions, such as Islam in the case of Senegambian slaves, which helped slaves navigate white society in Boston. All of this accumulated cultural knowledge from New England, Africa, and the Caribbean came together as a result of Boston's involvement in the slave trade. By the first quarter of the eighteenth century, the town's enslaved population was expanding and diverse. These slaves, equipped with knowledge of slavery and cultural traditions that allowed them to adapt to colonial conditions, had the flexibility and ability to integrate themselves into Euro-American society.

By examining the origins of Boston's slaves, we clearly see that the slave trade was an engine of Atlantic diaspora, shuffling enslaved populations to areas all around its littoral. Yet its significance was not simply about the movement of people to labor on distant shores but about the values, traditions, and knowledge those populations carried with them. Most important was the shared experience of slavery, as many slaves moved from one slave society to another. They accumulated knowledge on how to best navigate and contest enslavement and later employed that information once they arrived in Boston, eventually channeling their energies into acquiring concrete material gains and creating a space for themselves in Euro-American society.

The first group that composed Boston's eighteenth-century slave population was the relatively small group of Afro–New Englanders that had been in the region since the 1630s. Descendants of African-born slaves who most likely spent some of their time in the Caribbean, this population hovered around one thousand people for all of New England during the seventeenth century.[3] By 1700, about eight hundred of these people lived in Massachusetts, and it is safe to assume that two to three hundred lived in Boston, the colony's largest urban center and most diverse economy.[4] Although few in number, black New Englanders were fixtures in the social fabric of the region and constituted one of many classes of the unfree, which included indentured servants, apprentices, and Indian slaves. Like their descendants in the eighteenth century, they created multiracial communities and learned to navigate local institutions. Nevertheless, the relatively low density of slaves meant they did not reproduce at the prodigious rates of their white contemporaries, and their population always had to be reinforced with new arrivals.

In regard to slavery, seventeenth-century New England was quite similar to other seventeenth-century mainland English colonies such as New York and Virginia. Even in the latter case, Virginia was a not a full-fledged slave society until the passage of the Slave Code of 1705.[5] In Virginia, however, the slave code was not comprehensive and left many issues unresolved. About the only place where slavery had been organized in any systematic way was the Caribbean, where the sugar colony of Barbados passed an often-copied slave code in 1661.[6] As the early eagerness to adopt a slave code suggests, Barbados and the other English West Indian colonies were the centers of slavery in the Anglophone world. Given the close economic and social relationship between New England merchants and Caribbean planters, seventeenth-century slavery in Boston and the rest of the region was an extension of this relationship. In the course of trade and other forms of contact, New England and the West Indies became "one economic region," and a crucial link between the two "involved slave labor."[7] This relationship made New England not only a Puritan errand in the wilderness but also a slave-owning society.

Of course, New Englanders' close relationship with the West Indies did not force them to enslave Africans or to legally define slavery as an institution: it was a conscious decision. They had no problem enslaving Native Americans. After the Pequot War in 1636, they traded some of the war captives for African slaves in the Caribbean, who arrived in Boston in 1638, beginning the region's long history with African slavery. Three years later, settlers in Massachusetts made an attempt to govern slavery when they passed the colony's first legal code, *The Body of Liberties*. Article 91 ambiguously stated, "There shall never be any bond slaverie, villange or Captivitie amongst us, unless" someone captured those slaves in just wars, those slaves were "strangers" who sold themselves into slavery, or someone else captured, enslaved, and sold them to the colonists. Adding another layer of ambiguity, these slaves were to "have all the liberties and Christian usages which the law of god established in Israell concerning such persons doeth morally require."[8] At first glance, this clause seems to be a negative, declaring slavery illegal in all but three cases, yet it also opened the door to racial slavery. Most captives taken in so-called just wars would have been Native Americans captured in the vicious Indian wars of the 1630s. Strangers, on the other hand, primarily meant one group of people: Africans. While not many people would have sold themselves into slavery, except perhaps a few destitute English men and women looking for a better life abroad, most of the strangers sold to Massachusetts would have been blacks from the Caribbean and Africa. As for the sentence concerning ancient Israel, it is unclear if men and women could sell their daughters into slavery as suggested in Exodus, although masters probably liked the clause that considered all enslaved "strangers" (Leviticus 25:44–46) as permanent, inheritable property. The loopholes in the 1641 *Body of Liberties* allowed for the existence of racial slavery and possibly created chattel slavery.

Despite the backhanded legalization of slavery in article 91, the legal status of African slaves remained relatively ambiguous throughout the seventeenth century. It seems some masters considered slaves to be indentured servants. By comparing the wills of three seventeenth-century New Englanders, we can see this process. When the Boston merchant Antipas Boyse was composing his last will and testament on 3 July 1669, he took time to consider the fate of his slave Janemet.

After two additional years of service to Boyse's heirs, Janemet would be free, provided he served his masters "faithfully."[9] Unlike Boyse, who owned African slaves, George Alcock of Roxbury had two white servants, John Plimton and Joseph Wise. Like Janemet, both Wise and Plimton received their freedom shortly after Alcock's death, this time "after midsomer next."[10] Other slave owners gave their slaves their freedom shortly after their death as well. Mary Smith, the widow of Bostonian Abraham Smith, stated in her will why she freed her slaves Susan and Maria: for their "good care & diligence of me & my lat Husband." Nevertheless, the enslaved women still had to behave themselves for the remainder of Mary's life; otherwise "this Deed of Gift" would "be frustrate void & of none effect," indicating their freedom was provisional and not guaranteed.[11] Yet conditional freedom was not exclusive to African slaves. Alcock made Plimton pay five pounds to be freed along with Wise.[12] Although colonists bought, sold, and passed slaves on to their heirs, many seem to have considered their obligation to serve to be finite and, much like white servants, not lifelong.

The status of the children of enslaved Africans in seventeenth-century Boston was also problematic. English common law long held the notion of *partus sequitur patrem*, a belief that children took the condition of their fathers. For slave owners looking to increase the number of bondsmen and bondswomen they owned, this was not an issue if the father was a slave. Enslaved women who bore the children of free men, however, proved to be especially problematic for masters—who were sometimes the fathers. Virginian slaveholders solved this problem in 1662, eschewing English law and adopting the Roman law principle of *partus sequitur ventrem*, meaning children took the status of the mother. Interestingly, none of the New England colonies ever adopted this law, but as a historian noted, "custom and tradition achieved the same end."[13] Even in the eighteenth century, Massachusetts failed to pass a law clarifying the condition of enslaved children, leaving their slave status open to question.

Adding another layer of ambiguity, the seventeenth-century labor market was not always amicable to slavery. In early November 1661, the selectmen of Boston investigated Thomas Deane, who "employed a Negro in ye manufacture of a Coop." According to the town leaders, Deane's actions were "contrary to ye orders of ye Towne," suggesting the selectmen frowned on the use of slave labor in skilled trades. They then issued a cease-and-desist order, commanding that Deane "shall not employ ye sd Negro in ye sd manufacture as a Coop or any other manufacture or science after ye 14th day of this month." If the slave continued making barrels, his master would be given a "penalty of 20s, for euery day yt ye sd Negro shall continue in such employment."[14] Beyond official restraint regarding slave labor, it seems most enslaved workers in seventeenth-century New England either provided farm labor in the rural areas or worked as domestics or valets in their masters' homes.[15] Compared to the eighteenth century, when slave labor was an integral part of all sectors of Boston's economy, especially the artisanal trades, the selectmen's reprimand of Deane and the limited use of slaves in all parts of the economy demonstrate there was at least some hesitancy to employ slave labor.

While an uncertain labor market helped to confuse an already ill-defined institution, much of the ambiguity may have had to do with the behavior of the slaves themselves. Given the low population density of African slaves in colonial New England—by 1700, there were ninety thousand inhabitants in New England, only one thousand of whom were slaves—many slaves attempted to integrate themselves into colonial society.[16] This was especially true in Boston, a crowded cosmopolitan port town where Africans could easily mingle with whites, Native Americans, and other Africans. Consider Will, a slave belonging to Captain Prentice. In 1700, Will died after falling off a horse. Although dead, Will was not forgotten. Puritan magistrate Samuel Sewall took time in his diary to commemorate Will, a man Sewall obviously thought to be part of the community. Sewall remembered the slave "much delighted in Horses," and the irony was not lost on the justice that Will "now dies by a horse." Beyond Will's love of all things equine, Sewall also recalled an incident from nearly forty years before, in 1664. In that year, Will saved his "Master Prentice from a Bear." Will and Sewall had also spent considerable time together, as the bondsman traveled with the judge and Colonel Townsend to Albany, New York.[17] Nevertheless, while Will was obviously trusted and respected by Sewall, the magistrate's depiction of the slave suggests an obedient, docile paragon of service. Will's slavery lasted at least forty years, and his only memorial did not mention Will's friends, family, or community, only Sewall's.[18] Whether Will was as compliant as Sewall suggests will never be known, but his very mention in Sewall's diary suggests a slave ingrained in the community.

Slaves enmeshed themselves in white society in other ways as well. Seventeenth-century church records are full of enslaved people presenting themselves or their children to be baptized. The First Church of Boston recorded baptizing "William or William and Hannah Negro" in 1682 and "Lydia Pollow a negro Child" in 1697.[19] Likewise, John Winthrop, founder of the Bay Colony, noted in his diary in 1641, a "negro maid, servant to Mr Stoughton, of Dorchester, being well approved by divers years' experience, for sound knowledge and true godliness, was received into the church and baptized."[20] This enslaved woman received baptism only three years after the first slaves arrived in Boston, indicating that either slaves quickly learned the importance of religion in Puritan society, she had been exposed to Christianity before her arrival in Massachusetts, or some combination of the two.

Another indicator of how embedded slaves were in the social world of Boston was the frequency of interracial sexual liaisons. Court records attest to this trend. As fornication was a crime, interracial couples constantly appeared before the court, sometimes for sexual acts and at other times for having children out of wedlock. In late October 1672, the court found the English servant Christopher Mason guilty of "getting Mr. Rock's Negroe maide Bess with Childe." Mason received twenty lashes and had to pay a fine for his transgression. Bess, who appeared three months later, after having the "illegitimate Childe," received a whipping, and the court forced her to pay all legal fees.[21] Eight years later, Kathalina, a slave belonging to Thomas Dewer, accused Loftlan Loney of being the father of a "Bastard Childe born of her body about a month agone." Soon after the proceedings against Loney began, the child died. This tragedy became Loney's saving grace, as the court decided not to pursue the matter any further, knowing Loney would not stop "denying of it," and only forced him to pay court costs. Kathalina's ordeal was not over, however. Since she had approached the court claiming Loney was the father of her bastard child, she had also inadvertently confessed to fornicating, receiving fifteen lashes and a forty-shilling fine for her troubles.[22] These relations involved not only Africans and whites but also Africans and Indians. A Mr. Warren of Boston owned two slaves, one African and one Native American. In the same year as the case involving Bess and Mason, Jasper, the Indian slave, confessed to "committing Fornication" with Joan the African.[23] Not only do these fornication cases demonstrate how close slaves were with other Bostonians, but they also suggest that enslaved Africans associated with people of a similar social standing. Indeed, two of the three men involved in these cases were lower class. Mason was an indentured servant, and Jasper an Indian. While elites like Samuel Sewall could memorialize slaves they deemed worthy, it seems the enslaved were more comfortable interacting with people of a similar status.

Perhaps the most important part of slaves' integrating themselves into colonial society was their ability to learn the law. Most of this legal knowledge was experiential. As the fornication suits illustrate, despite the low numbers of slaves, they frequently appeared before the courts. In the 1670s, a slave woman named Hannah appeared before Suffolk County justices for stealing surgical equipment from Daniel Stone and selling it to Mary Pittum. The court found Hannah guilty and sentenced her to be whipped ten times and pay Stone ten pounds for the missing implements. Hannah accepted the lashes as just punishment but appealed the fine. On appeal, Hannah sought to defend herself under the "Law titell buglery theft page :13 section 2," stating that all fines incurred by servants and children would not be paid and that dependents could only be "openly punished," meaning corporal punishment. Since Hannah had already been whipped for her crime, she claimed she did not have to pay the fine. Although the court did not buy Hannah's argument and she lost her appeal, her understanding of the law was detailed and precise, especially given that she may have been illiterate—demonstrated by her signing the court documents with a mark.[24] How Hannah learned the law and how exemplary she was are both unknown, but it is safe to assume slaves' knowledge of the law was not as extensive as in the next century.

By the beginning of the eighteenth century, there was a small native population of slaves in Boston. In some ways, such as their attempts to integrate themselves into the community at large, this enslaved population resembled its eighteenth-century counterparts. In other ways, especially with respect to their role in the labor market, they could not have been more different. Moreover, slavery as an institution was legally ambiguous and ill defined. Legislation regarding slavery was sparse or, in the case of determining the status of slaves' children, nonexistent. Nevertheless, by 1700, slavery was firmly entrenched in Boston and was a customary institution, and new arrivals from the Caribbean and Africa became part of this slave society.

The new arrivals came in unprecedented numbers. Before considering the other two sources of enslaved Bostonians, it is important to examine the processes that brought black slaves to Boston and the demographic transformation they wrought. One of the biggest factors in bringing Africans to Massachusetts was the opening of the transatlantic slave trade to all interested parties. Beginning in 1660 with the Restoration of Charles II, a group of English merchants received a monopoly on slave trading. Their company, known as the Royal African Company, was notoriously inefficient and corrupt, depriving most peripheral regions of the English empire, including the Carolinas, Virginia, and New England, of slaves. The Royal African Company's monopoly affected how many slaves arrived in the Americas and the manner in which they arrived there.[25] In 1680, Massachusetts governor Simon Bradstreet wrote to the Board of Trade and Plantations in England explaining there "hath been no Company of blacks or Slaves brought into the Country since the beginning of this plantation." In nearly fifty years of being settled, only "one small Vessell about two years" before Bradstreet wrote the letter, "brought hither betwixt Forty and fifty Negro's" to the colony. Instead of receiving full coffles, "Now and then, two or three Negro's are brought hither from Barbados and other of his Majesties plantations." Bradstreet estimated that this ad hoc process of acquiring slaves brought "about one hundred or one hundred and twenty" slaves to the colony, a relatively low estimate.[26] Although Boston merchants occasionally attempted to skirt the monopoly and chartered their own voyages to buy slaves on the African coast, their attempts never brought more than a few slaves into the region.[27]

Following the fall of Charles II's brother James II during the Glorious Revolution, however, the Royal African Company lost its monopoly, and the slave trade opened to any merchant in the empire with the capital to charter a voyage. Bostonians were not big participants in the direct trade to Africa, but they did send at least thirty voyages during the period under study.[28] It must be noted, however, that rarely did these voyages bring a full shipload of slaves to Boston. While eighteenth-century white Bostonians were labor hungry, the market for slaves was never as large as that in the Caribbean or southern colonies. Ships from Boston would buy slaves in Africa and sell them in the West Indies, South Carolina, or Virginia. The leftovers would be sold in Boston. Many people made special requests to ship captains for slaves. Peter Faneuil, one of the wealthiest men in Boston and whose ship, the *Jolly Bachelor*, was a fixture in the Boston slave trade, asked the captain of one of his vessels, Peter Buckley, to bring him "for the use of [his] house," a "strait limbed Negro lad as possible

[Buckley] can about the age of from 12 to fiveteen years, & if to be done one that has had the small pox." The slave, "being for [Faneuil's] Own service," must "be one of as tractable a disposition as [Buckley] can find."[29] More important for the direct trade from Africa to New England were merchants in Rhode Island, the center of colonial slave trading.[30] Bostonians often took the journey to Rhode Island to purchase slaves. The jurist Nathaniel Byfield in his will remembered purchasing his slave Rose in Bristol after she arrived from the West Indies in 1718, when she was about thirteen years old.[31] While Boston was still not a preferred market for even its own merchants, the opening of the slave trade to all capable parties dramatically increased the number of slaves available.

Meanwhile, the older ad hoc process of merchants buying slaves in the Caribbean, especially Barbados, and selling them in Boston continued, only on a greater scale. Given the extensive commerce between Massachusetts and the West Indies, it is not surprising that slaves were also bought there and brought to Boston along with cargos of molasses and sugar. In the eighteenth century, however, slaves came to constitute a larger volume, especially in monetary value, of Caribbean trade. Hugh Hall, the son of a Barbadian planter and graduate of Harvard College who split his time between Barbados and Boston, ran an import/export business selling manufactured goods, fish, and timber from New England in exchange for sugar and slaves. Hall documented all of these transactions in his account book, but in 1729, the merchant attempted to record all "Negro's Received from Barbados," including ones he did not buy or sell. According to his estimations, Bostonians bought eighty slaves from the island in that year. A cursory glance at the names of the slaves listed suggests a couple of things. First, African names such as "Quaco," "Quashey," and "Bonabah" appear beside English names such as "Bess," "Betty," and "Tom" and the derogatory classical and biblical names that masters often gave slaves, like "Dido" and "Jupiter." This group of slaves may have been a mix of African-born slaves, who either were immediately shipped to Boston via Barbados or had only spent a short time in the plantation colony, and American-born creoles, whose masters gave them European names.[32] Not only does this mixture of origins make it difficult to determine where enslaved Bostonians came from, but it is also testament to the sheer diversity of slaves being brought into the town.

Hall's account book may be an artifact of diversity, yet it also taps into a much larger trend: the demographic changes brought about by such a wide-scale importation of slaves. As mentioned before, the black population in Massachusetts was 800 in 1700, but by 1776, there were 5,249 people of African descent in Massachusetts, a 650 percent increase. Although blacks only made up 1.8 percent of the population of Massachusetts, their demographic footprint in Boston was much greater and only grew during the eighteenth century.[33] In 1704, there were 400 slaves living in Boston, while in 1752, there were 1,541 slaves, an increase of over 350 percent.[34] In that latter year, there were 15,730 inhabitants of Boston, meaning African slaves made up nearly 10 percent of the town's population.[35] Yet that percentage may be low for a number of reasons. Slaves were taxable property, meaning it behooved masters to hide their chattel from census takers. Likewise, census records provide only a static picture of Boston's black population. Court records and other documents suggest a much more fluid and mobile population. Town officials commonly told "strangers" to leave Boston, a process known as "warning out." While most of the African interlopers tended to be free blacks, there are a number of slaves in the records. Most of the enslaved people sent out were from surrounding towns, as was a slave named Charlestown, who was unsurprisingly from the town of Charlestown across the Charles River from Boston.[36] Like the slave Charlestown, there seems to have been a large number of slaves from surrounding towns who came into Boston for recreation or to work, run errands for their masters, find a mate, or visit a loved one who lived in the colony's capital. Finally, given the large number of enslaved sailors who traversed the Atlantic world, almost every ship that came into port would either return enslaved Bostonians home or bring new ones into port. The black population of Boston grew dramatically during the eighteenth century, and although it is next to impossible to determine the exact number of slaves in Boston at any given time, it is safe to assume it was larger than what colonial censuses claimed.

Slaves who had spent considerable amounts of time or were born in other parts of the Americas, especially the West Indies and the American South, were an important component of this demographic transformation. As Hugh Hall's account book indicates, it is hard to discern which slaves were born in the Americas or were only transshipped from there. Nevertheless, on the basis of newspaper ads, we know that some slaves were born in the Caribbean and other places and sent to Boston. In November 1712, the *Boston News-Letter* ran an advertisement for a "Young negro girl born in Barbadoes that speaks good English."[37] The latter part of this ad indicates why American-born slaves were in such high demand. They could speak European languages, usually English and sometimes multiple others, making it easier for masters to command their chattel and teach them profitable skills. Likewise, they would have been familiar with how slavery functioned in British society, and potential owners believed them to be more docile. Even those who had spent a short time in the Americas were preferable to slaves fresh from Africa, as their exposure to Euro-American society was thought to make them better slaves. The slaves themselves, however, were trapped between two worlds, an African past and an American present, and used both knowledge sets to navigate eighteenth-century Boston.

By examining the lives of two slaves before they were sold away from the Caribbean to Boston, we will be able to see the slavery they experienced and the social worlds they inhabited before arriving in the place where they spent their final years. One slave, Mark, who we will meet again in the next chapter, belonged to Captain John Codman, a wealthy merchant from Charlestown. The second slave, Quaco, was already introduced at the beginning of this chapter. Both Mark and Quaco had Caribbean roots, Mark being born and spending his childhood in Barbados and Quaco residing for some time in Dutch Suriname. Both slaves had firsthand experiences of West Indian plantation society, giving them a deep understanding of slavery as an institution, their degraded place in European New World societies, and ways to resist that degradation.

"I was born to a reputable family" in Barbados in 1725, Mark told those who witnessed his execution in the summer of 1755, and left his "native Place very Young" and "came to Boston."[38] It makes one wonder if Mark, having just been convicted of murdering his master and sentenced to death, thought about his childhood and his parents, friends, and acquaintances in his tropical homeland. Maybe his memories were just a faint glimmer in his mind, but it is hard to imagine he forgot everything about growing up in Barbados. By his own description, he was "very Young" when he arrived in New England, but masters in Boston needed workers, not more children to raise, suggesting that Mark was probably between the ages of six and ten when he arrived, about the age boys went to work. Despite the short time living in the island colony, Mark's experience would have been formative.

To better understand why Mark's childhood in Barbados was so important for his later life, we need to better understand the history of slavery on the island. Barbados was one of the earliest colonies settled by the English, with settlement beginning in 1625. Although its white population grew steadily over the next two decades, its economy did not take off until the 1640s with the advent of sugar cultivation. Rather quickly, wealthier white Barbadians began to consolidate their ownership of the land and replace white indentured servants and free laborers with African slaves.[39] Less than twenty years later, blacks outnumbered whites on the island, and by 1680, they outnumbered European colonists by more than two to one.[40] While almost all of these slaves were native Africans during the first decades of slavery, by the early eighteenth century, a small native black population began to appear. Mark, a member of this creole class, and others like him indicated, according to the historian Jennifer Morgan, the "growing ability of men and women to navigate the social terrain of the island."[41] Being able to successfully reproduce themselves, these enslaved pioneers produced children who spoke English and came to be trusted by the master class. Owners elevated them to positions above African plantation workers and insulated them (to a certain extent) from the everyday violence and depravity of plantation slavery; many of the male creoles became artisans, fulfilling specialized labor needs. With this special treatment also came mobility.[42] Mark, then, was on track to become a skilled slave with a great degree of autonomy and perhaps observed adult slaves in a similar situation successfully navigate Barbadian slavery to obtain some level of material comfort. Nevertheless, Mark's ability to mitigate his slave status was something that came to fruition in Boston, not Barbados.[43] Why Mark's master would have sold away such a valuable slave is unknown, although there was no guarantee Mark, being a boy, would survive to adulthood and become a valued member of plantation society.

Despite Mark's creole status and all the benefits that came with it, he still would have had ties to his African ancestry. The bulk of slaves in Barbados were from Africa, and the miserable working conditions and disease environment meant that the slave population actually declined at a rate of about 5 percent a year.[44] Some masters even preferred to buy new slaves rather than allow their current chattel to reproduce, as, according to one planter, "it was cheaper to work slaves to the utmost, and by little fare and hard usage, to wear them out before they became useless and then to buy new ones."[45] This meant all of the slaves on the island, native born or African, constantly encountered new arrivals who brought African cultural and social practices with them. As Griffith Hughes, the author of an eighteenth-century natural history of Barbados, noted, the "Negroes in general are very tenaciously addicted to the Rites, Ceremonies, and Superstitions of their own Countries, particularly in their Plays, Dances, Music, Marriages, and Burials." "And even such as are born and bred up here," Hughes added, "cannot be intirely [sic] weaned from these Customs." All of the slaves stood "much in Awe of such as pass for *Obeah*," blacks who were essentially spiritual doctors and who "cured" slaves "when they [were] bewitched by others." In addition to the nearly universal belief in the supernatural, most Africans also liked to adorn themselves with "Strings of Beads of various colors."[46] Even in death, African slaves could not escape their cultural traditions, believing when they died that "they shall return to their own Country."[47] Although it is uncertain if creoles like Mark believed they returned to Africa upon death, they were nevertheless the product of two different cultural traditions, one that empowered them against slavery and another that allowed them to be part of the wider slave community. Both of these equipped Mark to decode the ambivalent and complicated world of slavery, skills he brought with him when he traveled to Boston.

Unlike Mark, Quaco arrived in Boston as an adult after spending a considerable amount of time living in the Dutch colony of Suriname. Why he was an attractive investment to any English person, especially given his reputation as a poisoner, is unknown, but the peculiar history of Suriname offers clues. The colony, located on the northeastern coast of South America and also known as the Wild Coast, had been a contested zone between the British, French, Spanish, Portuguese, and Dutch empires since the late sixteenth century. A number of colonial powers had tried to settle the area, including the English, who established a colony there in the 1630s and, after its failure, another in the 1650s. English control of the region did not last long, and the Dutch conquered the colony in 1667.[48] The Netherlanders quickly turned the colony into a productive center of sugar cultivation, and by 1700, the one thousand white settlers were heavily outnumbered by eighty-five hundred people of African descent.[49] Despite the Batavianization of the colony, however, the slaves continued to speak a dialect of English. Almost a century after the Dutch conquest, the botanist Edward Bancroft noticed, "at this time a species of corrupt *English* is universally spoken by the Negroes."[50] In fact, to this day, the lingua franca spoken in Suriname, Sranan, is derisively called *Neger Engelsche*.[51] As Boston merchants and ship captains began trading in Suriname in the eighteenth century, albeit illegally, finding slaves who were familiar with European slavery and could more easily learn English must have been an enticing investment.[52]

Quaco's experience in Suriname would have been markedly different from Mark's in Barbados. Although there was a small creole population in the Dutch colony, the slaves of Suriname were overwhelmingly African. The equatorial climate created a disease environment that killed off large numbers of all settlers, black and white. The brutal plantation regime exacerbated slave deaths. One of biggest differences between Suriname and Barbados is that the latter is a tiny island, while the Dutch colony was in the middle of the rain forest. Slaves could easily escape from plantations, retreat into the hinterland, and form their own communities. By 1700, there were more than one thousand of these so-called maroons in the colony, making up over 10 percent of the population.[53] They posed an imminent threat to Suriname's society, either by raiding plantations for supplies and women or by enticing other slaves to run away. Ever vigilant, Dutch authorities kept a close eye on slaves and meted out brutal punishments for the slightest offense. Upon first arriving in the colony to help put down a maroon rebellion, the Scottish-Dutch mercenary John Stedman saw a young woman "in chains, simply covered with a rag around her loins, which was, like her skin, cut and carved by the lash of the whip in a most shocking manner." After the slave woman failed to fulfill her "task," Stedman ambiguously mentioned, she was sentenced to receive "200 lashes and for months to drag a chain several yards in length, one end of which was locked to her ankle and at the other end of which was a weight of three score pounds." Captivated by both the horror and the woman's beauty, Stedman sketched an image of her (see figure 1).[54] Such an excessive punishment for such a minor offense indicates the paranoia of the master class and a willingness to sacrifice troublesome slaves to protect the plantation colony. Such high attrition through disease, absconding, and brutality ensured the constant arrival of new slaves from Africa.

Despite swift, vicious responses to affronts against whites, Surinamese planters and Dutch officials gave slaves considerable leeway in policing themselves, most likely to create an illusion that slaves controlled their own communities and would thus prevent others from running away to the maroons. Moreover, given the predominance of blacks and relative low number of whites, especially in the plantation zone outside

FIGURE 1 "A Female Negro Slave, with a Weight chain," from John Gabriel
Stedman, *Narrative of a Five Years' Expedition; against the Revolted Negroes
of Surinam, in Guiana, on the Wild Coast of South America; from the Year . . .*
(London, 1796)

the colony's capital, Paramaribo, slaves arbitrated legal matters themselves to ensure swift justice without cases having to go through the
Dutch bureaucracy. It was also probably how Quaco landed himself in
so much trouble and was sold out of the colony in the first place. Three
different groups administered justice on Suriname's plantations. The
first, enslaved drivers, known in Dutch as *bassia*, were slaves entrusted
by the master class to oversee workers in the fields. They were arbiters
by design, mitigating the abuses of the master class while ensuring that
slaves labored. Skilled slaves made up the second group. These slaves
could be Africans or creoles, male or female, and held positions of
power on the basis of their skills and supposed trustworthiness. Finally,
traditional African spiritual leaders and healers, similar to the Obeah of
Barbados and known as diviners, like their counterparts in the English
Caribbean, exercised considerable influence over the slave community.[55]
This triad held meetings among themselves and adjudicated disputes
on the plantation. They also decided what information about various
offenses the master class and local court, called the Court of Policy and
Criminal Justice, would hear. For minor offenses such as slandering a
fellow slave, the *bassia*, artisans, and diviners would arbitrate and mete
out punishment themselves. More serious offenses, however, would be
passed along to the white community, where the cases would be heard
by the Court of Policy and Criminal Justice.[56]

One of the most taboo crimes that a slave could commit, in the eyes
of Europeans, slaves, and maroons, was poisoning. Long-standing
African traditions dictated that poisoners, often thought to be practicing malfeasant magic, were to be punished with a cruel death or by
being sold into slavery. Maroons brutally mutilated the offender and
burned the body, while white authorities punished poisoners with
death.[57] Quaco, if Boar's story is to be believed, was found guilty of
poisoning along with the latter's mother. While it is unclear whom
Quaco poisoned, it was most likely not a white person. Unlike Boar's
mother, Quaco did not receive the death penalty. This sentence would
have been guaranteed, especially given Surinamese planters' penchant
for using savage displays of violence to make an example, for any slave
even accused of poisoning a white person. Instead, poisoning seemed
to be an interpersonal crime, one used by slaves against one another,
perhaps over a grievance, such as jealousy or a spurned lover.[58] Lending
credence to this accusation, the owners of Boston (the slave poisoned by
Quaco), James and Sarah Gardner, testified that Boston took sides with
a slave named Sambo, after Sambo and Quaco "had Quarrelled and

fought about a Negro woman they were acquainted with." According to the Gardners, some of Sambo's hogs had died mysteriously, giving them "Great reason to believe" Quaco poisoned the pigs "in revenge to Sambo."[59] Given Quaco's willingness to poison over a mate once, it is not a stretch to think he had done something similar in Suriname. Although his circumstances were unique in Boston, Quaco's case in Suriname, after being turned over by fellow slaves to the Court of Policy and Criminal Justice, would not have been unusual at all, as 36 percent of all cases heard by the court between 1730 and 1750 involved poisoning.[60] Quaco, then, hailed from a colony where slaves not only instituted their own system of justice but also commonly resorted to poisoning as a way of fulfilling their various agendas, something he took with him and later deployed in Boston.

After Quaco was accused by his fellow slaves and white authorities of poisoning in Suriname, the court condemned him to the traditional African punishment, being sold away as a slave, which is fitting because he was most likely born in Africa and not creole. His African day name suggests as much. More suggestive, however, is to compare his position with the relatively small number of native-born slaves residing in Suriname. Quaco remained enmeshed in a culture in which African norms, traditions, and supernatural forces—poisoning was considered a spiritual act—were part of everyday life. Creoles, however, lived at least part-time within the dominant European culture. *Bassias* and enslaved artisans tended to be creoles whom whites called on to protect the colony from the threat of maroons or recalcitrant slaves. Masters and white plantation managers commonly armed enslaved craftsmen and had them help track runaways.[61] Some creoles foreswore their African heritage altogether, fully embracing Dutch colonial society. Full-blooded Africans and mixed-race creoles understood the advantages of accommodating the planter class, especially females. As John Stedman observed, most "gentlemen . . . have a female slave (mostly a Creole) in their keeping, who preserves their linens clean and decent, dresses their victuals with skills, carefully attends them," and performed other wifely duties. "These girls . . . ," the mercenary continued, "naturally pride themselves in living with a European, whom they serve with as much tenderness, and to whom they are generally faithful, as if he were their lawful husband."[62] Stedman himself eventually fell in love with a mixed-race creole woman named Joanna (figure 2). Unlike the women Stedman documented or the plantation creoles who held positions of power, Quaco, by his African birth, was at a distinct disadvantage when

FIGURE 2 "Joanna," from John Gabriel Stedman, *Narrative of a Five Years'*
Expedition; against the Revolted Negroes of Surinam, in Guiana, on the Wild
Coast of South America; from the Year . . . (London, 1796)

attempting to navigate European society, which resulted in him in being sold out of the colony.

That said, however, there were plenty of opportunities for African-born slaves in Suriname to better their position, and the fact that Quaco did not suggests he was intransigent and unwilling to work with those who enslaved him. Although most slave artisans tended to be creole, a number of them were African, either bought as children from Africa and trained on the plantation or already knowing a trade when they arrived. Like their native-born counterparts, they would have participated in tracking down runaways. Surinamese authorities also deployed a free black militia to help fight against the maroons. These were African slaves who had been recruited and manumitted by the colony to fight. Stedman fought alongside a company of these so-called Rangers, generally having a good opinion of them, declaring, none "were accepted but such as were reputed to be of a very good character, and indeed they have since in my own presence given astonishingly proofs of their fidelity to the Europeans and their valor against the revolters."[63] Stedman, like on other occasions, took the time to sketch one of these free black militiamen (figure 3), noting that the soldier was "Coromantyn," or Coromantee, an ethnic group from the Gold Coast of Africa. Since Quaco was a slave, he was obviously not a militia member, and there is no evidence to suggest he was a craftsman. Instead, he resisted his enslavement using traditional African methods, not accommodating whites. To say this, however, is not, of course, to lionize Quaco. He was most likely a murderer, someone who resorted to poisoning to resolve disputes. Whether Quaco would have been a serial poisoner had he stayed in Africa we will never know. Nevertheless, it is obvious that the stress of enslavement, in both Suriname and Boston, made killing another human being through the use of poison a strategy that made sense to him.

Both Quaco and Mark are representatives of a particular class of slaves. They were either natives of or spent time in European New World colonies. Boston merchants and slave owners preferred these slaves, as they spoke English and were thought to be more docile and content with their enslavement. These slaves were anything but submissive, however. We have to look no further than the documents pertaining to these men to understand this. While there were certainly limits to the autonomy obtained by Mark and Quaco—both men eventually ran afoul of the law and were executed by the state—what we see instead of obedient bondsmen and bondswomen are

Figure 3. "A Coromantyn Free Negro, or Ranger, armed," from John Gabriel
Stedman, *Narrative of a Five Years' Expedition; against the Revolted Negroes
of Surinam, in Guiana, on the Wild Coast of South America; from the Year . . .*
(London, 1796)

slaves equipped to navigate enslavement. They had already been slaves in European colonies and understood how to exploit the customs and institutions of those societies to better their own lives. Despite their exposure to Euro-American norms, slaves like Mark and Quaco could also call on their African pasts, which connected them to other enslaved Bostonians, to form tight-knit communities and attempt to resist the degradation of enslavement.

Although New World creoles and Africans who spent a considerable amount of time in the Americas formed an important component of Boston's enslaved population, they also mingled with slaves who came directly from Africa. Some of these slaves had a short layover in Barbados, Jamaica, or other British West Indian islands, but it was not enough time to make a significant cultural impact. These "new negroes" came from all over Africa, even from as far away as Madagascar, but they mostly came from West Africa, especially Senegambia, Upper and Lower Guinea, and the Gold Coast.[64] Remarkably, slaves from this part of Africa would have been culturally equipped to decode Euro-American society in Boston. First, the region had considerable contact with Islam, a religion with some similarities to Protestantism. Likewise, traditional West African cultures, like European societies, also emphasized dependence as a way of binding society together and for children to learn the requisite skills for adulthood. Finally, and most importantly, West Africans were members of a society where slavery was firmly entrenched, a permeable institution where the objective was not freedom but integration into the enslaver's community.

To better understand the Africans who arrived in Boston, we need to examine the regions they predominantly came from. New England slave traders traded mostly with the northern part of West Africa. In 1760, the Boston merchant Timothy Fitch gave Peter Gwinn, the captain of Fitch's ship the *Phillis*, specific instructions for procuring slaves.[65] The captain was to sail to the West Coast of Africa, "Touching First at Senegall" and going to the slave "Facktory" there to sell some of his cargo—Fitch was hoping to double his returns—and buy slaves. Fitch hoped Gwinn could "Sell the whole of [his] Cargo thare to a Good Proffett & take Slaves & Cash & Cum Directly Home that would Shorten the Voyage Much," but this was "not Very Likely to be the Case." If he could not fill his hold with slaves and sell his cargo in Senegal, appropriately part of a region of Africa known as Senegambia,

Gwinn was to sail south to Sierra Leone, part of a region contemporaneously known as Upper Guinea. There, Fitch directed Gwinn, "make the best Trade you Can from place to place till you have disposed of all your Cargo & purcha[sed] your Compleat Cargo of Young Slaves which I sopose wil be about 70 or Eighty More or Less." If, and only if, the captain could still not procure enough slaves, he was to proceed to Portuguese-controlled central Africa. Otherwise, Gwinn was to stay away from that region and proceed to the Caribbean as quickly as possible to sell his human cargo.[66] Of the ten known slave-trade voyages Fitch commissioned, most of them captained by Gwinn, eight started in Senegal and worked their way south. The other two commenced on the Windward Coast, also known as Lower Guinea, and just south of Sierra Leone. One of these, in 1762, only started there to avoid Spanish privateers hanging around the Canary Islands.[67] As Fitch demonstrates, most New England slave traders preferred to trade for slaves on the northern edge of West Africa, and many Bostonians purchased slaves from that region.

Besides slave-trade merchants' letters, other documents indicate the African birthplaces of enslaved Bostonians. Slave-for-sale advertisements provide some of this information, but they need to be examined with one caveat. Before the 1740s, very few ads noted where in Africa a slave was from but instead noted only from where in the Americas the slave ship that brought them was arriving. Nevertheless, between 1704 and 1781, newspapers published for-sale notices for 128 African slaves and another 225 under the ambiguous moniker of "lately Arrived" or "New Arrival," suggesting a bondsman or bondswoman freshly arrived from Africa.[68] Of these, some were quite specific, listing the Guinea Coast, the center of the New England slave trade, as the place of origin. Robert Ball, a slave-ship captain, advertised a "Parcel of likely young Negro Boys and Girls" from the "Coast of Guinea" in 1744.[69] Others noted the exact region, such as one that promoted a "Number of Prime Slaves from the Windward Coast."[70] While none of the advertisements acknowledged the specific place or port of departure for slaves, it is obvious that most slaves originated from one swath of West Africa.

By examining the slave trade in this part of Africa, we can also discern the primary ethnic groups that the inhabitants of Senegambia captured and sold to English slave traders. Most were from the immediate vicinity, such as the Bambara people, located to the east in the middle Niger River valley. Two Bambara states in particular, Segu and Kaarta, were the targets of slave raids. Like other Senegambians, the Bambara were practicing Muslims and adhered to a strict caste system consisting of nobility, vassals, and slaves. In addition, local Wolof—a coastal Islamic group—kingdoms often preyed on their own subjects to sell to the Europeans. These included local non-Muslims subject to Wolof jurisdiction, such as the Sereer, but they also sold their own hereditary slaves.[71] While these groups were just a few of hundreds of language and ethnic groups that inhabited this region, the historian John Thornton has demonstrated that West Africa contained just two broad cultural groups, one in Upper Guinea inhabiting the region from modern Senegal to Liberia and the other in Lower Guinea, which stretched from the Ivory Coast to Cameroon.[72] These larger regions shared two common institutions: traditional forms of dependence and slavery. Before exploring those, however, we need to examine Islam, which predominated in Upper Guinea, and its influence on slavery in Boston.

Although relatively limited in other parts of West Africa, Islam had taken root in Senegambia, the northern part of Upper Guinea, as early as the tenth century. Prior to the arrival of Europeans, the Muslim Mali Empire controlled most of Upper Guinea. When the empire fell, its people, known as the Mandé, spread throughout Upper and Lower Guinea, carrying Islam with them. European travelers to West Africa noted the presence of Mandé, especially the Mandinka (Mandingo) subgroup. John Matthews, a lieutenant in the Royal Navy in Sierra Leone during the 1780s, encountered some Mandinkas, who boasted "Mahomet himself [could not] have wished for more zealous promoters of his law."[73] While surveying the Gambia River for the Royal African Company in the 1740s, the Englishman William Smith encountered African Muslims, who he noted were "strict in the external Observance of their Religious Ceremonies," although they drank alcohol in private.[74]

Both Matthews's and Smith's discussions suggest there was a high probability of New England slave traders purchasing Muslim slaves and selling them in Boston. The historian Michael Gomez argues that names may be indicative of Muslim slaves. The name "Sambo" for example, may come from the Pulaar word for "second son." Pulaar is the language of the Fulani, a predominantly Muslim West African ethnic group.[75] One name that was unmistakably Islamic was "Mahomet," the name of at least one Bostonian. In 1743, the Suffolk County Court of Common Pleas was set to hear the case *Pasmore v.*

Mahomet, but the defendant, Bashaw Mahomet, failed to appear—
hence we do not have many details about the case. There are a couple
pieces of evidence, however, that allow us to look into his life. The
court noted he was a mariner, possibly explaining his absence from
court. Moreover, Mahomet, the court readily acknowledged, was a
resident of Boston.[76] We know more about Roger Pasmore, the plain-
tiff, and he might provide a few more clues about Mahomet. Pasmore, like the African, was a sailor, and in 1740, he testified about a
smallpox outbreak onboard the ship he was traveling on from Bristol,
England, to Boston.[77] He was also charitable, housing foreign sailors
and one who was injured.[78] More important for his relationship with
Mahomet, however, was his religion. Pasmore married Mary Read in
July 1736, and the Reverend Elisha Callendar, the minister of Boston's
First Baptist Church, officiated.[79] While sailors were a quarrelsome lot
and would fight and sue one another over minor issues, religion may
have been a factor in whatever dispute arose between Pasmore and
Mahomet. Pasmore, a likely participant in George Whitefield's 1740
evangelical revival in Boston, would have been deeply offended had
Mahomet openly practiced his religion, especially if he behaved like
the Muslim slave in Pennsylvania who introduced himself by opening
with "Allah. Muhammad."[80] That alone was not enough for Pasmore
to file a civil suit, but Mahomet's faith was probably odious enough
that Pasmore may have opened litigation he otherwise might not have.
As the case of Mahomet and Pasmore suggests, Muslim Africans
resided in Boston, and their religion was almost certainly a driving
factor in shaping their lives and interactions.

The question remains how Islamic slaves would have adjusted to
their new setting.[81] Despite deep theological differences, Muslim slaves
would have shared some values with their Protestant masters. Both
religions emphasized education and literacy, and practitioners were
"people of the book." As we will later see, ministers in Massachusetts
exhorted slave owners to proselytize their slaves by teaching them to
read and write. The Puritan minister Cotton Mather even opened a
school for slaves to learn to read and published a catechism for slaves.[82]
Like Christians in Boston, West African Muslims attempted to bring
others into their faith. While observing the Mandinka people, Matthews recorded how they spread into surrounding villages, where
they would "erect schools, and teach their youth gratis, to read and
write Arabic." These schools proved to be part of a successful strategy
of increasing Islam's influence in the region, as in almost every village

where the Mandinka established a school, they also gained the "confidence of the chiefs and principal people" and even held positions of authority. One such position was what Matthews called a "*bookman*," most likely the village record keeper.[83] The tradition of reading and writing in Islam, like that in Reformed Protestantism, was a source of empowerment, one to be tapped in times of crisis. Islamic slaves in Boston would have had a special appreciation for literacy and possibly inspired them to learn to read and write English. It is no wonder that one of the first enslaved Bostonians—and African Americans—to publish, Phillis Wheatley, was born in one of the most heavily Islamized regions of sub-Saharan Africa, Senegambia.[84]

If Islam was relatively limited in the part of Africa under examination, almost all peoples living in West Africa lived in societies bound together by ties of dependence. As in early modern European cultures, dependency was ingrained in the very fabric of society. This dependence in both places was part of a child's transition to adulthood, in which they learned valuable lifelong skills, and was not a pejorative state of helplessness. Dependence in West Africa, however, differed from that in Europe and came from local notions of wealth and land tenure. In Europe, land and the ownership of it was the basis of all wealth. For Africans, a village or another corporate body such as a monarch controlled all of the land. The monarch or village elders would dole out land to those who were willing to cultivate it. But land in itself could not provide wealth; only the products of the land generated income. To produce those products, those who were given land needed labor. For that, they turned to unfree labor including, as we will see, slavery.[85] Dependency did not allow landholders to own labor like slavery did, but it did allow them to control it. One form of dependency was marriage, in which wives, as was customary in Africa, were under the control of their husbands, who also commanded their labor. In such a world, polygamy made sense, as more wives meant a larger labor pool to draw on. Not only did African women perform the traditionally female roles of rearing children and tending crops, but they were also involved in other forms of production. A monarch of the Kingdom of Whydah, an area slightly east of where enslaved Bostonians came from, allegedly had over one thousand wives, many of whom made cloth for export.[86]

Similar to the use of wifely labor, other forms of African dependency would have been familiar to Europeans. When the nearly seventy-year-old Venture Smith sat down to relate his life story to a

Connecticut schoolteacher in 1798, he vividly recalled his boyhood near the Gold Coast of West Africa. Smith, a nearly mythical figure in his own lifetime and one who continues to fascinate scholars to this day, was one of the few New England slaves who was born in Africa and lived long enough to find freedom in the United States. For all intents and purposes, before Smith was kidnapped, enslaved, and sent across the Atlantic, his experience in Africa was relatively conventional, including an event from his early childhood. When Smith was around five or six years old, his mother had a quarrel with his father over the latter's marriage to a third wife. While the couple later reconciled, she left her husband for a time, heading "eastward" with her three children, of whom Venture was the oldest. After traveling for a few days, Venture and his family encountered a "very rich farmer," and his mother left him with the farmer, "separate from all [his] relations and acquaintance." After his mother left, his "new guardian," who Venture often called his master, taught him the "business of tending sheep." Essentially, Smith's mother apprenticed him to a wealthy farmer, from whom he learned the basics of husbandry.[87]

Venture Smith, like so many English boys his age, entered into a dependent relationship to learn a skill. His master also fulfilled the obligations of those who took on apprentices, taking care of Smith. When two dogs attacked Smith and grievously wounded him, leaving him permanently scarred, his master intervened, "relieved" Smith of the attacks, carried the boy home, and nursed him back to health. Smith's apprenticeship would not have been as formalized as a European one, which was usually forged with a written contract, and his servitude was over when his "father sent" for him to "return home."[88] Dependence was an important cultural value that bound West Africans together, ensured a steady supply of labor, and taught children the requisite skills to become adults. When these Africans entered Boston, they would have found a world where dependence similarly regulated social and economic relations.

Despite the significance of dependency in African society, it did not allow African farmers and large landholders to command labor like slavery did. As such, slavery was in many ways the ultimate form of dependence, making slaves completely reliant on their masters for their survival and standing in the community, while ensuring that their owners had a steady supply of workers. Yet African conceptions of wealth as labor meant slaves were also the "most important avenue for private, reproducing wealth available to Africans." Unlike

Europeans, who bought land when looking to make money, Africans purchased slaves, which generated wealth and, as property, represented opportunities to increase one's own prosperity and could be passed on as part of an African man's patrimony.[89] As the only secure form of revenue-generating property, slavery became ingrained in the social fabric of most West African societies. Traditional law often condemned those who were convicted of major crimes to either death or slavery. As John Matthews observed, the "crimes of murder, poison, witchcraft, adultery, and theft, are always as capital, and have been punished with either death or slavery from time immemorial." In many instances, offenders had their death sentence commuted and were sold into slavery instead.[90] Even hardened criminals were potential workers in a society in which labor equaled wealth.

A large percentage of premodern Africa's population were slaves. While the numbers for the eighteenth century are next to impossible to discern, West Africa's use of slave labor was well recorded at later times. Some of the best statistics regarding this phenomenon are from Senegambia. In that region, late eighteenth-century travelers estimated that upward of three-quarters of the Mandinka states' population was enslaved. In a more recent study of the Fulbe people, anthropologists found that nearly 20 percent of the current population were the descendants of slaves. Finally, in 1906, French colonial authorities estimated that roughly 25 percent of all the people in French West Africa were slaves.[91] What these wildly different numbers suggest is that slavery existed nearly everywhere in Africa, but there were higher numbers of slaves in some places and next to none in others. This would have been a landscape of slavery similar to the one encountered in the Americas, with some regions, like the Caribbean, Brazil, and the American South, having large concentrations of slaves, and other places, like New England and the Rio de la Plata, having a smaller percentage of their population enslaved.

Despite demographic similarities with the Americas, slavery in Africa could be radically different from the institution in the Western Hemisphere. For starters, not all slaves were engaged in agriculture and artisanal enterprises. Many slaves served as bureaucrats and military officers, as they "were an ideal form of loyal workers, soldiers, and retainers," in multiethnic, composite states tenuously held together by conquest and alliance. Indeed, some African empires used entire armies and bureaucracies composed of slaves in order to check the power of the local nobility, often composed of the former autonomous rulers of the region.[92]

Even more familiar forms of servitude, such as agricultural slavery, were radically different in Africa. Given the nature of African land tenure, in which any person willing to cultivate a tract of land was given permission to use it, most slaves in husbandry tended to be like peasants or tenant farmers elsewhere. They worked either on their own or with other slaves on secluded plots of land, what Matthews called "slave towns," in many cases working one day a week for themselves and the rest for their masters.[93] As long as slaves recognized their dependent status, they were given quite a bit of leeway and elevated into trusted positions.

All of this is not to suggest that slavery was somehow more benign in Africa; but it was radically different, and those differences allowed African-born slaves to approach slavery in unique ways. African societies defined themselves through, as noted earlier, chains of dependence and kinship networks. Slaves lacked ties to the community and were outsiders, and their sole social function was to provide labor. In many societies, however, slaves had the opportunity to join their captors' society.[94] Matthews and Smith both observed this firsthand. Smith noted how African law allowed fathers to legitimate children born by his slave(s); if he did not, however, "his Heir" would look on these children as slaves, "and treat [them] as such."[95]

Matthews, for his part, saw differences between the various types of slavery. Those employed in agriculture were "held in no higher estimation than any other animal that contributes to its cultivation," while the "house slave" was "considered as a branch of the family." The latter also assumed their "master's name and calls him father." Yet Matthews could never understand the behavior of slaves in Africa because, unlike in the Americas, the enslaved did not seem to resist their enslavement. Instead, as slaves knew "no other situation" than slavery, they were "indifferent" as long as they received the "necessaries of life."[96] While Matthews, as an outsider, was not equipped to fully comprehend slavery in Africa, the traveler also missed the point of African slavery, in which even lowly agricultural slaves had certain rights, such as not being able to be sold except for serious offenses, and having considerable autonomy and mobility, ownership of at least some of their own time, the ability to marry, and even the opportunity to become trusted members of the community.[97] Under such conditions, the ultimate form of resistance was for slaves to overcome their outsider status and integrate themselves into their masters' society.

The Africans who arrived in Boston were primarily from West Africa, an area comprising Senegambia, Upper and Lower Guinea, and the Gold Coast. They brought with them a number of cultural traditions and institutions, the most important of which were Islam, dependence, and slavery. Each of these equipped Africans to navigate slavery in Boston, especially African concepts of slavery, in which slaves would attempt to incorporate themselves into their owners' community. When these Africans arrived in Boston, they did not bring with them notions of resistance built on abstract ideals such as emancipation but brought traditions rooted in their African past, in which assimilation was more important than freedom.

Enslaved Bostonians had diverse, polyglot, and cosmopolitan origins. Throughout the seventeenth century, New English colonists purchased a small number of slaves, whose descendants constituted a small number of enslaved Bostonians. While this first generation of slaves lived lives relatively similar to those of their eighteenth-century counterparts, even employing some of the same strategies that later slaves found successful, such as using the law, there were never more than two or three hundred in Boston. It was the town's integration into Atlantic slave-trade networks that caused a demographic explosion in the eighteenth century. Between 1700 and 1750, the enslaved population of Boston increased nearly eight times, and these new arrivals came from a variety of places in Africa and the Americas. American creoles were a significant component of this new population, either having been born in other parts of the Americas or having lived there for a considerable time. Two of these slaves, Mark, born in Barbados, and Quaco, from Suriname although most likely born in Africa, exemplify how familiarity with enslavement in the Americas helped them to carve out a space for themselves once they arrived in Boston. Like the American creoles, African slaves came from cultures deeply embedded in a tradition of slavery. Although they brought other experiences, such as Islam and dependence, with them, African notions of bondage largely shaped how they interacted with the institution of slavery and learned how to navigate it.

Origins mattered. Each of the groups explored earlier brought cultural baggage that equipped them to better navigate slavery in Boston. Boston's enslaved population was an Atlantic community, an assortment of peoples with diverse backgrounds and experiences. They channeled their collective pasts into creating a better life for themselves once they were in Boston. Understanding these histories is vital to understanding the lives of slaves. As almost all people of African descent in Boston had experienced slavery firsthand or came from societies where enslavement was part of the social fabric, we are forced to rethink what slavery and freedom meant to the enslaved. Freedom was amorphous, abstract, fickle, and ever changing, while slavery was deeply embedded in their own experience, something to be easily navigated and challenged. To say this is not to say that slaves wanted to be slaves but that these were people well equipped to deal with the pressures of slavery. As recent arrivals to a society undergoing its own cultural transformation, becoming a place where slavery, dependence, and unfreedom structured everyday life, the enslaved would need to muster all these skills to navigate Boston's peculiar brand of slavery.

2 /   Deference and Dependence

On 2 July 1755, the Middlesex County Court in Charlestown, Massachusetts, summoned the coroner and a jury to explore the suspicious death of John Codman, a prominent merchant and Charlestown native. Codman, the jury concluded, "Came to his death By Poison Procured by his negro man servant Mark."[1] Throughout July and early August, the court examined Codman's death and found that not only Mark but two of Codman's domestic slaves, Phillis and Phoebe, were also involved in the poisoning. After the investigation, the trial proceeded quickly, and the court found the three guilty of murdering Codman. Phoebe was sold out of the colony, while Mark and Phillis were sentenced to death. Their gruesome executions became something of local legend. Since the slaves were convicted of murder and petit treason—an old English legal statute that meted out severe punishments for servants who murdered their masters—Phillis was burned at the stake, the recommended punishment for female servants, while Mark was hung in front of the "greatest Number of Spectators ever known on such an Occasion."[2] That was not the end of Mark's punishment, however. His body was taken to Charlestown Common and "hanged in Chains, on a Gibbet erected there for that purpose," to serve as an example to any other slave contemplating the murder of his or her master.[3]

At first glance, the case of Mark, Phillis, and Phoebe was one that echoed the horrors of slavery everywhere: slaves, upset with their condition and wanting to be free, murdered their masters only to be gruesomely executed by the state. Upon further investigation, however, it appears that the murder of John Codman was anything but ordinary and certainly out of desperation. In the early 1750s, Mark had been living and working on his own in Boston with his wife and child, and Codman forced him to return to Charlestown after he repeatedly ran afoul of the law, while Mark's wife and child stayed in Boston. In 1752, a Suffolk County justice of the peace issued a warrant for Mark's arrest, which claimed he "had come to reside in Boston" and had been told repeatedly to leave but refused, and a Boston newspaper noted that Mark was "well known for his Roguery."[4] Phoebe had also been recalled in recent years from Boston, where she had been living with her husband, Quaco, but she never gave a specific reason. After the death of Codman's wife a few years prior to his murder, the slave owner had grown more distant from his family and abusive and domineering toward his bondsmen and bondswomen. To protest Codman's increasing heavy-handedness, the three slaves attempted to remove themselves from their master's presence and spend time with their families in Boston, but he forced them to stay in Charlestown. In an act of desperation, they burned down one of his outbuildings, hoping he would sell them to a new, more lenient and benevolent master. Only when this failed did the three slaves begin plotting Codman's demise. Instead of immediately murdering their master in the name of liberty, Mark, Phillis, and Phoebe engaged in subtler forms of resistance, ones that allowed slaves to negotiate the hierarchical, unfree world they inhabited.

The case of John Codman's slaves is important for understanding the world that enslaved Bostonians inhabited and how they adapted to that world. For white Bostonians, African slaves had a place in society that could not be altered. Changing one's status violated the social hierarchy and God's law. No matter how great the "Fondness of Freedom," in the words of Cotton Mather, it was intolerable for slaves to gain their liberty and freedom, which would threaten the very fabric and stability of colonial society.[5] Instead of violently and futilely challenging this paradigm, slaves like Mark, Phillis, and Phoebe carved out spaces for themselves and laid claim to a set of customary rights and privileges due unto them as a servile class, appropriating the hierarchical worldview of their masters to their own advantage. Only when this failed to produce the desired results did the slaves turn to violence and murder, making the case of Codman's slaves an exception, not the rule.

The form of resistance employed and the world inhabited by Boston's slaves was the product of a cultural transformation that had taken place in Boston beginning in the late seventeenth and early eighteenth centuries, just as hundreds of Africans began entering the town. The culture shifted from a hierarchical Puritan one, with an emphasis on equity, to a similarly hierarchical, divinely inspired, and monarchical culture obsessed with deference to one's social superiors and defined by ties of dependence. A parallel phenomenon happened throughout British North America, and Boston's experience both mirrored and differed from this bigger trend. As closer ties with Britain followed the Glorious Revolution, Bostonians began to adopt the monarchical culture of late Stuart and early Georgian England. These cultural ties led to an increase in trade and fostered an ever-growing economic rift between the merchants and gentlemen who had access to British goods and credit and everybody else, many of whom sank into a state of dependence. Increased commerce also brought a need for labor that could not be satisfied by local sources. Employers of all stripes turned to traditional forms of servitude in addition to African and Indian slaves to fill the void. The burgeoning Atlantic economy, however, challenged the monarchical order by enriching common people and making wealth, not birth, the basis for status. These social climbers, clinging to their newfound status, created and fostered legal categories of bondage and dependency for the laborers and others—unfreedom—to maintain this "natural" order.[6]

The cultural shift, economic stratification, and need for labor in Boston completely restructured society. Bostonians were now part of an artificially maintained order and a legally sanctioned continuum of unfreedom, with wealthy white men at the top and the classes dependent on their wealth, enterprise, charity, and patronage—women, children, artisans, servants, and the poor—below. At the bottom of this system were enslaved people of color, placed there because of their legal status as property and the color of their skin. Slaves fell into the chain of unfreedom in complicated ways and created their own adaptations to this Euro-American society.

Examining Boston through a lens of unfreedom forces us to reassess slavery in the town. While unique, slavery was nevertheless one of many forms of bondage and unfreedom in a complicated web of dependency and deferential relationships. Slaves were at the bottom of the hierarchy, but other factors such as gender, age, and wealth subordinated some people to others. In the end, for white Bostonians, slavery was a solution—and not always a preferred one—to the economic and cultural problems created by increased ties to Great Britain and imperial economic growth. By examining slavery as part of a complex and hierarchical continuum of unfreedom, we are able to eschew teleological, modern concepts of freedom. Moreover, it allows us to understand slavery not only as an exceptional denial of liberty in which skin color created a permanent and inheritable bondage but also as one of many ways to control labor in the American colonies.[7]

To better understand slaves, we need to understand the culture of their masters and the transformation that culture underwent in the late seventeenth and early eighteenth centuries. The Puritan settlers who came to New England based their society on a covenant with God. Families, dominated by the father—the patriarch of the household—provided the basic organizational structure. Servants, slaves, and other dependents were members of households and lived with New England families. Outside of man's subordination to God, the social hierarchy was expressed within the family, and male heads of household were effectively equal—aside from economic differences already present when the colonists arrived.[8] This system of patriarchy persisted in some places, especially in rural New England, until the mid-eighteenth century, but in Boston, a combination of factors caused a shift from a Puritan society to a monarchical one by the end of the seventeenth century. The key event that transformed Boston's economic and political culture was the Glorious Revolution. As the historian Brendan McConville notes, the revolution "forced local elites to accommodate an emerging imperial political culture, albeit one centered on a cult of Protestant Monarchy."[9] The complete Anglicization of Boston took some time and involved the adoption of not just monarchical culture but also imperial systems of measurement, time, and record keeping.[10] Closer ties with England also meant increased trade and incorporation into imperial networks. In 1700, for example, Boston had fifteen shipyards, supplied ships to other colonies and the mother country, and was the second-largest shipbuilding port in the empire.[11] By the first decades of the eighteenth century, most Bostonians would have agreed with the English jurist William Blackstone when he proclaimed that the king was "*pater-familias* of the nation."[12] The cultural shift in New England, then, could be seen as one of creating a new, imperial family in which the monarch was at the helm. Like the patriarchs of Boston's Puritan families, the king or queen structured relations within this newly enlarged household: the British Empire.

For Boston and colonials in other parts of British North America, the cultural shift manifested itself in a variety of ways. Most important was the establishment of a social hierarchy based on wealth. Considered by many people to be natural, this order was part of what the historian Gordon Wood calls a "great chain of existence that ordered the entire universe."[13] Arthur Browne, an Anglican clergyman who lived and preached in Boston and other New England seaports, noted in the middle of the eighteenth century that even in a place like Boston without an entrenched, titled aristocracy, one would see "proof how necessarily some difference of rank, some inequality must and ought to grow up in every society." Any attempt to overturn this system was "Ethiopian and ridiculous." Although Boston lacked an aristocracy, Browne reassured his audience that a superior order still emerged because of their "better property" and the fact that "more information" was available to them. In a sermon entitled "The Fall of the Mighty," Browne took his beliefs a step further and argued that the "supreme Governor of the World has been pleas'd to constitute a Difference in Families."[14] Browne laid out a divinely created natural hierarchy that, when not based on title, could be based on wealth. Even one who seeks wealth, according to one commentator, should not attempt to engage in trade "above his calling." Reaching too high could end in ruin because there "is no gracefulness in any motion that is not natural."[15] The belief in a rigid, natural social hierarchy came to dominate the cultural worldview of Bostonians and shaped interactions between the town's residents.

While Bostonians defined this order, they also became obsessed with their place in the structure, or what we call status. Most legal and official documents identified people by their occupation, their rank—gentleman or esquire—or, for women, their father or husband. Colonials viewed status as permanent and thus a useful means of legal identification. Basing one's social status on these criteria showed how society was structured. People of lower rank were expected to defer to those above them. As a young lawyer, John Adams quickly learned the importance of status, especially in the law courts. Lawyers had to be careful to "not call Esquires Labourers, and Labourers Esquires," and since society had established "Ranks and subordination . . . it [was] of Consequence that the Titles denoting those Ranks should not be confounded."[16] For an April 1761 case, for example, Adams tried to determine whether a Braintree man was a yeoman or a laborer.[17] This fixation on status, while not unique to the colonies, took on a special significance there. Lacking the institutional restraints and the large income disparity present in England, colonial elites used legal means of distinguishing themselves from their inferiors.[18] Using such methods had the effect of codifying the social hierarchy, although it remained much more permeable than that of Great Britain.

The problem with the acceptance of this order and legally establishing it was that by using the law, the hierarchy became unnatural and artificial. Economic forces, especially the rise of Atlantic trading networks, had the power to erode this order. Commoners could become wealthier than the nobility, behave like them, and intermarry with them. The deference that came with social position also began to break down. This was especially clear in the American colonies, where rustic provincials had few claims to title or status. John Hancock, who became the wealthiest man in British North America, was the son of a country minister.[19] It was Hancock and his recently enriched ilk, however, who believed most in "natural" hierarchy, despite knowing that the forces that enriched them threatened that very order. That is why they turned to an artificial, legally sanctioned system of deference, or categories of unfreedom. This legally prescribed dependency was a mechanism for maintaining an order that was quickly eroding.[20] The law, despite prolonging the system for a time, was ultimately an imperfect apparatus. Because of a long-standing English belief in equality before the law and the rise of natural rights discourse in the 1760s and 1770s, this system of unfreedom eventually generated more avenues for liberty than it destroyed.

Yet this order did not collapse completely until the American Revolution, and elites often used the ostentatious consumption of material goods to distinguish themselves. Gentlemen of the town bought all types of goods to display their wealth and superiority to the lower orders. They dressed in the finest silks, sat in custom furniture, and purchased exotic trade goods from all over the world. John Adams stood in awe when he visited a Boston merchant's house that contained "Turkey Carpets," a "Marble Table," and a "beautiful Chimney Clock," among other expensive items, and described them as the "most magnificent of any Thing" he had ever seen.[21] Craftsmen catered to the needs of the wealthy and appealed to their desire for prestige goods. One advertisement in the Boston News-Letter announced the arrival of a clockmaker and gave "Notice to all gentlemen" of the town that the artisan could repair old clocks or build them new ones.[22] The importance of consumption to status, however, was not lost on nonelites. Liberal credit from English financiers and local merchants allowed Bostonians of all classes to buy goods manufactured in both England and America.[23]

One of the best ways to display status was through the ownership of slaves. Being able to command the labor of enslaved Africans was a marker of status in the colonies that set gentlemen apart from others. One English traveler to New England noted that when the ladies of Boston "ride out to take the air," they always had a "negro servant to drive" their chaise, while the gentlemen rode on horseback "with their negroes to attend them." No matter if gentlemen were out for business or pleasure, their "black equipages" always accompanied them.[24] Like other luxury goods, slaves were marketed by sellers to the elite. One advertisement noted that the seller had a "choice Negro Man suitable for a Gentleman's Family."[25] Being able to fit into a family was an important prerequisite for a slave because many gentry brought slaves into their households and incorporated them into the patriarchal structure. John Hancock even paternalistically inquired after his slaves while away on business. He wrote his brother Ebenezer asking how his slave Molly was and whether his manservant Cato was behaving.[26] Hancock and other wealthy Bostonians had the ability to feed, house, and clothe their bondsmen and bondswomen—often in the latest London fashion—and the fact they owned another human being and that person's labor conveyed the wealth and power of Boston's leading gentlemen over not just their slaves but the rest of the town.

Artisans and other middling people, as with their consumption of other goods, often copied the gentry of Boston and bought slaves. Unlike their superiors, however, they did not use them as tokens of status but put them to work, and by midcentury, middling slave ownership matched that of the Boston elite. Probate inventories between 1700 and 1775 allow us to better understand slave ownership (see table 1). In this period, there were 601 estates that included slaves. Of those, 431 owners had an occupation listed or were widows. Of these men owning African slaves, 176, or 29.3 percent, were artisans and included trades such as blacksmith, gunsmith, housewright, shipwright, and one tobacconist. Another 179 were identified as mariners and merchants, occupations for which wealth could vary greatly. Other professionals included three ministers, three government officials, six physicians, three surgeons, and one schoolmaster. Eighteen

TABLE 1 Boston Slave Ownership by Occupation Listed in Probate
Inventories, 1700–1775

Occupation	Number	Percentage of total (rounded to nearest tenth of %)
Artisans	176	29.3
Merchants	96	16.0
Mariners	83	13.8
Widows	42	7.0
Gentlemen or esquires	18	3.0
Physicians	6	1.0
Ministers	3	0.5
Government officials	3	0.5
Surgeons	3	0.5
Schoolmaster	1	0.2
Unknown	171	28.4
Total	601	100.0

were either gentlemen or esquire, and it is safe to assume that many of
the unknown were also wealthier men. While each estate had a value
attached, the currency fluctuations and monetary uncertainty present in eighteenth-century Massachusetts make these numbers hard
to use.[27]

Occupation offers a better way of measuring these statistics than
wealth does. For many of the middling classes, slaves constituted a
large percentage of their estate. The mariner Newark Jackson died in
1744 with an estate valued at £2,433 Old Tenor, including three slaves.
One thousand pounds was real estate, meaning that his three slaves,
Warham, Siller, and Boston—worth £130, £80, and £130, respec-
tively—accounted for almost a quarter of his total movable property.[28]
Likewise, after accounting for real estate, Phillip Audebert Jr.'s slaves,
Prince and Guinea, constituted over 30 percent of the value of his
non-real-estate property.[29] In brief, slaves were important markers
of a family's fortune. As the imperial official Thomas Moore stated
in a letter to John Carteret, the future secretary of state, Bostonians
regarded "no labour [higher than] that of negroes," whom they and
their posterity "can keep as slaves for ever."[30] For the middling people

of eighteenth-century Boston, slave ownership ultimately created an important form of valuable, movable, fungible, and inheritable property.[31]

A series of laws promulgated from the late seventeenth century through the first half of the eighteenth demonstrates the ambiguous nature of slave ownership and how Boston officials integrated slaves into the monarchical order. On the one hand, African slaves were often considered servants under the law—colonials used the terms "slave" and "servant" interchangeably to describe their bondsmen and bondswomen—and like all servants, according to a 1741 law, had recourse against a cruel master. Local justices of the peace or the Court of the General Session of the Peace could fine the master five pounds for abusing a slave, and if the abuse was severe, the courts could free the slave.[32] In laws regulating crime, such as a 1698 law regarding the sale of stolen property, colonial lawmakers usually classified blacks with other "dissolute, lewd, and disorderly persons."[33] An act ordering tavern owners and victuallers not to sell liquor to "any apprentice, servant, or negro" indicates that blacks were to be regulated like other bound laborers. Nevertheless, slaves were different from other bound laborers in one key way: they were property. Masters had to pay an import duty on slaves, unlike white indentured servants, and the government enumerated slaves along with cattle, oxen, and other livestock in tax records.[34] Likewise, the selectmen of Boston singled out nonwhites—Indians, mulattos, and blacks—in a 1723 ordinance restricting their movement and prohibiting gatherings of people of color.[35] Even free blacks could not escape racial subordination. A 1707 act passed by the General Assembly required freedmen to work on public construction projects.[36] By triangulating cultural difference, class, and legal status, colonial and town officials used the law not only to situate Africans into an existing social order but also to place them at the bottom of that very order, where even legal freedom could not guarantee the autonomy enjoyed by free white men. That said, a man's place in society and legal status may have forced him to defer to his superiors, but deference did not create a culture of dependence. Rather, it took two other concurrent and intertwined processes, economic stratification and the need for labor, to create and define unfreedom in Boston.

Increased commerce with England and other parts of the Atlantic world beginning in the late seventeenth century enriched a small number of Bostonians and created, for the first time, significant economic stratification.

While these newfound trade connections created employment opportunities for laborers and artisans, most of the wealth went to the great merchants and owners of associated enterprises. According to the historian Gary Nash, in the fifteen-year period from 1684 to 1699, the wealthiest 5 percent of Bostonians controlled almost 26 percent of personal wealth, while in the decade before the American Revolution, they controlled over 46 percent of personal wealth, down from a high of almost 55 percent in the years 1726–1735.[37] Economic inequality was nothing new in Massachusetts, as Nash's seventeenth-century statistic demonstrates, but it took on special significance for two reasons. After the cultural transition discussed earlier, wealth mattered and became a marker of one's social class and place in society. Economic stratification was also key to accelerating the move toward slavery and coerced labor, as the market-based Atlantic economy also generated a level of poverty unknown in Boston before the eighteenth century. A new class of dependent poor emerged and helped to reinforce notions of hierarchy, deference, and status.

Given the boom-and-bust cycles of the Atlantic economy, devastating imperial wars, and agrarian problems, it is no surprise that the amount of poverty grew dramatically during the eighteenth century. Except for a few wealthy merchants, their sycophants, and royal officials, almost everyone, including skilled workers, lived on the precipice of poverty. This group, composed of "blacks, seamen, laborers, and poorer artisans who might dip below the minimum level of subsistence when unemployment increased," constituted between 30 and 40 percent of Bostonians by 1771.[38] Women also fell below the poverty line. Imperial wars and shipping disasters widowed a large number of Boston's women, both wealthy and poor, and by 1742, there were more than 1,200 widows in a population of 16,382.[39] For the more "respectable families," town leaders responded to female poverty by offering spinning classes and even opening a factory where the women could work and sell the cloth they made. While the factory required a large capital investment and "continuous and careful management," it was unable to compete with cloth manufacturers in Britain, and the Board of Trade in London looked down on such endeavors.[40] Such willingness to invest huge sums of money in a failed project and to raise the ire of imperial authorities indicated just how desperate Bostonians were for a solution to rampant and widespread poverty.

This class living at the edge of subsistence, called the "near poor" by the historian Allan Kulikoff, played an important role in defining the culture of dependence in eighteenth-century Boston.[41] Drawing on

English tradition, both the town and the Massachusetts General Court responded to increased poverty through the establishment of official institutions, notably the Overseers of the Poor. One of the techniques employed by the Overseers and other governing bodies to alleviate the worst effects of poverty was known as "binding out." Binding out involved placing the poor, usually children or widows but sometimes able-bodied men, into households in order to be cared for, gainfully employed, or taught a trade.[42] Not only does this solution illustrate the intersection of poverty and dependence, but it also demonstrates how immersed Bostonians were in the latter. Dependency was both a legally sanctioned status through which the state forced the poor to live with and serve their social betters and a solution believed to help the poor.[43]

If poverty and the culture of dependence were related, then slavery both influenced and was affected by this relationship. As noted earlier, the ownership of African slaves was a sign of a person's wealth and status. Slaves were also productive property who could work for wages and helped support their owners. Those same widows who worked in the cloth factory understood this. Many of them owned slaves or attempted to purchase slaves, as a white woman who could purchase a male slave, according to the historian Elaine Forman Crane, "could earn more by hiring him out than by working herself."[44] Widows, then, employed slave labor and were protective of their wealth-generating property. Mary Minott, a Boston widow, owned a slave woman, Parthenia, and was friendly with Parthenia's enslaved husband, Jeffs, a slave belonging to Elizabeth Allen, another Boston widow. Christopher Minot (his relation to Mary is unclear) accused Parthenia, Jeffs, and another slave, Richard, of stealing his seal-skin chest containing cash and "english coin."[45] Christopher made the charge on 13 December 1770, but Mary covered for Parthenia and her husband.[46] On that night, she claimed her slave went to bed around eight or nine p.m. after a "hard day at work" and "complaining she was not well." About an hour later, Jeffs came over to Mary's home and went into Parthenia's room. Mary did not go to bed until one or two in the morning and had no reason to believe Parthenia had left to burgle Minot. Likewise, she declared that she "never knew [Parthenia] guilty of any stealing."[47] Whether Parthenia robbed Christopher Minot or not, it is clear that Mary Minott defended her slave and that it was Jeffs, not Parthenia, who was later convicted.[48] Mary's deposition indicates she had a friendly relationship with her bondswoman. Moreover, had Parthenia, a hard worker according to Mary, been found guilty of stealing, Mary would have been deprived of her labor, as the slaves allegedly stole enough property to warrant jail time, if not capital punishment. Slaves like Parthenia were an important form of capital for widows living on the precipice of poverty and investments to be protected at all costs.

Poverty and the culture of dependence also affected how slaves became free and what life was like for free blacks. In 1703, the colony passed "An Act Relating to Mulatto and Negro Slaves," which required masters to post a fifty-pound security bond in order to prevent freed slaves from becoming a burden on an already overwhelmed poor-relief system.[49] Given the limited amount of specie and money in the colonies, it would have been hard for even the wealthiest masters to pay that amount to the state. Nevertheless, some slaves did become free. The majority of free blacks in Boston faced a life of racial degradation, lacked basic political freedoms, were coerced into laboring on public works projects, and faced other social limitations, such as a prohibition on carrying canes while walking about town.[50] Many free blacks were impoverished and part of the transient and dependent poor who traveled throughout eastern Massachusetts looking for work. Robert Love, a Boston constable, kept a diary of all the men, women, and families he "warned out" of Boston for the years 1765–1766. Of the seven people of African descent he ordered to leave, five were free.[51] Of the seventy-four blacks and mulattos warned out of Boston between 1745 and 1770, less than half were slaves warned out alongside their owners, while freed men and women made up a clear majority.[52] Boston's free black population did not fare much better than did the transients from surrounding towns. King's Chapel in Boston regularly distributed poor aid to congregants. Its rolls were full of free blacks who received money, including "Negroman Primus," who received more than sixteen pounds of aid from 1753 to 1756.[53] Likewise, Christ Church (Old North Church) gave aid to the Humphreys, a family of free black parishioners.[54]

The experience of the Humphreys and Primus could not have been more different from that of Cesar Lyndon. Lyndon was a slave belonging to the Newport, Rhode Island, merchant and future governor Josias Lyndon. Cesar's diary, the only slave diary known to exist, documented his life working as Josias's clerk and secretary.[55] Lyndon gave Cesar quite a bit of autonomy and control over his day-to-day life—not to mention access to the merchant's vast financial resources. Cesar was, in the words of one historian, "not reluctant to spend money either unnecessarily or extravagantly." Since Cesar's master provided for all of his living expenses, he used the profits generated from his many business endeavors, such as renting garden plots to fellow blacks, to buy silk gowns for his wife and luxurious silver buckles to adorn the clothing he received from his master. He engaged in Atlantic commerce and bartered for china teacups and a looking glass from Suriname. His generosity was something of legend, and he hosted a picnic in the 1770s for a number of his enslaved friends. In a hierarchical society where one's status was on public display, Lyndon successfully "asserted his ability to play the part of gentility."[56] Of course, Lyndon was an exceptional figure. Not all slaves had masters with vast reserves of financial capital or possessed the skills, knowledge, or autonomy to become successful entrepreneurs. Cesar's slave status, however, never seemed to be an impediment. He had to navigate a world in which he was technically chattel, but compared to many free blacks, Lyndon possessed a much greater degree of independence, despite his legal enslavement. Becoming free, then, was not necessarily an avenue for blacks to become independent. In many ways, free people of color were more constricted after "freedom," forced to rely on public and private poor relief and unable to escape dependence.[57] Likewise, not all slaves were confined to the bottom of the hierarchy, and socioeconomic diversity among people of African descent challenges our understanding of black Boston's social order and solidarity.

A final way that poverty and slavery intersected in colonial Boston was in the creation of an underground economy in which slaves stole goods from their masters and sold or gave them to people on the margins of colonial society, namely, free blacks and widows. Sarah, a slave belonging to the merchant John Powell, and Peter Saveton, a free black laborer, stole a pair of "Pattoons," a blanket, a "parcel of Wearing linen," six bottles of wine, shirts, and other various goods amounting to over five pounds from Powell on 20 December 1721.[58] The Court of the General Sessions of the Peace later found Exeter Turner, a free black porter, and his wife, Luce, guilty of receiving goods from Sarah and Saveton.[59] Likewise, the free black porter John Cuffy and his wife, Jane, received—most likely bought—a stolen rug from Primus, a slave of the upholsterer William Downes. Although the court acquitted Cuffy, his wife, Jane, received a twenty-pound fine.[60] It is important to note that slaves were not Robin Hoods stealing from the rich to give to the poor, because enslaved thieves often targeted marginalized people, as when Bristol and Hector stole a few "large fowles" from the widow Frances Banister, only to allegedly give them to Hester

Holt, another Boston widow.[61] Rather than serving a charitable purpose, Boston's slaves were able to take advantage of the underground economy, proximity to their masters' possessions, and the knowledge gained by working in the town's streets in order to profit—more than just economically—from theft.

We can see this process clearly in the case of Robbin, a slave belonging to John Jenkins and accused of robbing the merchant Samuel Greenwood. On 26 August 1734, Robbin allegedly broke into Greenwood's home "in the middle of the night" while the Greenwood family slept. The merchant claimed that Robbin stole more than eight pounds worth of bills of credit (paper money issued by the colonies) and "some other papers." Robbin had a history of theft; the General Sessions court had convicted him of stealing handkerchiefs from the widow Lettice Badgood in 1733. After being accused of robbing Greenwood, Robbin could not post bond and sat in jail until the next meeting of circuit court in February 1735. While he waited in jail, the court investigated the matter, summoned witnesses, and took a number of depositions. These documents give us insight into the role enslaved people played in the underground economy and how they benefited from it.[62]

The morning after being robbed, Samuel Greenwood asked his brother Joseph and his friend Joseph Snelling to help him find the thief. After Samuel interrogated his own slave, he traveled to a number of different shops in Boston and spoke with the proprietors, all of whom later testified. The shop owner Mary Mobberly claimed that a "Negroman came by the shop [to pick up] a pair of women's black shoes with red heels, two necklaces and a snuff box, which he had bought in the morning" from Mobberly's mother. Mobberly's mother noticed he was wearing new clothing, including a pair of blue stockings, which he informed Mobberly he bought "near the Mill Bridge." He then offered to buy a pair of garters with a New London Society bill of credit, but Mobberly refused to accept his payment. The storekeeper also informed authorities that her mother told Greenwood and his posse that she sold items to a "negro man she did not know" who paid the mother with a four-shilling bill that Greenwood later recognized as his own. The crew Greenwood assembled next stopped at the shop of Abigail Barker. Barker also noted that a black man had purchased a number of goods, including those that Mobberly questioned the slave about. She also testified that the African claimed to be a free black from Newbury and had a "number of large bills" on his person. Greenwood then returned to Mobberly's shop and met her mother,

Mary Howard, whose testimony matched that of her daughter, except she stated the man "Inform'd [her] he was going to Mistick," modern-day Medford, Massachusetts.

The shopping spree of this mysterious "negroman"—most likely Robbin—is telling about how the underground economy functioned. Once someone stole goods or money, he or she quickly sold the goods or spent the money at local shops, usually those run by women on the margins of colonial economy. Abigail Barker, for example, struggled constantly to make a living as a tailor and shop owner, especially because males in the same profession would usually make nearly twice as much for the same work.[63] These women, desperate for cash or goods to resell, were in a position to bargain for stolen goods or accept any cash on hand. Proprietors had to remain vigilant, as Mobberly's refusal of the New London note demonstrates, but her mother's ready acceptance of Greenwood's bill is illustrative that the allure of hard cash was sometimes too much to resist. The slave clearly understood this situation, because the first places he looked after being robbed were shops owned by these women.

It remains to be seen, however, why and how slaves participated in the underground economy, especially given the risk of fines, beatings, or even death if caught.[64] This reasoning can be extrapolated from the second half of Greenwood's investigation, when he traveled to Medford to find Robbin. Most of these details come from the depositions of Greenwood's companions, his brother Joseph and his friend Joseph Snelling. By the time the men arrived in Medford, they must have realized that they were looking for Robbin, because they inquired about him at the local tavern. The barkeep told the men that he was staying "at a Negro house" in town and that Robbin had purchased a pint and a half of rum. Greenwood immediately sent two men to find Robbin and bring him to the tavern. Once Robbin arrived, Greenwood's party searched him and "found nothing materiall about him to [their] purpose." Snelling then summoned a local justice of the peace, Simon Tufts, and they all traveled to the "Negro House," which belonged to Jack Hammon, a free black man.

While Snelling and Samuel Greenwood waited for Robbin to arrive at the Mistick tavern, Joseph Greenwood remained in Boston looking for clues. He spoke with a shoemaker's servant—it is not clear if he was a slave, apprentice, or indentured servant—who stated that Robbin had bought a pair of shoes and paid with a twenty-shilling bill of credit. But the cobbler could not make change, so Robbin "went out to change it" and returned to buy the shoes. The servant added that Robbin had on his person "another pair of small men's Shoes; that he said were for a lad at Mistick," and noted, like others, how Robbin carried a number of bills with him. After learning this information, Joseph Greenwood joined the others at the Medford tavern to interrogate Robbin and departed with Justice Tufts.

When the party arrived at Hammon's house, Jack's wife told the men that Robbin had been there and given a pair of women's shoes and a handkerchief to a black woman who "lived with one Mr. Whitmore" in Medford. The men then traveled to Whitmore's residence, where they met Margaret Anthony, a free black woman. At first, she was dismissive of the gentlemen, but Snelling informed her that Robbin was "suppos'd to have been guilty of Theft, and shee would be brought into Trouble if she Concealed" the items. Frightened, Anthony took Snelling and the others to a chest containing the handkerchiefs, blue stockings, and other goods that Robbin allegedly had bought with the stolen money. After four small bills fell out of the top of the chest, Anthony confessed that Robbin had given her the items that morning. Whitmore's daughter also told Joseph Greenwood that she saw Robbin give the goods to Anthony.

Greenwood and his companions, satisfied with what they had found, continued their investigation. The next stop was the home of a Mr. Patton, Robbin's employer. There they met a boy whom Joseph Greenwood later confirmed to be Robbin's son. On the "feet of [the] Lad," the men found a pair of brand-new shoes, and the boy, surrounded by three powerful white men, claimed that Robbin had given him the shoes that morning. Emblazoned on the shoes was "Mr. Greenwood," and Joseph Greenwood claimed these were the shoes that the shoemaker's servant claimed he saw Robbin carrying. The men wrapped up their investigation by inquiring at another shop and with Robbin's former employer, a shipyard owner. Once again, the group found incriminating evidence and thought they had amassed enough to convict Robbin of robbing Samuel Greenwood. They took Robbin to Boston and handed him over to colonial authorities hoping for a quick conviction.

But, alas, they were wrong. When the case went to trial in late winter 1735, the court found Robbin not guilty. The story of the theft had spread as far as Philadelphia, where the *American Weekly Mercury* reported that Robbin, despite being "thought by all" as guilty, was acquitted "for want of legal Evidence."[65] Despite all of the detective work conducted by Greenwood and his compatriots and all the damning evidence against Robbin, none of the shopkeepers ever identified him by name, and the two people who did, Margaret Anthony and Robbin's son, did so out of fear. Moreover, by the time of the trial, Robbin had already spent nearly six months in jail, meaning that the court may have considered that punishment enough.

Even though Robbin was not convicted for robbing Greenwood, the not-guilty verdict resulted only from a lack of evidence, allowing him to avoid sentencing. Given his prior conviction for theft, we know that Robbin had a reputation, according to one Boston newspaper, as a "Negro Fellow of ill Fame" and a capable and cunning thief. The editor of the newspaper was almost certain that Robbin would "Swing" for his crimes but did express concern that "some People are full of Fears lest the Affair should be huddled up, and so the Fellow escape Justice." If this happened, the editor feared that Robbin's actions "would greatly encourage others in the like ill practices."[66] And he was right. Not even a year after being found not guilty, Robbin, "an old Offender" who "should have been hanged last Winter . . . or sent out of the Country," had his "Master . . . been as good as his Word," stole a shirt. Justice Savage convicted Robbin of theft and sentenced him to be whipped ten times. Since the notorious thief still resided in Boston, his whipping would at least "make a Holiday for abundance of People."[67]

Why, then, would Robbin commit such crimes? The most obvious reason is that theft and participation in the underground economy allowed Robbin to provide for his family. While we cannot establish a romantic relationship between Margaret Anthony and Robbin, he did give his son a new pair of shoes. We know from a deposition by Whitmore's daughter Mary that Robbin had been a sailor, a story confirmed to her by another slave.[68] Robbin would have made a decent salary as a sailor, but much of it would have gone to his master. Perhaps the only way he could provide shoes for his son was by stealing. Likewise, the types of goods he gave to Anthony were not saleable goods but gifts. He used the money stolen from Greenwood not to buy merchandise that could be resold for a profit but for goods a woman would need to be respectable—silk ribbons, handkerchiefs, stockings, garters, and the like. The fact that Robbin gave her these things indicates some sort of relationship, if not an attempt at courtship. Robbin's black-market activities, then, were a way of combating poverty and establishing relationships. His behavior conforms to the patterns established earlier. He pilfered the money only to spend it on other marginal people, in this case, his enslaved son and a free black woman, while also using his ability to acquire, disperse, and use these luxury goods to improve his own social standing.

Slaves served a role in pilfering the goods or money that fueled the underground economy. One letter to the editor of the *Weekly Rehearsal* noted how slaves were "much addicted" to stealing and that their masters were wont to punish them and even "screen[ed] them from the Hands of Justice."[69] As frustrated as this letter writer was, it was not an innate proclivity to crime and unwillingness to punish that drove theft perpetrated by slaves. Rather, it is indicative of a desire to resist the social degradation of slavery and poverty in colonial Boston. Luxury goods, even ones purchased with stolen money, helped to improved one's status. Although illicit economic activities aided marginal Bostonians in their resistance to the poverty and unfreedom generated by the economic stratification, it was ultimately futile. There was never any real change, courts thoroughly and effectively chastised thieves and the recipients of stolen goods, and participation in the black market only reinforced negative stereotypes of the lower classes, especially the bound laborers working in the town's burgeoning economy.

In the early spring of 1723, a group of slaves burned buildings across Boston, leading the imperial official Thomas Moore to note how "masters will rather be burnt in their beds by [their slaves] than suffer English servants to come hither to work."[70] While Moore undoubtedly exaggerated Bostonians' love of slavery, he did understand their desire for bound labor or labor of any type, and this need created legal dependence. The number of laborers required fluctuated with Atlantic economic cycles, but increased trade activity in the eighteenth century demanded a larger, more specialized, and more dynamic workforce. Manual labor in premodern societies was, according to Gordon Wood, considered problematic, however, "associated with toil and trouble," and most people, or so the "better sort" believed, "would not work if they did not have to."[71] This alleged difficulty led to a legal code that "subjected manual wage workers, not merely indentured servants, to legal compulsion in fulfilling their labor agreements."[72] Laborers at the bottom of the colonial hierarchy, like African slaves, Native American servants, and non-English servants, were even easier to legally coerce into working. In New England, many of these bound laborers were young and born in the Americas. They accepted servitude as part of a passage to adulthood, while simultaneously possessing limited rights and recourse against an oppressive labor regime. As Moore noted, however, very few European indentured servants arrived in Boston, and most imported laborers were African slaves.[73] The labor force of the town contained myriad forms of bound labor, all with varying rights and liberties within the system. Boston's labor demands, then, created a continuum of unfreedom that literally bound workers to employers, and slaves and servants to masters.

Despite the increase in nonwhite bound labor in the early eighteenth century, some Bostonians realized there were long-term negative consequences. Samuel Sewall's condemnation of slavery, *The Selling of Joseph*, acknowledged this preference. "All thing[s] considered," Sewall began, "it would conduce more to the Welfare of the Province, to have White Servants for a Term of Years, than to have Slaves for Life." Sewall understood that Boston needed labor but expressed his concern about the difference between white servants and African slaves: "[Slaves] can never embody with us, and grow up into orderly Families, to the Peopling of the Land: but still remain in our Body Politick as a kind of extra-vasat Blood."[74] A stable, cohesive, and ultimately white society concerned Sewall more than slavery did. While Sewall offered many critiques of African slavery, one of his main concerns was not about the type of labor—he did advocate bound labor after all—but the kind of laborer and the length of servitude.

It was only with the rise of a free-labor ideology among white, working-class Bostonians in the mid-eighteenth century that race and status became popular issues. John Adams, writing after the American Revolution in response to a number of questions about slavery in Massachusetts, believed it was the "multiplication of labouring white people" that stopped wealthier Bostonians from hiring African slaves and taking away white workers' jobs. While Adams was not known to be a man of the people, he claimed that his class-laden argument was popular among the "common people," who "would not suffer the labour, by which alone they could obtain a subsistence, to be done by slaves." He concluded with an ominous prediction that had it continued to be the case that gentlemen were allowed to own slaves, "the common white people would have put the negroes to death, and their masters, too, perhaps."[75] Working-class resentment toward slavery—most likely exacerbated by the unstable economic situation in eighteenth-century Boston—enforced a racialized free-labor regime, but not until the late colonial and revolutionary era.

The antislavery and anti-African ideologies conveyed by Sewall and described by Adams were ultimately ideas adopted slowly, while slaves and other unfree laborers multiplied prodigiously in Boston. In fact, the largest number of slaves entered Massachusetts after Sewall published his tract, despite laws passed with Sewall's support to prevent their entrance and bring in white indentured servants. In 1705, for example, a clause attached to an act preventing interracial liaisons forced anyone who imported a slave to register the slave with the impost office and post a four-pound bond.[76] Slave owners flagrantly ignored the law, forcing the provincial legislature to reissue it several times throughout the colonial period. Likewise, the government passed "An Act to Encourage the Importation of White Servants" in 1709, to no avail.[77] Moore, characteristically exaggerating, noted how Bostonians would force ship captains carrying white servants "to carry them back again upon their own charge, or else they must not trade in this country."[78] Free-labor ideology was just as ineffective at deterring bound labor as statutory law was. Runaway-slave and servant advertisements appeared throughout the 1770s and 1780s.[79] These failures illustrate that in a hierarchical society where the possession of bound labor was demonstrative of one's status and there was a need for any labor, free or unfree, ideology lost to cultural norms, pragmatism, and cold, calculated economic decisions.

Examining runaway advertisements in the local press provides a better understanding of the composition of bound labor in eighteenth-century Boston.[80] Between the years 1700 and 1750, over ninety unique, Boston-based runaways appeared in the town's newspapers.[81] While the sample size is relatively small and the data subjective because not all servants ran away, it reveals some trends about the bound workforce in Boston. Over 40 percent of the runaways, or thirty-eight, were African slaves, confirming that they represented one of the dominant forms of unfree labor in the eighteenth century. More surprisingly, the second-most-common type of runaways were Irish indentured servants, who made up about 26 percent of the sample. From the mid-seventeenth to early eighteenth centuries, the English shipped large numbers of Irish to the West Indies to labor in the sugarcane fields. Given New England's close trading relationship with the Caribbean, it is not surprising that many indentured servants arrived in Boston.[82] The third-most-common type of runaway laborers were Indian servants, who came from both local tribes and from the Carolinas. The rest of the servants were either English, from other parts of the British Isles, French, or unknown (see table 2). Despite the preponderance of free labor, then, Boston's workforce contained a large and ethnically diverse group of unfree laborers.

While most working Bostonians were technically free, there were many who were not and, as demonstrated earlier, were bound in a

TABLE 2 Runaway Servant Advertisements in Boston, 1700–1750

Ethnicity	Number	Percentage of total (rounded to nearest %)
African	38	41
Irish	24	26
Native American	8	9
English	6	7
Other British (Scottish, Welsh)	4	4
French	2	2
Mulatto	1	1
Unknown	9	10
Total	92	100

number of ways. Traditional forms of English servitude existed in Boston. Apprenticeship for children and adolescents, boys and girls, was quite common. There were two types of apprenticeship, according to the historian Carl Bridenbaugh: voluntary and compulsory.[83] Besides teaching adolescents a trade or important life skills, apprenticeship was a way of maintaining the status quo and reaffirming hierarchy and deference. This latter purpose is important for understanding compulsory apprenticeship. Also known as pauper apprenticeship, this form of indenture allowed the state, usually town officials, to bind out poor children to masters, who would help these children, as the historian Ruth Wallis Herndon notes, "take up their place in society." The forced removal of these poor children from their homes and into apprenticeship was common throughout the American colonies and England. It was particularly common in New England because potential masters and government officials worked together to ensure the "proper place of poor children in a hierarchically organized society."[84] Pauper apprenticeship, then, was not only a vital labor source but a way to integrate the poor into monarchical society. It was less of a solution to poverty than a way of ensuring order and stability in a volatile economic climate.

Colonial law bound people of color, just like the poor, in a variety of ways to harness their labor and enforce the status quo. From the beginning of settlement in the 1630s, New Englanders bought and sold Indian slaves and servants.[85] Although Indian slavery was eventually outlawed in the late seventeenth century, the historian Margaret Newall notes these laws were often "short-lived and unenforceable," and before 1700, "Native American servitude was the dominant form of nonwhite labor." By the eighteenth century, however, Indian servitude had become the second-most-common form of unfree, nonwhite labor after African slavery and transformed into an entirely different institution. Large numbers of nonnative Indians from northern New England, the Carolinas, and Spanish Florida entered New England port cities as part of the growing pool of bound labor. Colonial officials designed new ways to regulate these Indians, often lumping them with African slaves in laws regulating slave behavior. Likewise, for the native Indians remaining in southern New England after King Phillip's War, judges and other magistrates sentenced them to servitude for minor criminal offenses. Many of these newly imported or newly indentured Indians mostly served in New England's urban centers, namely, Boston.[86] Once there, these slaves became enmeshed in the same networks as bound African laborers. Titus, an Indian servant belonging to the Charlestown merchant John Hay, "formed a Correspondence" with James, an Indian servant living in Boston, and another James, a black slave belonging to John Fisher in Dedham. These three men created a theft ring that stole eighteen pounds worth of bills of credit and "one half pound of the best Virginia Tobacco" from Indian James's master, Richard Draper.[87] Like African slaves, Indian slaves participated in the underground economy and interacted with other unfree and marginal peoples.

Nonetheless, the most important source of bound, nonwhite labor in eighteenth-century Boston was African slavery. Enslaved blacks were readily available given the town's connections to the Atlantic market and its merchants' participation in the transatlantic slave trade. This availability meant that the ideological justifications for African slavery echoed those of other British slaveholders throughout the empire.[88] The clearest illustration of these justifications for slavery came from John Saffin, in his reply to Samuel Sewall's *Selling of Joseph*. In this tract, which refuted Sewall point by point, Saffin used the Bible to justify slavery. Sewall may have noted God's prohibition on "man Stealing" in Leviticus, but Saffin argued that the "*Israelites* were forbidden (ordinarily) to make Bond men and Women of their own Nation, but of Strangers they might." Africans, as strangers, were eligible for enslavement. Likewise, once again echoing early racial thought, Saffin justified the enslavement of Africans because they were the "seed of *Cham* [Ham] or *Canaan*." Slavery was actually good for blacks, Saffin reasoned, because Europeans brought them "out of their own Heathenish Country, where they may have the Knowledge of the True God, be Converted and Eternally saved." Saffin continued listing these common eighteenth-century justifications for slavery and even agreed with Sewall that all men, no matter what their race, were descendants of Adam, but their common humanity did not rule out slavery.[89]

More importantly, however, and perhaps unique to New England, Saffin ended his tract by successfully integrating the hierarchies of race and class. He began by acknowledging how "we are to love, honour and respect all men according to the gift of God that is in them." Nevertheless, it would be a "violation of common prudence, and a breach of good manners, to treat a Prince like a Peasant," and a gentleman "would deem himself much neglected, if we would show him no more Defference than to an ordinary Porter." Saffin agreed with Sewall that all human beings were God's children, but that did not mean they should violate the natural, divinely inspired hierarchy to enforce this spiritual equality. Even more problematic were the slaves themselves. If one could not violate the social order for other Christians, then Bostonians should be careful not to "tender Pagan Negroes with all love, kindness, and equal respect as to the best of men."[90]

Saffin's warning illustrates the intersection of class and race in colonial Boston. He acknowledged that all Christians were equal as God's creation and Adam's descendants and also part of a social order inspired by that same God. White Bostonians regarded Africans, as non-Christians and foreign strangers, as culturally inferior, placing them at the very bottom of Boston's social order. Black slaves, then, unlike pauper apprentices, were never really meant to be incorporated into the colonial body politic. Rather, they were always outside and thus at the bottom of an oppressive hierarchy designed to harness unfree labor. Europeans could not conceive of a life outside of labor for Africans. Saffin's retort to Sewall's insistence that Bostonians free their slaves clearly sums up this perspective, as it was "to be feared that those Negroes that are free, if there be not some strict curse taken with them by Authority, they will be a plague to this Country."[91]

Cultural transformation, economic stratification, and a need for labor may have forged the chain of unfreedom that defined relations and the social order in eighteenth-century Boston, but it remains to be seen what slaves thought of, and how they lived in, this world of deference and dependence. Both of these issues can be understood by returning to the case of Mark and Phillis, the two slaves from Charlestown, Massachusetts, who were convicted and executed for murdering their master, John Codman. The high-profile nature of the case and the large number of people involved means that there is a large documentary record, including testimony and depositions, where we can hear the slaves' voices and see how they understood the world they inhabited. Issues that concerned white colonists, such as status and reputation, also concerned their African counterparts, but in different ways. More importantly, however, slaves adopted the monarchical value system and interpreted it as giving slaves a set of customary rights and privileges, including the right to marry and have a family, live where they pleased, and labor on their own terms, while also being protected from abuse. Masters sometimes tried to keep slaves outside the hierarchy and deny them the customary privileges of living in an Anglo-American society, but slaves insisted they were indeed part of that class system.

The legal proceedings provide interesting insight into how Boston's slaves adapted to monarchical culture. Most importantly, the enslaved appropriated a set of rights to benefit themselves, their families, and their communities. Codman's murder reveals some of these liberties that slaves viewed as traditional and as coming with their place in the natural order. Never once throughout the trial did Mark, Phillis, or any of the other slaves mention their desire for freedom as a motive for killing Codman. Rather, Mark and Phillis both claimed they were unhappy with Codman as a master and desired a new one. Phillis acknowledged this when confessing to burning down Codman's "Workhouse." Mark, she related, believed that Codman would have to sell his slaves as punishment for destroying his property.[92] Since that measure failed and Codman became much more draconian after it happened, his slaves resorted to murder not to be freed but to "have another master."[93]

This desire to have another, perhaps better, master suggests that slaves believed masters had certain duties to their chattel, and enslaved people had rights, ones that Codman—at least as Mark, Phillis, and Phoebe understood them—neglected. Before moving forward with an exploration of these rights and duties, however, it is important to remember that this section concerns how slaves conceived of rights and duties, not how these actually worked in law. Indeed, if we follow the common law, some of Codman's actions were justifiable. As Justice Oliver Wendell Holmes later explained in his 1881 *The Common Law*, "duties are logically antecedent to legal rights." Following this legal formulation, the relationship between Codman and his slaves, especially Mark, would have functioned something like this: Codman had a public duty to control and closely monitor his slaves, ensuring they did not endanger the public good, and that duty superseded any of his slaves' alleged rights.[94]

Common law aside, Codman's slaves felt that their master neglected a number of rights and duties. These fall into four broad categories: the ability for them to labor on their own terms, the ability to live away from their master's home, the right to maintain a family, and protection from abuse. The first two, the right to labor and be mobile, seem to have been Mark's chief complaints. In his confession, Mark noted how Codman had been nice enough to let him live in Boston with his wife, but, as Phillis's interrogation reveals, he was quite upset with Codman for making him move back to Charlestown.[95] As Mark's run-ins with Boston authorities demonstrate, however, Codman could not risk allowing Mark to remain in Boston, or he might be held responsible for his slave's actions. Nevertheless, Mark felt bitter about the whole ordeal, and the "Reason he gave" Phoebe and Phillis for burning Codman's outbuilding was that "he wanted to get to Boston." It also seems that someone had offered to purchase Mark for £400, but Codman had refused.[96] By refusing to accept the offer, Codman only added insult to the violation of Mark's belief that he had the right to live and work where he pleased.

The right to live away from one's master was also tied into the liberty to maintain a family. Both Mark and Phoebe married slaves living in Boston, which complicated their relationships when Codman would not let them reside there. Mark also had a child, whom he could not visit, and when an apothecary's slave named Robin delivered the arsenic to poison Codman, he told Phillis he was there to "see Mark very much about his Child." Mark told Robin to use that alibi as a way of avoiding suspicion in case he encountered anybody else in the Codman household. His subterfuge indicates that the other slaves, if not Codman, knew that Mark cared about his child and that the separation bothered him.[97] Phoebe, on the other hand, did not have children and wanted to live in Boston with her husband, Quaco. The enslaved man often visited Phoebe in Charlestown, although it is unclear whether

Codman approved. Quaco claimed in his deposition that the poisoning was Mark's idea and that he told Phoebe "not to be concerned wth. Mark about Poyson on any accot. whatever."[98] Mark's confession, however, offers a different, more plausible explanation. Mark implicated Quaco. It was Phoebe who first decided to poison Codman and approached Carr, another apothecary's slave, but he refused to give her any arsenic because she confessed she "had a Design to Poyson somebody in the House." Carr also told Quaco, who pretended to be angry with her when he later spoke with Mark. Nevertheless, Mark believed Quaco "was as knowing in this Affair" as he was himself and wanted Codman dead so he could get Phoebe "over to *Boston* to live with him."[99] Only Codman's death could restore Phoebe and Quaco's right to have a proper family life.

Finally, Codman failed to adequately protect his slaves and could be an abusive master. While his earlier life is not well documented, only three years prior to his death, Codman's wife, Parnell, died. He never remarried and instead turned the management of his household over to his two daughters. He was also "free to indulge his darkest moods."[100] Shortly before his murder, Codman struck another one of his slaves, Tom, in the face and severely damaged his eye. Tom later told Mark he "did not care" that Phoebe poisoned Codman and hoped his master "wou'd never get up again for his Eye's sake."[101]

Even more disturbing, however, was Codman's relationship with Phoebe. Although it is never explicitly stated, it is clear that Codman had a coercive sexual relationship with Phoebe and perhaps also Phillis. Mark noted how Phoebe was Codman's favorite slave, and he "treated her better than any of [the] Servants."[102] It is possible that this preferential treatment came in return for sexual favors. Likewise, when asked why Mark would poison Codman, Phillis replied that not only did Mark want a new master, but he was "uneasy and . . . concerned for Phoebe and [her] too."[103] Phillis did not comment on the matter further after her ominous statement, nor did the authorities ask her to, suggesting that Codman was doing something—most likely sexual—to his female slaves that caused Mark to contemplate murder. The final piece of evidence that suggests sexual abuse was Phoebe's punishment. Unlike Mark and Phillis, she was not convicted of petit treason and sentenced to death but was sold out of the colony, most likely to the West Indies. Caribbean slavery may have been a death sentence unto itself, but Phoebe never appeared in the summons, indictment, conviction, or writ of execution. Unlike the other

main actors, her deposition and interrogation do not exist. Quite simply, authorities muted Phoebe and ordered her sold to avoid embar-
rassing Codman. Had she received the death penalty, she would have
had to meet with a minister, who would offer spiritual guidance and
serve as a confessor. Like Mark, she would have confessed her sins
publicly, giving her the perfect forum to describe Codman's sexual
crimes. Phoebe became a liability to Codman's reputation as a respectable gentleman and had to be removed from the colony. Codman, by
abusing and raping his slaves, violated the very essence of a dependent
relationship—that the strong protect the weak and the weak labor for
the strong—and paid with his life.

These "rights" claimed by John Codman's slaves were not recognized by whites except in the few statutes protecting slaves. Rather,
enslaved people adapted their conceptions of rights and liberties from
dominant British culture. They confronted this aspect of monarchical culture on their own terms with their own interpretations. There
was also no coherent set of rights to which slaves laid claim. Mark,
Phillis, and Phoebe wanted a new master, the ability to labor and live
away from their master, the right to a family, and protection from
abuse. What they wanted, however, is not indicative of what other
slaves wanted. In fact, the customary rights that slaves came to believe
they held could be highly individualized. Nevertheless, understanding the slaves' interpretation of traditional liberties and status helps to
understand how they adapted to an unfree world and explains slave
rebellion, running away, and even murder in the absence of modern
conceptions of freedom.

In early eighteenth-century Boston, newly arrived African slaves
entered a place that had undergone a dramatic cultural transformation over the previous decades. That these societal changes and slave
importation coincided was no accident. Colonists' eschewing their
Puritan hierarchy in favor of a traditional English monarchical model
brought them closer to the mother country. These close relations fostered commercial development but only enriched a few and created
serious economic inequality. Boston's social elite, not having landed
nobility like their English counterparts, turned to legal mechanisms,
consumption, and ostentatious displays of wealth, one of the most
important being the ability to command the labor of slaves, to display their status. Middling artisans and professionals quickly copied
their social superiors, and slave ownership became commonplace

throughout the town. Moreover, increased trade also created a demand for labor, one that Bostonians filled from any available source. Despite growing demands for free, white labor, merchants, business owners, and artisans turned to bound labor, the most important being enslaved Africans.

Cultural transformation, wealth disparity, and a need for labor created a stratified, unfree world built on deference to social superiors and dependence. Everyone had a place in the natural and divinely inspired hierarchy and had liberties fitting their station. Status determined one's place in society, but it was race that pushed Africans to the bottom of this order. Legal statutes defined Africans as servants but also singled them out as somehow irredeemable, prone to crime, and unable to be incorporated into colonial society, thus forever confining them to the lowest tier of the social order. While it is hard to discern how slaves interpreted and adapted to this changing world, it seems that African slaves, like every other class of people in this society, believed they possessed a set of defensible, customary rights.

In early eighteenth-century Boston, chattel slavery, an Atlantic invention, and traditional European conceptions of class intersected and merged to create a distinctive social order.[104] The combination of these two structures produced a hierarchy built on varying degrees of unfreedom. By conceptualizing slavery as one of many forms of bondage, we are forced to think beyond simplistic dichotomies of slave/free and white/black. Moreover, it forces us to historicize the meaning of freedom. Slavery was a legally defined and codified institution. Freedom, however, was amorphous, ever changing, and defined by its context. In a system meant to command and control labor, degrees of freedom and unfreedom were glaringly apparent, but only the latter was legally defined. What is obvious, however, is that even in such a seemingly unfree place, the people at the bottom of the hierarchy could push back, asserted their own autonomy, and fought for the rights they believed they possessed. Boston's slaves did this by laying claim to an identity outside of being chattel, creating families, and fostering a dynamic community.

3 / Social Worlds

On the night of 9 May 1752, William Healy, a poor white laborer, and Robin, a slave belonging to the Cambridge merchant Henry Vassall, broke into the home of Vassall's neighbor, William Brattle. Despite knowledge of a smallpox outbreak in the Brattle household, one of the men sneaked into the house at the behest of the owner's slave, Dick. They stole a chest containing 603 Spanish dollars, 170 pieces of eight, silver dining ware, and English and colonial currency amounting to over £350. After they burgled the Brattle home, Robin and Healy had trouble hiding the chest because Joseph Luke, another poor white laborer who was supposed to show up, was too drunk to help. Nevertheless, the thieves believed they could get away with their crime, and Robin buried the chest in his master's yard. He also gave some of the money to another Vassall slave, Toney, who in turn traveled to Boston and exchanged some of that money for usable copper coinage. When finally caught, Healy told the court that the men hoped to use the money to "go to Cape Breton and from thence to France." Instead of running away, the men were sentenced to be whipped, and since they could not recover all of the money, the court awarded Brattle the right to sell Healy into servitude for twenty years and Robin permanently.[1]

The case of Robin and Healy demonstrates many of the factors that characterized the social world inhabited by enslaved Bostonians. First, poor whites and enslaved men worked together to rob Brattle. While the cooperation between Robin and Healy suggests a degree of interracial solidarity, especially among the downtrodden and unfree, the fact that they were willing to cast blame on each other before the court belies any belief in a universal class struggle against elite colonials. Likewise, Healy and possibly Luke embedded themselves in enslaved communication networks, as Robin and Dick originally devised the plot. Toney, living in the same household, was probably part of the plan too. The latter slave's coin exchange also shows how mobile many enslaved Bostonians were. Finally, the punishment meted out to Healy and Robin shows the violent, unstable, and unfair world inhabited by the people on the margins.

Living in an inherently unfree world shaped the social lives of Afro-Bostonians. Most importantly and perhaps also due to demographics, slave communities were not racially exclusive but were multiracial, cross-cultural networks comprising poor, working-class, and other dependent classes of white people along with enslaved and free people of color. The idea of a slave community, pervasive in the historiography of slavery, especially plantation slavery, since the 1970s, should be eschewed for a more expansive definition of community, what I call a social world.[2] Many of the interracial encounters were in the master's household, either with the owner and his or her family or with white servants and other dependents living in the home. The only racially exclusive institution was marriage, legally codified in 1705 and limiting the marriage partners of black Bostonians to other Africans and Native Americans, which allowed them to create formal and legally recognized families.[3] Family was a troubling prospect, however, as many slaves lived away from their spouses in their own masters' homes, and few had free time to spend with their families. Most of the socializing occurred after work, and given slaves' high degree of mobility—allowed and clandestine—it happened all over Boston itself and in the immediate vicinity.

The social world created and maintained by slaves consisted of layers. The outer layer in which slaves participated was outside the home, such as going to taverns or cavorting around town. If that layer is peeled back, it reveals the family, an institution dictated by circumstance, which forced couples to live apart. Nevertheless, they managed to court one another and have children. The final layer was in the slaveholder's household, where slaves spent much of their nonworking lives. Within the home, they formed relationships in this enlarged "family," not always antagonistic, with their masters and other dwellers.

Interspersed at every level, however, was violence. Slaves were a downtrodden class living in an unstable world full of social, economic, and cultural pressures. Masters and authorities employed violence as a way of disciplining dependent classes. Interpersonal violence erupted at all levels but especially between slaves and other unfree and impoverished persons frustrated by their condition. Many were driven to crime to survive or drank themselves into a stupor to dull the pain of enslavement. Suicide was rampant, while intimate violence haunted even the happiest of marriages. In some cases, the callous treatment that slaves received hampered the formation of real, substantive relationships. Nevertheless, this violence did not prevent them from forming families and communities, many of which were across racial lines, and to manipulate their situation to better serve their own interests.

One of the most important spaces in the social world of a slave was the master's household. Enslaved Bostonians spent many of their non-working hours in their owners' homes and formed relationships with the other dwellers. The master's house was both a physical space and a place of social interaction. Given the expansive early modern definition of family as all of those who lived in a patriarch's household, slaves were part of an extended family that included multiple generations of family members, servants, and other dependents. Households were multicultural and multiclass gathering spaces where slaves and others fostered lifelong connections and grew close to those they lived with. That said, heads of household, usually men, ruled their domestic domains with an iron fist, punishing those who stepped out of line or challenged their authority.

In order to better understand the domestic sphere inhabited by Boston's slaves, the physical space they lived in needs to be considered. There were usually only one or two slaves in a household, and unlike in plantation regions, most slaves did not live in their own quarters, unattached to those of their master. One exception to this rule was Isaac Royall Sr. Royall, an émigré from Antigua who settled in modern Medford, Massachusetts, brought twenty-seven slaves with him when he moved. Despite buying and enlarging an already large house in the early 1730s, Royall nevertheless lacked the space for all his slaves. In 1732, he constructed a large outbuilding that served as a slave quarters for all of his bondsmen and bondswomen. The Royall family employed many of these slaves as they would have done in the Caribbean, having them work in agriculture and domestic tasks on Royall's estate, Ten Hill's Farm.[4] Unlike the Royalls, most Boston

slaveholders accommodated slaves within their homes. As demonstrated in chapter 2, the majority of slave owners were either wealthy
or middling freemen, meaning they owned homes large enough to
contain their entire expanded family. The wealthy Borland family of
Boston built an extra story on their home to accommodate their slaves.
This pattern seems to be similar to most other living arrangements of
families with slaves. While not all slaves lived on a special floor built
just for them, most dwelt upstairs, out of sight from the main parts of
the home. In that regard, the slaves were like other servants, living in a
segregated space within the home, only in sight when coming, going,
or serving the master.[5]

Outside of slaves' own dwelling spaces, both male and female
slaves spent considerable time in the kitchen of the home, even
when not working. This seems to have been the room where enslaved
Bostonians received guests, usually their spouses. Jenny, a slave
belonging to Thomas Hubbard, entertained her husband, Quaco,
and another black couple, Flora and Boston, in Hubbard's kitchen.
Two other members of Hubbard's household went into the kitchen
where the slaves congregated and thought nothing of them meeting
there, suggesting that Jenny regularly entertained in the kitchen.[6]
It is unclear whether slaves like Jenny thought of the kitchen as the
slaves' domain, but she nevertheless used the space to make the most
of her leisure time.

While the physical space inhabited by slaves provides a context for
home life, the relationships they formed with other members of their
household were more important in shaping their social world. The
most important of these connections was between masters and slaves.
Enslaved Bostonians were in regular contact with masters, for better or worse. Sometimes slaves had amicable relationships with their
masters, even if only to secure special privileges and, in rare cases,
their freedom. Other times, relations were much more contentious,
especially when slaves demanded autonomy that owners were unwilling to give. Likewise, the disposition of the master often mattered as
well. Masters could be benevolent or abusive, friendly or adversar-
ial, or some combination of these. At the end of the day, Bostonians
owned slaves as property, investments that would at the very least help
around the house but would also become valuable commodities to
be passed to heirs. The willingness of bondsmen and bondswomen
to assert their autonomy and demand privileges in the face of this
adversity frequently resulted in violence.

Most masters provided for slaves, but not out of benevolence. Rather, they looked to protect their property and investments. The merchant John Usher often recorded the food and other consumables he bought for his slaves, including corn, "chese & Bread," tobacco, and meat.[7] Of course, Usher was a wealthy man and could afford tobacco and other luxuries for his slaves, unlike poorer masters, who could barely provide for themselves, let alone their slaves, especially as food prices rocketed and shortages occurred throughout the eighteenth century.[8] Slave owners also provided for their chattel's medical care. Dr. Elisha Story of Boston commonly treated slaves. Between April 1766 and May 1775, Story treated around twenty slaves, many of them multiple times. Joseph, who belonged to Captain John Tyley, received ninety visits from Story between April and August 1773, almost every day. Most of those who were treated by Story were male slaves belonging to artisans, suggesting that the profitability and value of a slave dictated whether he or she would receive medical attention.[9] Sometimes a slave's visit to the doctor would result in a noteworthy occurrence. The Boston sawyer Thomas Smith purchased a slave in late 1717. For months, the African man, who had an "extraordinary Stomach," complained about "something within him, that made a Noise Chip, Chip, Chip." Smith finally called for a doctor, a German man named Sebastian Henry Swetzer, who informed Smith and his slave that the black man had "Worms." Swetzer put the slave on a regimen of powders, and five days later, a Sunday, the powder took effect. The slave vomited "up a long Worm, that measur'd a hundred and twenty eight Foot, which the Negro took to be his Guts." Swetzer and other interested Bostonians took the worm, most likely a tapeworm, to investigate and provided a complete description, even analyzing it under a microscope.[10] Not all slaves had such distressing medical conditions or encounters with doctors, but the willingness of Boston masters to provide for their slaves, even if done solely because of economic self-interest, is important to understanding the master-slave relationship in Boston.

Another part of basic care was the coverage of a slave's legal costs and fees. There were no special slave courts in Massachusetts, and slaves appeared before justices of the peace like any other Bostonian. Provincial courts only met periodically, meaning when the justice decided a slave would go to trial, the defendant waited in jail until the next meeting of the Court of the General Sessions of the Peace, Boston's criminal court. Whenever a slave committed a crime, masters were quick to post bond and ensure their slave's good behavior, most likely in order to regain their slave's labor instead of letting him or her sit idle in the town prison. Justice of the Peace Richard Dana's record book is full of masters posting bond for recalcitrant servants. Cato, a slave belonging to John Knight, broke into the painter Jonathan Singleton Copley's home "diverse times" in February 1761. Dana ordered Cato to appear before the General Sessions court in April, and his master posted a twenty-pound recognizance for his good behavior, ensuring he would not sit idly in jail. Likewise, when James Lamb's Cato broke into and hid in the home of Thomas Pitts "with intent to steal his goods," Lamb posted the twenty-pound bond promising his slave would appear at the next meeting of the General Sessions court. Masters also paid slaves legal fees, as when Hugh Moor paid his slave Tom's fine for breaking James Maltman's glass windows.[11] These legal fees, while not incurred by all slaves, were surely a point of contention between masters and their slaves.

Rudimentary care aside, there was a wide range of relations between owners and their bondsmen and bondswomen. While many masters were benevolent toward their slaves and gave them considerable leeway, that did not make slavery in Boston somehow more benign or less taxing than in other parts of the Americas.[12] New England masters, especially the older generation still influenced by their Puritan forbears, believed slaves were part of the patriarchal family.[13] As Cotton Mather reminded himself in his diary, "I will always remember that my servants are in some sence my children, and by taking care that they want nothing which may be good for them, I would make them as my children."[14] Slaves were, in the eyes of their masters, perpetual children, to be provided for and used as the head of the household saw fit. And if they stepped out of line, they could be "corrected," punished, usually by whipping, for their transgressions.

It was not only about how heads of households organized their families' labor, however, but also how good, Godly societies functioned. In the Puritan worldview—an epistemological framework that still had some sway as late as the American Revolution—the father was the head of a "little commonwealth," creating, fostering, and protecting the family, an institution that served as the bedrock of any functioning society. Families were the building blocks of stable communities, which were the foundations of functional polities. The king may have been the head of this great chain of being, but families were the foot soldiers of order. Slaves, as strangers integrated into the patriarchal family, needed to be taught, cajoled, and coerced into conforming to this system, even if it meant perpetual infantilization.[15]

Being treated as children may have been less overtly brutal than being driven like livestock on a Caribbean sugar plantation, but it also prevented slaves from ever becoming independent of the master class. While slaves may have had certain expectations about how masters were to treat them, white Bostonians' conception of slaves as children prevented autonomy within the household. Sambo, a slave belonging to James Smith, ran away and most likely had good reason, given that Smith described his bondsman as having "smooth Skin, with a down look, mark'd with a Whip on his Neck." Nevertheless, Smith did not expect Sambo to have run away to another colony, jumped ship to another seaport, or fled into the wilderness but expected him to have run to Peter Papillon, his former master, who lived in Newton. It is possible that Sambo was trying to reconnect with family members still residing with Papillon, but he may have also found better living conditions with his former master.[16] Even manumission could not distance slaves from the family, as demonstrated when Samuel Sewall freed his slave Boston. After Boston obtained his freedom, he continued living and working in the Sewall household.[17]

Like the lack of independence, manumission was an important piece of the relationship between masters and slaves and for understanding the nature of freedom in eighteenth-century Boston more generally. Ezekiel Price, a Boston notary, recorded a number of manumissions over his almost fifty-year career, spanning from the late 1740s until 1794, although he recorded most of them before 1775. Most of the manumitted were like Violet, freed by her mistress, Ester Perkins. Perkins freed Violet because the slave "faithfully Serv'd [her] as a Slave from her Childhood."[18] Likewise, Susannah Ellis of Hopkinton freed her "Trusty Negro Man" Charles.[19] Words like "faithful" and "trusty" appear in all of Price's manumission records, indicating that freedom for slaves was conditional and masters dictated the terms of freedom. They had a subjective measure of what it meant to be well behaved, as indicated when Jeremy Green offered his slave Cuffee freedom in return for his loyal service for two additional years of work but warned, "if my said Servant Shall not faithfully serve me and my heirs the time aforesaid then this Instrument to be void."[20] Although Cuffee served out his time loyally, Green's terms indicate that freedom was a reward for trustworthy slaves, not an inherent right. Enslaved people had to conform to their master's standards, making manumission more about accommodating the whims of their owners than resisting enslavement in the name of abstract notions of freedom.[21]

Examining the relations of two slaveholders with their slaves will allow us to better understand the master-slave relationship. Both men were exceptional but provide a general guide for the ways in which owners governed their human property. The first, John Wheatley, a wealthy Boston merchant, was a benevolent master toward his slave Phillis. When John and his wife, Susanna, purchased Phillis in 1761, both were over fifty years of age, and Susanna was looking for a female domestic to care for her and her husband as they grew older. Yet, when she went to purchase a slave, she was drawn to Phillis, a young, sickly girl freshly arrived from Africa. They most likely chose Phillis because just a few weeks before the purchase, the couple commemorated the ninth anniversary of the death of their youngest daughter, Sarah. Phillis would have been about the same age as Sarah when she died. The frightened, sick girl reminded the Wheatleys of their daughter. Once purchased, the Wheatleys' domestic became more like a child of a wealthy family than a slave. She did not have to do menial household tasks. In fact, it is unclear if she ever learned to keep house. She may have even eaten at the table with the Wheatleys. Meanwhile, John taught Phillis to read and write English, Greek, and Latin. They gave the little girl free rein in the household, and she even had a private room to herself. But the Wheatleys' benevolence only extended to Phillis, not their other servants. One, an adolescent indentured servant named Abner Wade, ran away from John. Another, an African slave named Prince, received a severe reprimand from his mistress for sitting on the same seat as Phillis when he brought her home in the family chaise.[22] The Wheatleys favored and treated Phillis like their own child. As for Wade and Prince, they were chattel to be used for the advancement of the Wheatleys' own fortune. Even within one household, a master's munificence could vary from one unfree laborer to another, with some receiving preferential treatment.

A more disturbing example is the New England slave owner Samuel Johnson, a farmer from York County (modern-day Maine), and Toney, his slave. Toney murdered his master's five-year-old daughter because the slave "had received several abuses" from his master. At first, Toney contemplated suicide to escape his cruel master, but he had been taught that "there was no Hope of Mercy with God for self mutherers." Instead, he considered killing Johnson or those who had assisted in "Tying him while his master beat him," in order to "be brought to Justice and be hanged and so get rid of his Servitude." Toney finally decided to kill his master's young daughter, Mary, "Immagining she was more fit to Die" than the others, and thus, according to Toney, her murder was "less Sinful." After planning the murder, Toney went to bed with his clothes on, determined to kill Mary Johnson. The next morning, while it was still dark out, he went into Mary's room, grabbed the child, ran out of the house with her, and threw her down the farm's well. He then ran as fast as he could to the town of York to turn himself in to the authorities. Toney was later executed.[23] The "several abuses" Johnson meted out to Toney pushed the slave to his breaking point, and he eventually inflicted horrific violence on the Johnson household.

As the examples of John Wheatley and Samuel Johnson suggest, some slaveholders could be benevolent to some of their slaves, but overall, masters saw slaves as wealth-generating property to be controlled at all cost. Most slaves lived in households where they were purposefully socially isolated. Even when enslaved Africans lived with other unfree laborers in the household, as Phillis Wheatley demonstrates, masters played favorites, dividing dependents into factions. Likewise, even the best-treated servants were still property, owned by another, subject to the degradation of unfreedom.

This callous world produced serious social pathogens among the enslaved, the worst of which was suicide. Coroners' reports, court records, and newspapers are full of slave suicides, many of them performed in reaction to their masters' treatment. On 18 November 1733, James, a slave, grabbed his owner's pistol and shot himself in the neck, dying instantly.[24] Likewise, Maria, a slave belonging to Roger Hardcastle of Boston, hanged herself in "an upper Chamber in the House of her said Master." Maria not only killed herself but did so in her owner's home, leaving her body to be discovered by another member of the household.[25] Some suicides were more public, as when a "new [a recent arrival to Boston] Negro Boy about 12 Years old, belonging to a Gentleman in this Town, upon some disgust" jumped into a well, hoping to drown himself. When he landed in the cold water below—perhaps the first time the boy had ever experienced biting cold before—he "bawl'd" for help, but he died from being "chill'd with the Cold."[26]

Suicide, although the ultimate form of resistance and dehumanization as it denied the master his or her human property entirely while destroying a slave's personhood, was not the only way slaves challenged their masters' control. Toney's case, cited earlier, indicates that sometimes slaves targeted their owners' family members. Phillis, a teenage slave belonging to the apothecary John Greenleaf, poisoned two of Greenleaf's children with arsenic from his pharmacy before being caught. Greenleaf made Phillis care for the children, and Phillis, finding her master's demands onerous, killed the children, hoping to free up her time.[27] Although Phillis was eventually executed for her crimes, her case shows that no family members—not even infants— were safe around vengeful slaves. A master's power was never absolute, and attempts to enforce that control could lead to incomprehensible levels of destruction.

Family members could exacerbate already tense relationships with slaves and perhaps faced slaves' destructive wrath without the master being involved. In late October 1729, the "Heads of a Family" (husband and wife) of a household in Mendon had business to attend to away from home. They left behind a young woman, two small children, and their "Negro Man," a household slave. After a while, "some difference" arose between the slave and the woman. The argument escalated, and the African man went into another room in the house and grabbed a gun and, "full of Revenge," chased after the woman and children, who fled the house. When he caught up with the fleeing group, he aimed and pulled the trigger, but the gun misfired. Before he could reset the firing mechanism, the woman fled to a neighbor's house and explained the situation. The neighbor gathered a posse to "secure the Negro" and went to the master's home to search for him. When they arrived at the house, they found the slave "stretch'd out upon the Bed with the Gun lying upon him, the muzzle of which was placed under his Chin." Upon further investigation, they discovered he had "shot himself to Death," the musket ball going in his neck and exiting the top of his head.[28]

At the other end of the spectrum, not all relations between slaves and the master's family were unfriendly, and some formed relationships that lasted a lifetime. A good example of this is Benjamin Jacobs and his father's slave Primus. Years after the death of Primus, Jacobs came to the aid of Primus's widow, Dinah. After his master freed him, Primus Jacobs (he took his master's last name) fought in the American Revolution, entitling himself and his wife to a pension. Although Primus had died before the United States passed the Pension Act, Dinah applied for the money. Testifying on her behalf was Benjamin

Jacobs, claiming he was "well acquainted" with Primus, that Primus had served honorably in the Continental army, and that Dinah, whom he was also "acquainted" with, was indeed Primus's wife. The relationship between Benjamin and Primus not only made it possible for Dinah to collect Primus's pension—not a small sum at $520—from the American government but also illustrates the amicable, deep bonds that could form between slaves and the master's children.[29]

Of course, immediate family members were not the only ones living in the household. Many families owned multiple slaves, servants, or apprentices. This underclass of dependent workers served the family and in many cases grew up together. Of the 601 Bostonians who left probate inventories enumerating slaves, 253, or 42 percent, owned more than one. Of those, 13 owned both African and Indian slaves. Although servants and slaves often received different treatment from the master and his or her family, they nevertheless shared a common experience of not enjoying the fruits of their labor and lacking autonomy. That said, white servitude usually came to an end, while African and Indian slaves were "servants for life." The length of servitude, however, is not a good measure of how slaves and other dependents cooperated. Relations varied greatly, as sometimes slaves within the same household quarreled, while white, black, and Indian servants befriended one another and lived in peace.

White servants and slaves often grew up in the same household. We can see this trend by corroborating the lists of pauper apprentices with probate inventories. Between 1700 and 1775, town officials bound out 237 poor children. Of these, 24, or 10.1 percent, of the masters who received pauper apprentices also owned slaves, meaning a significant number of poor children and slaves lived in the same household.[30] One such master, John Stirling, a Boston wig maker, owned two slaves, Glasgow and London, both listed as boys in Stirling's 1764 probate inventory. In 1760, he received James Melvin, a seven-year-old pauper, from the almshouse. Until Stirling's death four years later, all three boys would have lived together in their master's home, learning the rudiments of wig making. These boys had little in the way of a childhood, as Stirling did not purchase them to play but to labor, learn how to make periwigs, and increase the value of his estate. Considering that Stirling's estate was worth only seventy-nine pounds when he died—the value of Glasgow and London constituted sixty-six pounds of it—he needed the boys' labor to build wealth. Nevertheless, they were still boys, and if they were anything like an "Apprentice

Lad" and a young "Negro Fellow" who belonged to the merchant John
Clark of Salem, they would have made time to play together.[31] While
it is unclear how much free time Stirling gave the boys, his death permanently separated them. The two slave boys would have gone to Stirling's heirs or been sold to cover his debts, while Melvin returned to
the poor house, to later be bound out to Richard Carpenter of Boston.[32]
Being separated may have severed a deep, abiding friendship among
the three boys. John Clark's servant and slave were friends. While
playing in Clark's yard, a horrific accident occurred. The apprentice
was playing with a loaded musket, and the gun accidently went off,
killing the slave boy. When the death was being investigated, the
court interviewed a woman named Sarah Bartlett about the relationship between the two boys. The apprentice, named Walter Hamilton,
Bartlett alleged, would have never intentionally shot the slave, named
Cuffee, because there were "never angry words" between the two boys,
and she believed "they loved one another," lived together, and went
"a gunning" all the time.[33] Although there is no direct evidence for
Stirling's three servants, the story of Cuffee and Hamilton suggests it
was possible for these young unfree laborers to form friendships that
transcended race and shaped their childhoods.

Not only did these slaves and servants live with one another, but
they also worked together to change the conditions of their servitude.
They often collaborated to challenge the authority of their masters,
and while these attempts were not always meetings of equals, both
white servants and black slaves took charge of these conspiracies. In
October 1737, Peter, an African slave "about 27 Years old," and Daniel Davis, a nineteen-year-old English servant, ran away from their
master, William Mirick. The runaway advertisement noted that Peter
spoke French, Spanish, and "pretty good English," suggesting that the
men might run away to a non-Anglophone colony. Peter also would
have been useful to ship captains sailing around the Atlantic, which
led Mirick to remind "Masters of Vessels" that "harbouring, concealing, and carrying off" the servants was a crime. Davis, although
"pretty slow of Speech," was wise to team up with Peter, whose lin-
guistic skills created opportunities for Peter and those who joined
him.[34] Like Peter and Davis, Joe and Peter, African slaves belonging
to James Taylor, collaborated against their master. According to a fellow servant, an indented man named Hopestill Stone, he often heard
the slaves say that they would make trouble and force their master
to dispose of them. He added that both men were a "great charge" to

their master and that Peter was an "Idle Boy" well "Practiz'd in Theiv-
ing," indicating that both the slaves were willing to prove troublesome
enough to be sold to a new master.[35]

A final example demonstrates the dynamics that existed in households with multiple unfree laborers. In a place where masters, slaves,
direct family members, and other dependents mixed, the situation
could become volatile, even when relations on the surface looked
fine. Bristol, a slave belonging to John McKinstry of Taunton, arrived
in Massachusetts in 1755 at about the age of eight and was first purchased by McKinstry's father, John Sr. When the elder McKinstry
died in 1760, his son John inherited Bristol and took him to Taunton
to live with his family and other slaves. Most sources acknowledge
that John and Bristol had an amicable relationship and that Bristol
was, at least according to the lawyer and family friend Robert Treat
Paine, an ideal slave. He "always appeared happy in his Situation, and
shewed an uncommon Readiness to do his Business, and Faithful-
ness to perform what he undertook, without the least Appearance of
Sullenness or Malice." About a year after McKinstry received Bristol,
McKinstry's younger sister, Elizabeth, moved in with her brother,
and both she and John treated Bristol with "all the Tenderness and
Instruction that could be desired." Moreover, Bristol and Elizabeth
had already lived together at John McKinstry Sr.'s home before his
death. On the morning of 4 June 1763, however, something went
awry in the McKinstry household. Early in the morning, Bristol,
then about sixteen years old, Elizabeth, and one of John's daughters
were the only people awake. When Elizabeth went upstairs to place
flat irons in the fire so she could do laundry, Bristol grabbed one of
the irons and struck Elizabeth on the head, knocking her into the
fire and burning her face. He delivered another blow and "immediately dragged her down the Cellar Stairs, where finding an old Ax, he
struck her with it on the Head." Bristol immediately fled the scene,
stealing one of McKinstry's horses. He was eventually apprehended
in Newport, Rhode Island, from whence he was sent back to Taunton
for trial. McKinstry's daughter found Elizabeth's body—after hearing
groans coming from the cellar—shortly after Bristol fled. When Paine
arrived to investigate the matter, he eventually got Bristol to confess
to his crime.[36]

As we have seen, household situations were already tense and the
potential for violence great, but Bristol's case was a bit different. When
he confessed, Bristol admitted he "never had any Anger against the

deceased, nor any of the family." Nor had he ever been ill treated by Elizabeth or her brother. Bristol did not live just with McKinstry and his sister, however. John owned a number of slaves, one of whom had a grudge against Elizabeth. Instead of doing the dirty work himself, he pressured Bristol into killing her, threatening to kill Bristol if he did not. Both Paine and later the *Boston Evening Post* blamed the murder on two factors. First, all of those who had the "Care of Negroes" had to be "very vigilant in removing their barbarous Disposition by Instruction." They had a duty, one John McKinstry neglected, to "instill into" their slaves' "Minds such Christian Principles as may influence their Actions when absent from the Eye of their Masters." Slaveholders had a responsibility to their families and communities to ensure slaves were well behaved. Second, masters had to monitor the activity of their slaves in order to mitigate the "bad Effects of Negroes too freely consorting together." In these complex, diverse households, patriarchs had to closely monitor the behavior of their charges, for as the death of Elizabeth McKinstry demonstrates, lax behavior endangered the immediate family and community at large.[37]

Households in eighteenth-century Boston were multicultural, multiracial, and multistatus institutions all under the moniker of "family." Male heads of households took charge of these families and formed relationships with their dependents, usually built on the exploitation of their bondsmen and bondswomen for personal gain and from the cultural power they received from being "masters," whether of dependent servants or women and children. As such, these relations were volatile and potentially violent, although some slaves did eventually receive conditional freedom. When relations broke down, the master's family members were often targets of the slaves' rage. Nevertheless, slaves and other unfree persons did form relationships with one another, but as the case of Bristol demonstrates, these were not always healthy. Boston masters maintained households of unfreedom, creating a home life meant to maximize control over their wealth-producing property. Given the confining household environment, it is no surprise that enslaved Bostonians took every opportunity to create their own families apart from those of their masters.

Although homes tended to be interracial meeting places where free and unfree alike formed relationships for better or worse, family life for many of Boston's slaves was one of the few activities they engaged in that, outside of their masters' oversight, exclusively involved people of color. By law, African slaves were forbidden to have sex with and marry whites—a possibility given the close contact between slaves and other dependent whites—but it was legal for slaves to marry. Many slaves married other Africans and nonwhites, free and slave, who lived outside of their master's homes, meaning black families did not generally live in contiguous units. Moreover, many black men worked onboard ships or in professions that removed them from their families for extended periods of time, while any slave could be sold away from Boston. Nevertheless, enslaved men and women still formed long-term relationships that produced children. Once again, violence was omnipresent, usually between men who were trying to court the same woman, when masters, as demonstrated in chapter 2 with the murder of John Codman, forcibly distanced slaves from their families, and from the stress of maintaining a marriage in such an oppressive environment. To better understand black families, the process of familial formation from courtship to childrearing and married life are all important factors. The act of marriage, a religious ceremony, and its meaning to slaves is examined in chapter 5 and not part of the discussion here. Nevertheless, enslaved Africans, despite all the restrictions against them and in the face of incredible odds, still formed family units, albeit ones that were often unstable, still under the control of the master class, and different from those of their white contemporaries.

Before moving forward with the analysis of slave marriages, it is important to note the limitations of the sources available. Most of the materials concerning matrimony are legal records or other documents produced after violence or a criminal act occurred, perhaps skewing our perceptions of slave marriages. Well-functioning and blissful slave families, while they certainly existed, rarely produced historical records. It is not my intent to depict slave families as pathological but rather a reflection of the source material.

Almost all marriages, except the few arranged by masters, started with slaves courting each other. Slave courtship is hard to discern, but there are some circumstantial pieces of evidence. Since there were more black men than women in Boston, courtship could quickly turn competitive and violent. When Quaco, the Surinamese slave we met in chapter 1, poisoned Boston, the latter's master and mistress, James and Sarah Gardiner, believed that Quaco "owed [Boston] a spite." Allegedly, Boston took sides with a fellow slave named Sambo. Sambo and Quaco had "Quarrelled and fought about a Negro woman they were acquainted with." Given that Quaco was already married to an enslaved woman named Jenny, either he was engaged in extramarital courting; he held a grudge for a significant amount of time; he practiced polygamy, as many West Africans and Surinamese blacks did; or Jenny was the woman, and despite his victory, he was still angry over the whole situation. Not only did Quaco target Sambo's allies like Boston, whom he poisoned to death, but Sambo's property as well, killing all of his hogs.[38] Quaco was more than willing to kill—and later die—in his quest for a mate.

As if the violence of Quaco was not enough to suggest that courtship was a serious endeavor, other slave behavior substantiates the importance of finding a mate. This was especially true when masters objected to or otherwise tried to prevent slaves from courting. Brazill, a slave belonging to Thomas Plaisted and known "by his Legs," ran away to, in Plaisted's derogatory language, "his Whore." She lived in New Town (Newton), and Brazill's affection for her drove him to run away from his master because he was possibly forbidden from marrying her.[39] An even more disturbing occurrence in Boston's North End indicates the degree to which two slaves courting each other were committed to their relationship. Neither slave's name appeared, but the man lived in the North End, while his girlfriend lived in the South End with her master. The two had "contracted an intimate and strict Friendship together"—courting each other exclusively—but the man learned the woman was to be sold out of Boston. Instead of being separated by her master, the two slaves took matters into their own hands and "resolved to put an End to their Lives, rather than be parted." Such an act suggests not only despair and desperation but the ultimate defiance, with the couple denying two masters of their labor and control over their lives in the name of love. On an early-December night, the couple went into the garret of his master's house, where the male cut his lover's throat with a razor and "then shot himself with a Gun prepar'd for the Purpose."[40]

Despite some courtships ending in tragedy, many slaves did end up getting married. In order to understand slave matrimony, Boston's marriage records need to be examined. Although most marriages occurred in churches, in provincial Massachusetts, marriage was legally a civil institution governed and regulated by the state. As such, marriages had to be reported to the civil authorities in each town. Between 1700 and 1775, churches and town officials reported 223 marriages involving people of African descent (see table 3). Of these,

TABLE 3 Black Marriages in Boston, 1700–1775

Type of marriage	Number	% of total (rounded to nearest tenth)
Slave—different household	91	41
Slave—same household	19	9
Slave—unknown	52	23
Free black	26	12
Mixed slave/free	31	14
Mixed—male/free	10	4
Mixed—female/free	21	10
Indian/black	4	2
Total	223	100

162, or 73 percent, were between two slaves. Of these slave marriages, 91 involved slaves who lived in different households, 19 who lived in the same home, and 52 unknown, most of which occurred early in the eighteenth century. There were another 26 free black marriages and 31 mixed-status weddings between free blacks and African slaves. In the latter, enslaved men married free women at a ratio of more than two to one, indicating that even if the husbands could not escape their bondage, their children would be born free. Unsurprisingly, most of these mixed marriages occurred in the fifteen years before the American Revolution, when ideas about natural rights and freedom became part of public discourse. The records also include four Indian-black marriages, a number that seems low given the extensive contact between enslaved blacks and Indians.[41]

The data also demonstrate that a majority slaves who married other slaves did not live together in Boston. Of the 162 slave marriages, 91, or 56 percent, married slaves in different households. This high number suggests that most slave marriages would have been attenuated and must have been difficult, challenging, and uncertain. Moreover, a slave would now have a second master to contend with—that of his or her spouse. Having two white men with tremendous power over slaves' lives and marriages was certainly an added layer of stress on already tenuous relationships.

Of course, the state and churches did not solemnize all slave marriages. Many African slaves were part of an institution known as "Negro marriage," the equivalent of common law marriage for whites.

Masters often considered slaves who maintained long-term relation-ships, regardless of whether they lived with each other, to be married.[42] Flora, a slave belonging to John Clough, and her longtime compan-ion, Boston, who belonged to a miller named Payne, exemplify this trend. In late November 1757, Flora gave birth to a child, although she claimed she did not know she was pregnant. Even numerous mid-wives and a doctor told her she was not. When she went into labor on November 30, she was bewildered after the child "came from her," and thinking it excrement, she went to the privy and threw the newborn into the pit. Flora then cleaned up, only to realize a short time later it was a child. A number of neighbors later testified, including Elizabeth Atwood, to whom Flora had confided a fear of being pregnant a short time before delivering the child. Although Clough and a couple of other neighborhood men retrieved the child from the "Vault," it later died.[43] Flora was later brought up on infanticide charges for killing her child. Despite all of the evidence of murdering her own child, the court found Flora not guilty. Her exoneration was a technicality. Under an obscure seventeenth-century law protecting bastard children from being murdered, Flora was not guilty of any crime because Boston "kept her company with her masters Consent for above a Year and an half," and so they were considered married and the child legitimate.[44] Since the courts never charged Flora with infanticide, but rather the murder of a bastard child, her relationship with Boston was enough for her to be acquitted. Even though legal marriage was possible for slaves, many chose not to marry, and as Flora's case demonstrates, the courts often recognized long-term relationships as legitimate.

Behind these matrimony statistics and informal "Negro mar-riages" hides an institution that, despite being initiated by slaves, was still controlled by masters. Masters often dictated the terms of marriage, and slaves needed the permission of their owner and that of their spouse to marry. They even redefined the terms of marriage. Samuel Phillips, a minister and slaveholder from Andover, modified vows for slaves to include clauses acknowledging subjugation to their masters. When the minister would marry slaves, they would have to have "ye Consent [of their] Masters & Mistrress," had to "continue [their] Places of abode," had to behave themselves "as it becometh Servants," and were reminded that they "as really and truly as ever" remained their "Master's Property."[45] Even marrying a free person did not guarantee a slave any greater degree of autonomy from the mas-ter. Patience Boston, also known as Samson, was a formerly enslaved

Indian woman who received her freedom because her master could not control her "lewd practices." When she married her husband, an enslaved African, Boston could only marry him on the condition that she "bound [her]self a Servant with him [her husband] during his Life Time." She must have really cared for her husband because she agreed and quickly became a domestic servant owned by her husband's master.[46] Not all of the control masters had over slave matrimony was oppressive, however. When Tom, a slave belonging to the Reverend Joshua Gee of Boston, wanted to marry Jenny, who belonged to a Reverend Thatcher, Gee made arrangements to buy Jenny. While this gave Gee more control over his slaves' marriage, it also ensured they could live together in the same household.[47]

Outside of the jurisdiction masters exerted over their slaves' marriages, other factors made maintaining a meaningful relationship difficult. Most couples lived in different households, meaning one of them would always have to travel to see the other, and they could only do this with the leave of their master or after the workday ended. Limitations on slave mobility, such as a 1703 statute threatening any "Indian, negro, and molatto" caught in the street after nine p.m. with a whipping, made visiting a significant other that much harder.[48] Even if the spouses did find time, legally or illegally, to visit each other, they were still chattel. Slaves could be sold away at any time if their owner landed in financial difficulty, completely destroying the family. Enslaved children belonged to neither parent but to the master of the mother. These children could also be sold away for a profit or given away because a master could not support another servant.[49] All of these restrictions on marriage and family life suggest that slave families were relatively unstable and hard to maintain.

The stress of sustaining a family can be seen in the testimony of various slaves. After Patience Boston married her African husband and bound herself to her husband's master, her relationship with him was anything but blissful. Shortly after their marriage, Boston "was drawn in to the Love of strong Drink." When drunk, she would abuse her husband in "Words and Actions." Eventually, Boston became pregnant, often "had tho'ts of murdering" the child, and even ran away while "big" with child, drinking more and breaking the "Marriage Covenant" while away. When she finally gave birth to the child, it died a couple of weeks later. The death of Boston's child changed her outlook on life, because not long after the death of her first child, she became pregnant again and decided to reform herself. She sought counsel from a minister and stopped drinking for a few months but soon fell back into her old ways. The second child died within two months. After losing two children in a short period of time, both her personal life and marriage had reached a breaking point. None of this could have been helped by the fact that her husband was an enslaved sailor serving on a whaling ship and gone for long periods of time. While the husband was home from a voyage and about a month after losing their second child, Patience became drunk and started a fight with her husband. In the course of the argument, she told her husband she had murdered both of their children. Horrified, the husband threatened to turn her in to a justice of the peace, which he eventually did. Patience Boston finally went to trial, in which the jury acquitted her, but her husband's master and presumably her husband could no longer live with her. The feeling was mutual, and Boston desired to be sold to Joseph Bailey, who lived in Casco Bay (present-day Maine). We know Patience Boston's story because she eventually murdered Bailey's grandson, but her earlier life and rocky relationship with her husband, while in some ways exceptional, demonstrated the instability of slave marriages and the difficulty in balancing the demands of enslavement and family life.[50]

Along with the volatility and abuse highlighted by the case of Patience Boston, abandonment was a persistent problem. William Banks, a slave belonging to Eleazar Robbins of Groton, married Hannah Wansamug, a free Native American woman of Natick, in 1719. As part of the marriage, Hannah purchased William's freedom from Robbins for fifteen pounds. Their marriage was brief and unhappy. Shortly after the wedding, Banks absconded—possibly part of a plan to gain his freedom—abandoning Hannah and leaving her financially destitute. She purchased Banks on credit and could not repay Robbins. The former master filed suit when she could not pay, landing her in debtors' prison in Boston. From prison, Hannah petitioned the Massachusetts House of Representatives for relief, and eventually Edward Ruggles of Roxbury paid off her debts and court costs, which amounted with interest to twenty-five pounds. Ruggles did not act out charity, however, as the House empowered him to sell off an equivalent amount of Hannah's ancestral tribal land in Natick.[51] Like Hannah Banks, the free black woman Lydia Sharp's enslaved husband abandoned her. According to Sharp's 1773 petition, Boston, her husband, abandoned her three years prior, "cohabitated with divers other Women of infamous Character," and had contracted the "terrible and infectous disease commonly called the Pox." Worst of all, she accused Boston of being a philanderer who lived in "constant Violation" of their marriage vows.[52] Examining the cases of Patience Boston, Hannah Banks, and Lydia Sharp reveals the relative instability of slave marriages, which were marred by physical and emotional abuse, abandonment, philandering, alcoholism, and other social pathogens.

Much of the evidence presented suggests that enslaved people were unable to create meaningful relationships or form stable families, but these nevertheless did exist. Mary Minot allowed her slave Parthenia's husband, Jeffs, to have regular visits and even spend the night at her home. Jeffs even went to Minot's home to take care of his wife when she "was not well."[53] On top of taking care of each other, spouses often defended each other from criminal allegations. Jenny, the husband of the Surinamese slave Quaco, claimed that the slave whom he supposedly murdered, Boston, had not been poisoned but had injured himself in a workplace accident.[54] Boston's wife, Flora, on the other hand, believed that she, like her husband, had became ill and vomited from drinking the same concoction that killed him.[55] They also tried to maintain as normal a family life as possible, entertaining other couples in their masters' homes, frequenting gatherings of other slaves and unfree peoples, or going out to one of Boston's many taverns as a couple. The fact remains, however, that "almost nothing is known about the internal relations of [enslaved] family members" that did not come to the attention of the courts, although there are enough pieces of evidence that some slave marriages were loving and that the enslaved worked hard to create some semblance of family life.[56]

Many enslaved and mixed-status couples, no matter whether their relationship was stable or not, had children. Most children resided with their mothers and their mothers' masters if they were enslaved. Masters named the children, although parents may have referred to their children by different names.[57] Masters could also sell children away from their parents for a profit, although they sometimes sold female slaves and their children as a package deal, like one owner who advertised a "Negro woman age about 24 years, and her child, a girl about five years."[58] In many instances, especially in tough economic times, masters would just give away children. One master was so desperate that he offered a "fine Negro child of a good healthy breed to be given away."[59] Nevertheless, many slave parents attempted to have some control over the lives of their children. Between the years 1725 and 1775, ministers at Christ Church (Old North Church) in Boston baptized eighty people of African descent. Of these, twelve were the children of enslaved parents. Richard, slave of John Jon, and his wife, who belonged to Mr. McDaniel, had their son, Richard Jr., baptized in 1746. Cuff and Rose, described as "Negroe Servants," presented their daughter Joanna in 1774. Although these baptisms may have been at the behest of slaveholders, the church entered the record under the children's parents' name, not those of their masters.[60] The act of baptism, then, created an official record of a child's parentage, especially that of the father, and might have, in a small way, tugged at the consciences of devout masters looking to separate children from their parents. Moreover, slaves could be highly protective of their children, especially if sale was threatened. The Connecticut slave Silvia proclaimed that she would "spill her last drop of blood" rather than see her daughter, Hagar Merriman, sold away.[61] Unfortunately, outside of this bold proclamation, there is not much evidence concerning the relationships between enslaved parents and their children in New England.

Despite the instability and uncertainty of slave families, they were, whether legally ordained or common law, an important part of the social lives of enslaved Bostonians. It was a space occupied exclusively by people of color, although the white master class exerted influence on their chattel's families. Many marriages were between people of different statuses, and many Native Americans married African slaves. Although little is known about the children who resulted from slave marriages, slaves attempted to be protective and exert control over their offspring. Family formation, despite its inherent precariousness and being replete with abuse and other forms of violence, was nevertheless significant in shaping the social world they lived in and helped to influence the communities they formed.

While slaves married only other people of color, they formed multiethnic and cross-cultural communities and social networks. Enslaved Bostonians regularly interacted and formed relationships with Euro-Americans of all classes, although most of them tended to be other servants and poor workers and free people of color. This dynamic social life constituted an important part of the social world inhabited by slaves, as it was one of the few areas, outside of work, where bondsmen and bondswomen could escape their master's gaze. To understand this social world outside the home, we must explore the social life of Afro-Bostonians, which allows us to see where they spent their time and the types of activity they engaged in outside of work. Many of these activities led to the creation of intimate relationships in the form of friendships and sexual liaisons. Moreover, African slaves in Boston participated in a number of public ceremonies and held their own, simultaneously stupefying and horrifying white observers. Although violence was a part of the social life of slaves, it was not woven into the fabric of other relationships as it was woven into those inside the home or within the family. This life outside the home, then, was a way for slaves to ameliorate their condition and find autonomy, fleeing from the violence and exploitation within many of Boston's homes. These interracial communities were a powerful form of resistance, in which enslaved Bostonians defied law and social convention to forge deep, abiding relationships with Bostonians of all races and classes.

Slaves often inhabited a social space outside the house where they were in close contact with other Bostonians. They congregated with other slaves and unfree peoples in Boston's many churches, where they sat in segregated spaces, wharfs, public places such as the Common, and after 1742, Boston's town market, Faneuil Hall. The most important of these places, however, were taverns, which could be venerable institutions where gentlemen drank wine and talked high politics or, at least from the perspectives of those same gentlemen, wretched hives of scum and villainy. Slaves tended to congregate in the latter, despite laws prohibiting blacks from purchasing liquor. Although meant as drinking establishments, taverns served diverse social functions. Men and women gathered to dance, sing, play games—usually games of chance and gambling—have discussions of politics and other issues, and sometimes hear the newspaper and other pamphlets read aloud, an especially important function for the illiterate.[62] One Boston master, whose bondswoman disappeared a few days before, went looking for her, and when he arrived in neighboring Roxbury, he was alarmed by a "Noise" in a local tavern. When he entered, he found a "Dozen black Gentry, He's and She's, in a Room in a very merry Humour, singing and dancing, having a Violin." Of course, there was also a "Store of Wine and Punch" to keep the slaves in libation. The newspaper that published this account expressed concerns about "Nocturnal Frolicks," which were very expensive, despite slaves not having access to much money, and asked how and why their masters gave them leave at night.[63] Despite the concerns expressed by this newspaper, slaves continued to congregate in taverns until emancipation, when they gathered there as free men and women.

Most taverns frequented by slaves were barely legal establishments themselves. Between 1720 and 1728, Boston magistrates charged over ninety people for selling alcohol without a license. Many of these people ran illegal drinking establishments, sometimes called "disorderly houses." In 1727, William Cox and James Habersham were both convicted for keeping these types of houses and entertaining women, slaves, and white servants. The situation became so bad that by 1765, Joseph Coolidge had to promise that he did not "intend to make the least profit in his new business by supplying negroes and other servants with liquor." Many of these marginal tavern owners welcomed business from slaves and servants, no matter what the law said, as a way to make money.[64] Many women kept these establishments, especially widows who had no other source of income. Alice Oliver, a Boston widow, was accused of "keeping bad Orders and bad Company in her House White and Black at unseasonable time of Night to the great disturbance of the Neighborhood." Although later acquitted, Oliver most likely did keep a disorderly house, as a slave named Ned was later caught breaking into her home to steal alcohol.[65] Unlike Oliver, Sarah Newman, the wife of a Boston mariner, received a fine for keeping a "lewde disorderly House in Boston" and entertaining "loose, idle, and vagabond persons Negroes etc."[66] These illicit taverns, run by the marginalized for the similarly marginalized, were some of the most important sites for the poor and unfree to congregate, enjoy time away from the master class, relax, and form bonds with one another.

Although slaves frequented taverns, legal and illegal, it was technically against the law for them to be out after nine p.m. Justice of the Peace Richard Dana commonly handed out fines to slaves he caught on the street after their curfew. While practicing in Charlestown in the late 1740s, Dana caught Caesar, a slave belonging to John Codman, outside after nine and sent him to the town jail for being "away from his said Master's Family."[67] When the justice moved to Boston in the 1750s and 1760s, he likewise caught slaves outside after hours, like Kuff and Dick, two slaves he sent to jail after they were caught in the streets after one a.m.[68] The curfew was always a point of contention. Slaves and the others targeted in this way never bothered to follow it, while some whites believed the statutes needed to be enforced to ensure public order. A letter to the editor of the Boston News Letter in 1738 expressed dismay at the lax enforcement of the curfew, even going so far as to reprint the statute in its entirety. The author believed "due Execution of that law would much tend to promote good Orders" and hoped that "all Masters or Owners of any Indian, Negro or Molatto Servants" would "take effectual Care that such their Servants may not be unnecessarily abroad after Nine a Clock."[69] Nevertheless, the arrests, fines, and lobbying by white Bostonians was not enough to enforce the curfew or prevent enslaved Bostonians from roaming the streets at night.

Perhaps one of the reasons town officials imposed a curfew on African slaves, especially men, was their penchant for fighting duels and engaging in other affairs of honor with other blacks, whites, and Indians. Interestingly enough, West African and English conceptions of manhood were remarkably similar in their commitment to patriarchy and independence, especially, as we saw when examining courtship, when it came to choosing a spouse.[70] The slightest offense to one's honor could result in a quarrel or duel. In late November 1728, an Irishman had a "quarrel" with a slave belonging to a Mr. Sweetser of Malden. The Irishman struck the slave and gave him such a grievous wound that he later died.[71] Many fights, however, involved African slaves exclusively. Richard and John Billings's bondsman Cesar stabbed John Parker's slave Boston with a penknife in the course of a quarrel. Although Boston nearly died from his wounds, he later recovered, leaving the Billings brothers to petition the court to release Cesar, claiming he was only in jail "in case . . . Boston had dyed of his wounds."[72] Although the quarrel between Boston and Cesar was informal, slaves also fought actual duels. Another Cesar, this one belonging to the gunsmith Samuel Miller, challenged Tom, the slave of Daniel Bell, a Boston mason, to "fight a Duel with him." Tom agreed to a small sword duel and on 16 March 1742, and the two men met on Boston Common. With "their private malice, fury, and revenge . . . [they] voluntarily Engaged" in a duel that endangered both of their lives.[73] These slaves appropriated not only the notion of dueling from Euro-Americans but also the method, agreeing on a place, time, and certain weapon to settle their dispute. While the court never stated why the men had fought each other, their use of the word "revenge" suggests that either Tom or Cesar had affronted the other's honor.

Not only did male slaves engage in duels when someone affronted their honor, but some wrestled, a masculine sport popular in West Africa. Wrestling presented the opportunity for otherwise oppressed slaves to prove their manliness and almost always involved only people of African descent.[74] Boston, a slave belonging to Lidia Daggert, left work at a local shipyard one day in September 1731 and joined up with Sharper, who belonged to a widow named Hood. As they walked home together, they encountered Minto, a slave belonging to Dr. Francis Archibald, by Archibald's home. Minto took hold of Boston and told him "he would wrestle with him." Minto and Boston wrestled until the latter "threw" Minto, upon which Minto decided to wrestle Pompey, another slave who gathered to watch the match. Minto began his contest with Pompey but lost again, being thrown multiple times by the better wrestler. Infuriated, Minto "offer'd to beat . . . Pompey," but Boston intervened, telling Minto the match was over and to go into his master's shop and leave the other slaves alone. When Minto refused, Boston, obviously perturbed, "gave him two blows in the face."[75] Dr. Archibald later brought charges against Boston for assaulting his servant, and the court sentenced Boston to be whipped ten times and to pay a twenty-shilling fine.[76] Wrestling was a racially exclusive way for African men to exert dominance and an important—and less lethal way—of displaying one's manhood.

Like some affairs of honor, many crimes committed in Boston were interracial, especially theft. Not only were whites often the target of black crime, but enslaved criminals often joined with Indians, poor whites, and other unfree peoples in attempts to achieve their goals. While not all slaves or dependent people were criminals, crime was, as demonstrated in chapter 2, an important survival strategy. By teaming up with others and dividing the risks, slaves were able to achieve their goal of stealing goods to resell or distribute. Although many thieves were caught—that is how we have records, after all—crime and criminal activities were an important part of the slaves' social world.

As indicated by the story of William Heley and Robin, cited earlier, interracial theft was quite common. In May 1724, an Irish servant, two black men, and a black woman, all most likely slaves, stole a ship docked in Boston Harbor in the middle of the night. It was apparent that the four servants did not have much maritime experience, as they ran the ship aground on an island in the harbor. A local "Man of War" tracked the thieves down and found they were also armed with two "Firelocks" (muskets), although "their Design (or wheather any others were concern'd with them)" was not known.[77] Similarly, on 13 March 1744, four thieves stole over four hundred yards of cloth of various types from two Boston merchants' warehouse. When authorities finally tracked down the robbers, they found a polyglot group that included a poor white man named Eleazer Newall; two African slaves,

Harry and Dover; and an enslaved mulatto woman named Parthenia.[78] While slaves were more than capable of stealing small items on their own, both of these examples demonstrate that larger thefts, such as a ship or an enormous amount of cloth, required multiple people, cutting across racial and class barriers.

No matter what the race or class of potential thieves, they had to tread carefully, as there was no guarantee of solidarity with other servants or protection from vigilantism. In 1723, town authorities busted the Native American slave Titus's theft ring. Titus worked with James, an Indian slave who belonged to Richard Draper, and another James, a black slave living in Dedham. Titus would team up with Indian James to rob Draper and then give the goods to black James, who would stash them. When the three men were finally caught, another servant named Primus was called to testify against them, suggesting that slaves and other servants did not always cooperate.[79] Even if these interracial bands could get away with the theft, they would sometimes have to answer to the community. A slave residing in Roxbury, "suspected of stealing some Money," was "by divers Persons ty'd" to a tree and whipped in order to extract a confession. After the beating, the mob released the slave, leaving him on the grass, and although he was later taken to his master's house, he died shortly thereafter.[80] Facing such dangers, slaves' willingness to participate in these theft networks speaks to the desperation fostered by enslavement.

Not all relations between the unfree revolved around crime, as many formed strong bonds with one another. This trend can be most clearly seen in the sexual relations between slaves and other Bostonians. Interracial sex between blacks and whites was illegal from the early eighteenth century, but the town's records are full of women and men being punished for interracial fornication. Most of the cases involved black men with white women, although white men also had sex with women of color. Between 1763 and 1771, the Boston Overseers of the Poor recorded births in the almshouse, and of the seventy-three women who gave birth, five had mulatto children. One of those, Abigail Glover, bore a mulatto girl, who the Overseers "presented to the Grand Jury" in order to bring charges against Glover. Taking a cue from Glover's plight, when Nancy Storey gave birth to a mixed-race boy, she "Went away from the [alms] house."[81]

Although enslaved Bostonians sometimes had sex with whites, intimate encounters with Native Americans were much more common. As indicated earlier, a number of African men married Indian women. Demographically, this made sense. By the mid-eighteenth century, many Native American men had either been killed in war or fled Massachusetts to escape debt collectors. Meanwhile, most white Bostonians preferred to purchase male slaves, who provided the hard work and heavy lifting needed in a bustling Atlantic port town. Native American women also controlled some of their tribe's land, an enticing prospect to enslaved African men seeking independence.[82] This seemingly perfect match had one problem: geography. The enslaved men lived in and around Boston, while Indian women lived in their tribal communities throughout eastern Massachusetts. Joseph Bills, a free black man, seems to have found a solution. In 1765 and 1766, Robert Love, the town constable we met in chapter 2, was in charge of warning out unwanted visitors. Love was a frequent visitor to the house of Bills, who often harbored Indian women. One, Lydia Horton from Stoughton, visited in "town Last Week and offen before" her 24 February 1766 warning out and always lodged with "one Joseph Bills." Two other Native American women, Masthen Legen and Sarah Burney, lived with Bills and were warned out on the same day, 22 July 1766. It is safe to assume that Bills was illegally housing Indian women so they could find mates. Further suggesting Bills's role as facilitator was Patience Peck, a free "Matato" (mulatto) woman who stayed with him. Peck, according to Love, was a "Bad woman and Comes after Negor fellows." Love later caught Deborah Jennins, an Indian woman, with Peck, who was "offen with Gentlemen Negors." Seemingly acquainted with the black men of Boston, Peck would have been able to help these Indian women find a companion, while Bills provided the housing.[83]

Those whites who engaged in interracial sex, especially with Africans, alienated most of Boston's white population, ensured their scorn, and disrupted communal life. Some were publicly ridiculed for giving birth to mulatto children, as was Nell Donahue, whose name suggests she was Irish. The court found Donahue guilty of fornication and sentenced her to be whipped ten times, and the *Boston Evening Post* published her crime for all to read.[84] These types of relations could also rip apart marriages. Sarah Foster filed a divorce petition against her husband, Benjamin, in 1755 for adultery, desertion, and bigamy. Her most damning charge, though, was the accusation that her husband had fathered a mulatto child with a "Negro Girl." Although the outcome of this case is unknown, the legislature ordered Benjamin to appear and give them good reason why Sarah's petition should not be granted.[85] Finally, the sexual proclivities of slaves or masters could disrupt household relations. The prominent Bostonian and future governor James Bowdoin wrote to a friend in 1763 that his slave Cesar had "engaged in an amour with some of the white ladies of this Town." These revelations horrified Bowdoin's wife, who locked Cesar out of the house and refused to let him back in, despite Bowdoin acknowledging the relations as consensual. Eventually, Bowdoin sold Cesar to the West Indies to placate his wife.[86] Although there is very little direct evidence that Boston masters had sex with female slaves, there are a number of slave women who gave birth to biracial children without fathers listed, suggesting that the owners may have been the fathers.[87]

The question remains, however, whether these interracial relationships were based on love, lust, or coercion. Surely all these existed, but some blacks and whites clearly built loving relationships with one another. In 1705, the court convicted a different Cesar, this one belonging to a Captain Hill of Boston, of fornicating with a white woman, Mary Goslin, a relationship that produced a child. Both Cesar and Mary were to be whipped, but when it was Cesar's turn, "he behaved himself impudently." Cesar refused to accept the punishment and swore to the court that he "would be again guilty of the same crime." Not only was Cesar defiant—the court sentenced him to an additional twenty-five lashes for his intransigence—but a network of marginal whites helped Cesar and Goslin. Abigail Trott received a fine for allowing the mulatto child to be born in her house, lying about the identity of the child's mother, and receiving money and goods from Cesar to take care of his child. Another woman, the widow Sarah Wallis, bought stolen cheese from Cesar, which "she knew he had stolen in order to raise funds to pay for the child."[88] Although Cesar was punished by colonial authorities, his stubbornness and dogged attempts to provide for Goslin and his child indicate that some mixed-race couples had loving relationships that they attempted to maintain in the face of adversity.

Intimate encounters of all sorts shaped the personal lives of enslaved Bostonians, but their participation in public events and ceremonies allowed them to carve out their own social world within the dominant culture. Slaves participated in white ceremonies, such as muster and election days, while also holding their own ceremonies, usually funerals. The most well-known and well-studied exclusively African ceremony, held throughout all of Afro–New England, was an event called Negro Election Day. Beginning in the 1750s, African and African American slaves and free blacks would gather for a day of celebration, where they would elect a "governor" or "king" to represent them. It was a major celebration, but there is little evidence that this event ever occurred in the town with New England's largest black population.[89] There are a few explanations for its absence. First, many Afro-Bostonians were born either in New England or in the Caribbean, whereas Negro Election Day had distinctly African roots. Many people of African descent celebrated this holiday, no matter how many generations removed, because of an alleged "Africanization" that occurred after the introduction of so many African-born slaves after 1750.[90] Given the continued presence of large numbers of Afro-Caribbean creoles and Afro–New Englanders in Boston, African traditions such as this holiday may have been subsumed into the dominant black culture in different ways. Second, there was a large Negro Election Day celebration in nearby Lynn, Massachusetts, and considering how mobile Afro-Bostonians were, there is a possibility they traveled there to participate.[91] Finally, almost fifty years of statutory law, at both the town and provincial level, regulating slaves and free blacks in Boston may have prevented the huge gatherings of Africans required for Negro Election Day. While enforcement of these laws was quite lax, hundreds of blacks gathering on Boston Common would have caused considerable alarm.

Instead of holding Negro Election Day, Afro-Bostonians held other celebrations and commemorations. Funerals were among the most significant of these events. When the "Consort of Mr. James Carlington," a free black, died in 1723, she had "six Blacks of the first Rank" as pallbearers. Her funeral procession must have stretched a considerable distance, as 270 more African Americans attended the funeral.[92] When a freed man named Boston died in February 1729, according to Samuel Sewall, a "long train follow'd him to the Grave, it's said about 150 Blacks, and about 50 Whites, several Magistrates, Ministers, Gentlemen &c." Furthermore, Sewall added, "his Funeral was attended with uncommon Respects and his Death much lamented." Not only does Sewall's lamentation indicate that Afro-Bostonians could be held in esteem, but many funerals involved both blacks and whites in the mourning process.[93] As the funerals of Mrs. Carlington and Boston indicate, black funerals could be large. While these were common in West Africa and later in the Caribbean, town officials in Boston were not impressed with and were intolerant of the large funerals that paraded through the streets for hours and could be boisterous affairs. Eventually, the selectmen limited the number of bells that could be rung for the dead and passed an act "for Preventing and Reforming Disorders at the Funerals of Negroes."[94] Despite attempts to regulate black funerals, however, they continued to be important occasions for the enslaved. Unlike the funerals of white Bostonians, which became more private occasions as the eighteenth century went on, African funerals were still public affairs on which the participants spent large amounts of money to commemorate the dead. During some of the early protests against British imperial authority in the 1760s, a newspaper commended "those Patriots" who had stopped giving English manufactured goods, especially mourning gloves, out at funerals. In the many months before the July 1765 article, there "had been but one Burial for many Months past" that handed out gifts, "and that [for] a Negro."[95] Funerals were important public ceremonies for people of color, especially for the enslaved, where any friends or acquaintances—no matter what their race—of the deceased could gather and mourn.

Even though slaves held their own celebrations, they could be found at almost every public activity in the town of Boston, either on the sidelines or as participants. Town ordinances testify to their ubiquity. The town selectmen forbade slaves from "selling liquor or provisions" during muster days and other public ceremonies. Spontaneous street festivals were banned not because they disturbed the peace but because the selectmen assumed that the "tumultuous companies" contained "children, & Negroes."[96] Public gatherings almost always included seedier elements on the margins, leading the General Sessions Court to uphold a law banning "Young People, Servants, and Negroes" from "playing in the streets with money, pawpaws etc."[97] All of these restrictions suggest that slaves used public events as a way to misbehave, gamble, or make a little extra money, but they also participated in these occurrences. When the Reverend George Whitefield preached in Boston over a ten-day period in 1740, enslaved Bostonians turned out in huge numbers. On Saturday, September 27, Whitefield preached on the common to "about 15,000 people," leaving him to exclaim, "Oh, how did the word run!" The word must have run to the many black faces in the crowd, because the following day, after addressing a "very crowded auditory" in Joseph Sewall's meeting house, Whitefield "went and preached to a great number of negroes," eager to hear about the "conversion of the Ethiopian."[98]

The world outside of the home and family for Boston's slaves was interracial and a space where the slaves could exercise some degree of autonomy. Many spent time in Boston's taverns, where they drank, cavorted, and sometimes committed crimes with and against people of all races and classes. Despite restrictions on movement and curfews, slaves still enjoyed considerable mobility throughout the town. Their lives outside of the master's home frequently led to interracial relationships, many of which were sexual. While black Bostonians held their own public ceremonies and commemorations, they were also involved in almost all public events either at the margins or as active participants. Slaves forged their own communities with people they interacted with, forming long-lasting relationships and creating a place for themselves in public life.

Enslaved Bostonians occupied a social world that was inherently multiracial. Indians, Africans, and Europeans were in close, intimate contact with one another, despite class and racial differences. The master's home, a place where slaves spent many of their nonworking hours, was a multicultural space where the unfree and other dependents lived beside the master and his or her family. Although relations between masters and slaves were often antagonistic, slaves had healthy relationships with other servants and even their owner's family. Family life for enslaved Bostonians was as ambivalent as household relations. Confined by law to marry only people of color, slaves took other Africans and Indians, both enslaved and free, as spouses. Relations were often tense, as the majority of slaves lived away from their spouse and the demands placed on spouses by their obligations as slaves and the demands of family life were often stressful. Children resulted from these relationships, although they were the property of the mother's master and little is known about how slaves interacted with their children. Outside of the home, slaves interacted with whites, Native Americans, and other blacks in a number of public forums, and these sometimes resulted in long-term relationships. And slaves were ubiquitous fixtures at almost all of Boston's public events. Despite the vitality of this social world, it was fraught with violence, speaking to the instability and volatility of enslavement.

Such a multicultural, cosmopolitan, and unstable world forces us to rethink slave communities and the nature of resistance. Instead of confining themselves or being confined into distinct and exclusive enclaves, enslaved Bostonians created a social world inhabited by those who were racially and culturally diverse. In an early modern, unfree place like Boston, status was more important than race. Slaves built communities that included poor colonials, white dependent classes, and people of color. While there were activities and events exclusive to Afro-Bostonians, we need to expand the definition of community to include these multiracial, multiclass structures. Moreover, in the context of this social world, the definition of resistance changes. Slaves often resisted in the face of an immediate threat of violence or the treatment they received from masters. Most violence perpetrated by slaves did not challenge the institution of slavery but was a futile attempt at survival or frustration, usually aimed at a spouse or the master's family and rarely at the masters themselves. Instead of violence, community formation and the ability to create relationships with people across class and racial divisions proved to be a much more powerful form of resistance for enslaved people. These communal structures allowed slaves to ameliorate the horrors of enslavement by working with other similarly unfree people.[99] Rarely did enslaved Bostonians protest for freedom or emancipation, but they worked to gain more autonomy from the master class or to protect their families or communities. While this form of resistance often led to violence, the working lives of Boston's slaves offered more than ample opportunity to challenge the boundaries of slavery.

4 / Laboring Lives

In Boston, slaves were part of a dynamic and versatile labor force.[1] Given the chronic labor shortages that plagued early modern port cities like Boston, slaves there were able to exert significant control over their working lives. Many slaves held skilled and semiskilled positions, which enabled them to navigate and negotiate Euro-American society. Rather than confronting the master class and fighting for freedom and liberty, Boston's slaves worked hard, found common cause with fellow workers both enslaved and free, and protested working conditions, all to carve out an autonomous space in which they could live their lives and protect the interests of themselves, their families, and their communities.[2]

In order to better understand enslaved labor in Boston, we need to understand three key factors. First, as discussed in chapter 2, there was a need for labor of any type, especially skilled labor. This led many masters to train their slaves in a trade or at least to have them labor in artisanal workshops. Even if slaves were not formally skilled, many specialized in certain types of labor. Enslaved Bostonians learned these skills, became important to Boston's economy, and, in turn, gained a degree of self-sufficiency and autonomy. Second, slaves labored for their masters; were hired out; performed myriad jobs; interacted with coworkers, owners, and bosses; and, in general, lived dynamic working lives. Third, analyzing the meaning of this independence and the working lives of slaves allows us to see how they embraced and exploited workplace conditions to ameliorate the dehumanization of slavery and create a space for themselves in Euro-American society. This autonomy sometimes turned violent as slaves protested working conditions, terms of employment, or the treatment they received. Independence was mostly limited to skilled male slaves, however, while others, such as the unskilled and women, did not have the same opportunities.[3]

Examining slave labor in Boston, especially in the context of slavery throughout the early modern Americas, illustrates how enslaved men and women could use labor to challenge their enslavement without undermining slavery as an institution. Autonomy and the opportunity to enjoy the fruits of their labor permitted enslaved Bostonians to defy their legal unfreedom while not openly challenging the master class.

The great need for workers in provincial Boston led to the use of bound laborers and the importation of large numbers of African slaves. According to the historian William Towner, by the mid-eighteenth century, enslaved blacks "were more important as a source of bound labor than any other type—apprentices, indentured servants, criminals, poor, or Indians."[4] Local sources and white European servants could not satiate Boston's economic demands. Moreover, Boston was unlike other regions of the Americas where bound laborers primarily worked in agriculture. The town had a sophisticated mercantile economy that needed not only laborers but also skilled workers who could provide specialized services such as shipbuilding (which required around thirty different trades itself), blacksmithing, coopering, and printing.[5] Artisans and merchants trained their slaves in these skills not only to fill their economic needs but also to increase the value of the slaves and the labor they provided. Likewise, even if slaves were not formally trained in a craft, many were versatile laborers who could earn extra money for their masters and themselves. How these slaves came to be skilled and the importance of enslaved skilled labor is important for understanding the nature of slave labor in Boston.

Many of Boston's slaves learned a trade. Although how they learned can be hard to discern, there are a few clues. Artisans owned the largest number of slaves in Boston, suggesting they most likely trained slaves in their own trade. John Butler, a Boston cooper, owned four male slaves, all of whom were worth more than £400 apiece, including his enslaved boy, Prince Eugene. Their exceptionally high value indicates that Butler trained all four to be coopers.[6] Other masters provided for their slaves' training. The ship captain Peter McTaggart apprenticed his slave boy Caesar to himself, and he taught his bondsman how to sail.[7] Ephraim Burrell of Weymouth gave specific instructions in his will about what to do with his slave Tom and looked after the slave's "improvement," most likely craft training.[8] Similarly, Sarah Forland, a Boston widow, ensured that her "Negro Boy Caesar" would be provided for until he was sixteen, get an apprenticeship in some trade, and then practice that trade for at least seven years. Although Caesar eventually would be freed per Forland's will, between his apprenticeship and years of service, he would have been an enslaved artisan into his early thirties.[9] A number of slaves also knew a trade before arriving in Boston, as did Quaco, supposedly a cooper who was sold from Barbados to Boston (see later in this chapter).[10] Senegambia, the region of Africa where many of Boston's African-born slaves came from, had a local tradition of blacksmithing, leather making, and boat building that may have crossed the Atlantic and made slaves from there more marketable upon arrival.[11] However Boston's enslaved population acquired knowledge of a craft—either before arrival, through apprenticeship, or in their masters' workshops—they constituted one part of a highly versatile and skilled slave population.

Even slaves not trained in a formal trade often possessed other specialized knowledge and skills, as colonial newspapers attested. This trend was especially true for women. The *Boston Evening-Post* advertised two young enslaved women for hire who could "handle their Needles very well."[12] Another was a "very good Cook" and came highly recommended.[13] Men also had skills to draw on. One of the most interesting was fiddling. A 1754 issue of the *Boston Gazette* advertised for hire a "Negro Man that plays well on the violin."[14] Enslaved violinists were often hired to play at parties, in taverns, and at various public ceremonies.[15] Some Bostonians raised concerns about the skills and degree of training that African slaves supposedly possessed. In a letter to the editor in the *Massachusetts Spy*, an anonymous Bostonian worried that an enslaved chimney sweep was not "sufficiently cautioned to be faithful in the discharge of his duty" after the chimney of a house that the slave had recently cleaned caught fire.[16] As the concern over the enslaved chimney sweep indicates, skilled slaves were not always to be trusted, but they were certainly instrumental to the function and social and economic life of Boston.

The legal identity of almost all early modern Britons was tied to their occupation, but this took on a special significance with slaves.

Whenever people of African descent appeared in print, the article or advertisement made note of their profession. For-sale and hiring-out advertisements mentioned occupation, which increased the slave's marketability. One ad mentioned that the slave was a "good House Carpenter and Joyner," while another noted how "A Stout likely well set Negro Boy, about seventeen years of age," had been "five or six years at the Cooper's business."[17] Likewise, another ad for slaves to be hired out mentioned that one was a tailor.[18] While we can expect advertisements to mention a trade, other articles discussed slaves' occupations in ways unrelated to their labor or market value. In July 1741, the *Boston Post Boy* contained an article about a "Frolick" gone horribly awry. Seven slaves took a small ship into Boston Harbor to spend the day relaxing on Spectacle Island. Upon their return, "the Wind being against them, and blowing very hard," their boat capsized, and four of the slaves drowned. The newspaper went out of the way not to describe the slaves but only to mention their owners and the slaves' occupations. Two of the drowned men belonged to Barrat Dyer and were coopers, while another belonged to a Captain Compton and "has been used to the Lightering Business many Years."[19] This obsession with a slave's occupation, mentioned even in the face of disaster, indicates skilled slaves' economic importance, not just to their masters but to the town itself. While the death of Dyer's slaves many have been a personal financial setback for the master, it deprived Boston of two coopers—artisans who took time, effort, and money to replace.

Two case studies help to illuminate the importance of slavery to Boston's mercantile economy. The first involved an enslaved man named Quaco (see earlier in this chapter), who was sold from Barbados to Boston as a "cooper." The details of Quaco's time in Boston come from a court case filed by the man who purchased him, John Coleman, a distiller, and against a Barbadian merchant named Benoni Waterman. Most of the narrative comes from the depositions of Richard Barnard, a Boston cooper and business partner of Coleman, Coleman's workers, and a Barbadian planter named Edward Denny, who was the original owner of Quaco. In the summer of 1730, Waterman approached Coleman about buying the slave. Coleman took an interest in buying him, but Waterman demanded £100, an exorbitant sum. Taken aback and thinking about walking away from the deal, Waterman informed Coleman that Quaco "was a cooper." As a distiller needing workers and barrels, Coleman immediately became interested again and asked Quaco if he knew how to make rum casks, to which the slave replied that he could and that he could make molasses casks too. When asked how many he could make a day, Quaco replied that he could make two. Coleman judged Quaco "a very good Workman" and tried to bargain with Waterman.[20]

Throughout the process, the distiller drilled both Quaco and Waterman with questions, asking, for example, if the slave "liked Drink," to which Quaco replied in the negative. When Coleman became suspicious as to why such a valuable slave would be sold away, Waterman informed him that masters "often sent [slaves] away for a Small Fault" and "that if he thought it would not Dislodge the Gentleman that sent [Quaco] to [Waterman], he would give that money for [Quaco] and carry him back to Barbados." Convinced, Coleman bought Quaco. According to Nathaniel Belknap, who witnessed the sale, Coleman wanted to pay on credit, but Waterman demanded cash, which Coleman paid. Despite two major warning signs—such a valuable slave being sold away and the demand to be paid in cash—Coleman purchased Quaco, only to find he had been bamboozled.

Although Quaco's original owner later insisted Quaco was in fact a cooper, Coleman quickly learned that Waterman fooled him. Coleman offered Richard Barnard, a cooper who did contract work for the distiller, an opportunity to see Quaco in action and lent him to Barnard. When Barnard took Quaco to his shop and put him to work, he discovered that the slave "understood very little of being a cooper." Barnard returned Quaco to Coleman, informing him that Waterman had tricked him. A little while later, when Barnard visited Coleman's distillery, he witnessed Coleman return Quaco to Waterman, claiming that the slave was not a cooper. An argument broke out between the two men, with Coleman shaming Waterman by stating that he "thought he had to do with a Gentleman who would not have sold him a false thing." After the encounter, Waterman disappears from the record, evidently leaving Coleman with an enslaved "cooper" who could not make casks. In the months leading up to the September 1730 court case, Robert Walker, a worker at Coleman's distillery, "often spoke" with Quaco, inquiring why he lied about being a cooper. Quaco always answered that "Waterman told him to do so." Walker probed deeper into Quaco's life, asking him the real reason that he was sold away from Barbados, to which the enslaved man replied that it was "for being Drunk" and "very commonly in Drink." Coleman's need for a cooper led him to foolhardily purchase a deficient worker. The distiller understood the importance of skilled labor both to his personal wealth and to the town's economy as a whole. An alcoholic plantation slave had no place in Boston, but a cooper would never lack work, would provide a steady income for his master, and would contribute to the town's economy in dynamic and constructive ways.

The second case involves the Boston merchant William Blair Townsend's slave-trading activities. As a young man in the 1740s, Townsend sold a few slaves to help establish himself as a merchant. In 1745, Townsend wrote to the South Carolina merchant planter Colonel Benjamin Payton, offering him an enslaved man named Paris and informing him, "you cant but like [Paris], to be sure he is as likely a fellow as any in Boston, he is Two & twenty years of age, & is sold for no other Reason but because he is impudent & his master being in years cant manage him, he is guilty of no Vice & he is also very Cheap."[21] Payton must have agreed to the sale, most likely enticed by the good deal that Townsend offered, because seven months later, Townsend wrote Payton to inquire about Paris. A "Gentleman" met with Townsend to discuss Paris, and Townsend wrote to Payton, "[The man] desired me to write that if you would send him here again he would" pay Payton fifty pounds over the initial buying cost. The gentleman desired Paris for "his being a good workman at the Glaziers business," which, Townsend continued, "perhaps you might not value him the more for."[22]

Unfortunately, Townsend's surviving correspondence with Payton ends after that letter, so there is no indication if the planter sent Paris back to Boston. Townsend's letter nevertheless indicates something interesting about skilled bound labor in Boston. South Carolina required, despite having a need for artisan labor on its plantations and in Charleston, agricultural laborers to work on its burgeoning rice and indigo plantations, but any slave could work in agriculture. Boston, however, needed glaziers, a specialized craft, and Paris, as enslaved glazier, was much more suited—and thus useful—to Boston's merchant economy than South Carolina's plantations. While it is unclear where Paris would have worked in South Carolina, the threat of his talents being wasted was too risky for Townsend. Even if the gentleman wished to purchase Paris for his own profit, the tone of Townsend's letter established a notion of "value." South Carolina could not benefit from Paris's skill, but Boston understood his true value and economic importance.[23]

As these two case studies suggest, skilled slaves played an important role in Boston's economy and made significant contributions to the workforce, and Bostonians saw slaves and the labor they provided as valuable. Whether formally trained in a trade or having mastered a set of skills, such as cooking or sailing, slaves worked in almost every part of the town's economy. In fact, occupation became an important way to identify a slave and assess his or her worth. It is still unclear, however, how many of these slaves acquired skills, although some may have learned them before arriving. Likewise, it remains to be seen who hired slaves, the conditions of their employment, and their workplace behavior, topics that will allow us to better understand the dynamics of enslaved labor in Boston.

Although learning a trade allowed slaves to become an important part of Boston's economy, masters needed to deploy these slaves effectively in order for their chattel to generate income. Moreover, the working lives of slaves—their day-to-day experience, their workplace environment, and relationships between the enslaved and their masters and white workers—remain elusive and need to be addressed.

There were three ways in which enslaved laborers in Boston worked: hiring out, self-employment, and under their master's direct control. The third is the easiest to identify because most slaves worked for their masters, either in the household or in the workplace. Almost all female slaves worked in their masters' households, although some would be hired out for short intervals. Robert Desrochers found that 71 percent (282 of 397) of all female slaves offered for sale in Massachusetts newspapers were advertised as being employable in some sort of "household service."[24] Men also performed work for their masters but were not always confined to the house. London, a slave belonging to the merchant Peter Luce, carried produce and other goods from Luce's farm in Dedham to Boston.[25] London and his fellow male slaves were often employed outside the home, but male bondsmen skilled in domestic tasks such as gardening, working in stables, and waiting tables, still made up 27 percent (140 of 518) of all male slaves advertised for sale in Massachusetts.[26] These statistics demonstrate that the workplace experience could vary widely for slaves engaged in work for their masters, with female slaves mostly confined to the house, while those like London had a certain degree of mobility and independence. The type of service, then, is not a good measure of autonomy, which depended on both the type of work being performed and whom slaves were working for.

Although most slaves worked in their master's service, some slave owners chose to hire their slaves out to others. This process, known as "hiring out," is not as well documented for Boston as for the American South, but some details can be discerned.[27] The best sources for understanding this process are newspapers, in which owners often advertised slaves whom they were willing to hire out. Sometimes, masters hired slaves out because they did not have enough work for them or, in eighteenth-century parlance, "for Want of Employ." That was the case for one Bostonian, who offered a boy for sale and a "sober young Negro fellow to be hired out."[28] Slaves for hire were often bundled with other goods or property for sale or rent, such as in an advertisement for "Two genteel CHAMBERS furnished or unfurnished, at a pleasant part of the town. Also a young Negro Fellow to be hired out."[29] This advertisement was quite clever, as a servant and a nice place to stay were enticing offers to long-term visitors looking for comfortable accommodations in Boston. The length of the hire also varied depending on the master, with some slaves, like one twenty-year-old female, being "hired out by the Month," while others were hired out by the year.[30] Some owners were even willing to compromise on the hiring terms. A master offered two female slaves in their twenties who could "do all sorts of Household Work, and handle their Needles very well," for thirty pounds a year. If the person who hired them agreed to clothe them, however, the price was only twenty pounds a year.[31] Such a deal would save the master money and transfer even more responsibility to the person who hired his or her slaves. Finally, some Bostonians in need of labor advertised for a hired slave. One potential employer posted an ad in the *Boston News-Letter*, desiring "A Negro Man of Character, to be hired to serve in a Family," and was willing to negotiate on the length of service.[32] All these advertisements demonstrate that there was a vibrant and dynamic hiring-out system in Boston, even if it did not enter into the official record.

Even though newspapers allowed masters to advertise slaves for hire, the actual hiring process remained highly informal and personal, usually arranged by word-of-mouth agreements made between two parties. Zachariah Johonnot, a merchant and distiller from a prominent Boston family, lent his slave to Hopestill Foster, a lumber merchant, in order to pay some of his debt to Foster.[33] Given colonial New Englanders' litigiousness, the informality is surprising, and few hiring contracts survive. One of the few in existence deals with an enslaved sailor named Toney. During Queen Anne's War (1702–1713), the British government authorized the Province of Massachusetts Bay to issue certificates of marque to privateers. One of these legal pirates,

John Halsey, hired Toney from his master, Samuel Lynde, in 1702. Per the contract, Lynde allowed Toney to serve aboard the brigantine *Adventure* as a cook, and Toney was "Entitled unto one full and whole share of all prizes plunder which . . . Shall take upon their Expedition as much as any able Saylor on board not being an officer." The contract concludes with Halsey agreeing to return Toney to Lynde and pay the master "what shall be do and belong" to Toney.[34] Toney's contract was an exception, however, and the record suggests that masters hired out slaves on an ad hoc basis and without formal contracts.[35]

The final way in which slaves found work was by hiring themselves, usually with the permission of their masters. Like hiring out, very little evidence of this practice exists, and most of what we have is circumstantial. Briton Hammon, for example, explained that on Christmas Day 1747, "with the leave of [his] Master," he left his owner's home in Marshfield, Massachusetts, and went to Plymouth, where he "immediately ship'd [him]self on board of a sloop." Hammon needed permission to leave his master's service and work on his own, but other than that, the enslaved man was in charge of finding work for himself. As an experienced sailor, Hammon did not have any trouble.[36] More evidence of self-hiring can be gleaned from other sources. Cotton Mather's diary tracks the development and progress of his slave Onesimus, whom Mather desperately tried to Christianize. After Onesimus learned to read and write and was tractable toward his master and his master's family, Mather rewarded him with "great Opportunities to get money for himself."[37] Another example comes from the case of Mark, the slave executed for murdering his master, John Codman (see chapter 2). In his gallows confession, Mark discussed how Codman allowed him to live with his wife and work in Boston. There was also an arrest warrant issued for Mark when he did not leave Boston after being warned out. Neither of these documents mentioned him laboring for someone else, suggesting that Mark worked on his own as a day laborer for cash. Furthermore, before being sold to Codman, Mark belonged to a number of other owners, including a brazier, meaning that Mark could have acquired this trade. It can be inferred from these sources that Mark worked on his own and hired himself out, most likely remitting some money to Codman, before Codman forced him to return to Charlestown.[38] All of this evidence suggests that there were a number of slaves who were able to negotiate much, sometimes all, of their own working conditions in eighteenth-century Boston. Nevertheless, Mark's case demonstrates that there were limits to the autonomy granted by self-hiring, as all slaves were still chattel compelled to follow the whims of their masters.

Occupation, then, is another way of understanding workplace conditions, the independence those conditions granted, and the limits of that independence for enslaved Bostonians. The historian and legal scholar Christopher Tomlins argues that Boston's growing slave population, which doubled in the first half of the eighteenth century, demonstrates the importance of slavery to "artisanal and proto-industrial production."[39] While this is correct, we should recognize that enslaved labor was significant for the domestic and maritime trades as well. Taking these trades together, Boston's slaves fell into four broad categories of laborer, including domestic (household) workers, unskilled workers (Tomlins's "proto-industrial production"), enslaved craftsmen, and sailors, each featuring its own unique skill set, working conditions, and interactions. Uncovering the day-to-day lives of common white people in the eighteenth century is difficult, and that of enslaved Africans is even more so; but by contextualizing the lives of specific slaves in Boston with what we know about labor in early modern Britain and its American colonies, we can garner a fairly accurate picture of slave employment. Given that slaves were in Boston to work in the first place, analyzing workplace conditions helps to decode an important facet of their lives. It also helps to understand both the possibilities and limitations the workplace afforded. The liberties available depended on occupation. These liberties were not codified into law and certainly were not inalienable rights, but they could create an incredible degree of independence.

The first category of labor was domestic servitude. Lawrence Towner cautions that this "term embraces much more than its present use would indicate," as the unclear division of labor in colonial society meant that many household tasks were considered domestic. These included tending livestock (many Bostonians kept pigs and sometimes cows), spinning yarn and other thread, soap and candle making, gardening, child care, food preparation and cooking, and making and mending clothes. Likewise, wealthier families usually maintained servants as butlers and coachmen. By the late seventeenth century, the people who became servants changed dramatically. Before, most tended to be neighborhood girls, usually in their early and mid teenage years, whose servitude was like an apprenticeship in which they learned to take care of a household. After 1700, however, enslaved Africans and Native Americans took the place of white teenage girls, and instead of being bound for a short period, they entered a new domestic servitude that became a form of permanent and inheritable slavery.[40]

It was also not uncommon for some masters to have both African slaves and white indentured servants in their households working side by side. We can see this trend by cross-referencing the probate records and tax-evaluation records of slave owners with recent research examining pauper apprenticeship (see chapter 2) in colonial New England. The merchant Oxenbridge Thatcher noted the ownership of two slaves in his will, Cesar and a "Negroe Woman." Cesar most likely worked on Thatcher's farm in Milton, but the woman resided with Thatcher in Boston. In 1753, Thatcher received Mary Guillion, a poor, white fifteen-year-old girl, from the Boston Overseers of the Poor as a pauper apprentice to work as a domestic and be trained as a spinster for three years. Guillion's time most likely overlapped with that of the enslaved woman in Thatcher's household.[41] Despite doing similar tasks and both learning to spin, the relationship between the two women cannot be discerned.

Demographically, most enslaved domestics tended to be women, although men often served as butlers, drivers, and sometimes as cooks, and all played an important role in Boston's economy. Household servants tended to be some of the most versatile slave laborers, even serving as couriers, carrying messages between their master and his or her acquaintances. Mark, a slave belonging to Andrew Belcher, carried the money that David Jeffries owed Belcher, not only securing communication between the two men but facilitating trade and commerce.[42] Others, such as Chloe Spear, a house slave belonging to Captain John Bradford, engaged in a number of "domestic avocations," even being dispatched by her mistress to take care of a sick neighbor.[43] Moreover, we can assume that unfree laborers made a large number of goods produced in Boston homes, such as cloth and beer. Almost 25 percent of all Bostonians who had an estate inventory taken between 1700 and 1775 owned slaves, many of whom would have been engaged in domestic production, meaning that much of the clothing and other homemade goods consumed by slave owners was slave made.[44]

Despite the versatility and importance of domestic workers, that category of labor gave slaves the least chance to create space for themselves. Many were under the constant surveillance of their master and mistress, unless they went to fetch water or pick up goods at the market. Being confined to the home, it was much easier to catch slaves doing clandestine activities, as when Chloe Spear's master caught her teaching herself to read and threatened to "suspend her by her two thumbs" and severely whip her if she was caught again; he proclaimed that reading "made negroes saucy."[45] Living in close proximity to the master and his or her family could also bring unnecessary harm and violence. Violet, an enslaved maid belonging to Samuel and Priscilla Royall of Dorchester, received a grievous wound one evening when the Royalls' son returned home drunk and threw a large stone, which struck Violet in the head.[46] On top of the surveillance and abuse, domestic servants were also the most commonly sold slaves, constituting 46 percent of all slaves advertised for sale in Boston, indicating that they were not as valued and thus were more disposable compared to skilled bondsmen.[47] Although every master was different, domestic servitude generally condemned slaves to confined lives under the control of their owners.

Enslaved day laborers or "common laborers," as they were sometimes called, unlike household servants, had a degree of mobility and the opportunity to earn their own wages. Most of these laborers tended to be men and usually did not perform tasks different from enslaved male domestics, but they were usually hired out to perform those duties. Some were also hired as porters, as stevedores, and for other menial, yet grueling, labor. These workers also had the least amount of job security, especially if their master could not secure regular employment for them or there was an economic downturn. In times of plenty, however, these unskilled workers were ubiquitous throughout the diaries and account books of Bostonians and visitors to the town. While residing in Cambridge, Edward Augustus Holyoke noted that he paid "Snoden's Negro 16/ for sweeping 2 Chimneys" in mid-December 1747.[48] The Boston merchant John Briggs hired a "Negro for Work abt ye house" for six shillings on 16 May 1718.[49] Artisans and established tradesmen in Boston always needed additional help and commonly employed enslaved laborers, as when the housewright Benjamin Eustis hired "boston Jackson & bilings Negero" to clean Andrew Oliver Jr.'s "litel house."[50]

Not all unskilled enslaved workers labored independently, and many worked for and beside their masters. Of special note here are the slaves owned by Boston tavern keepers. David Conroy examined these enslaved men and women and found that of the forty-one tavern owners licensed between 1680 and 1720, nineteen owned African chattel. Slaves "worked on close terms and in close quarters with their respective masters," leading some masters to care for them in retirement or manumit them when they died. These slaves performed all the duties needed in a drinking establishment, such as serving refreshments and cleaning. In elite establishments like Thomas Selby's elegant Crown Coffee House, Selby's four slaves waited on some of the leading gentlemen of Boston and served them spirits from their master's extensive and rare collection.[51] While both types of these laborers, those hired out and those who labored with their owners, served a vital function to the town, examining where they appear in account books and taverns does not help to demonstrate their day-to-day lives.

Like unskilled white laborers, unskilled enslaved laborers lived rough-and-tumble, unpredictable lives. The historian Gary Nash notes in his description of labor in the early American seaports how unstable and transient this workforce was. Workers drifted job to job, performing the "essential raw labor associated with construction and timber." They were "the diggers of basements and wells, the pavers of streets," Nash continues, "the cutters and haulers of wood, and the carters of everything that needed moving."[52] Enslaved laborers may have had more stable lives, as they could not easily jump aboard a ship and travel to the nearest port to find better work—although a few tried, and fewer succeeded. Some performed multiple tasks, especially if they self-hired or their owners hired them out as a general laborer. They also faced unemployment and job instability, but unlike white workers, they could not leave to find work elsewhere and faced the possibility of being sold for "want of employ."

Black laborers also engaged in the same debauchery as working-class whites, usually right beside them. They drank, gambled, and philandered. And they fought, leading to trouble with the law. On 17 November 1752, Thomas Chub, a sailor, and Abraham, a slave, assaulted and killed John Crab, another laborer. Although the details are sparse, the case seems to be either a bar brawl taken too far or a workplace dispute. Chub struck Crab with an oak pipe stave, leaving a wound on his head "three inches long and half an inch deep." Abraham followed up with a second blow using a spruce pole. Despite the two men proclaiming their innocence, the court found them guilty of murdering Crab. The case of Chub and Abraham is interesting because it involves two working-class laborers of different races and legal statuses who came together to fight and kill someone of a similar socioeconomic standing. While there is not enough evidence to draw conclusions about race and class, this case suggests unskilled African laborers, like Abraham, were in a similar, if not the same, position—both economically and culturally—as white unskilled workers.[53]

The third category, sailors and other maritime workers, were most similar to enslaved laborers, in terms of both flexibility and lifestyle. W. Jeffery Bolster estimates that up to 25 percent of "male slaves in coastal Massachusetts" by the 1740s had been involved in some type of shipboard work.[54] When not at sea, many of these slaves probably worked on the docks as porters and stevedores. This flexibility can be seen in an advertisement from the *Boston Gazette*. The article described a "strong healthy Negro Man" who was capable of doing "Household Work, us'd to the Cooper's Business, and a very good Sailor."[55] Furthermore, wealthier sailors and ship captains in Boston owned slaves, many of whom served alongside their masters.[56] When at sea, however, slaves generally served as sailors and cooks—although those roles could be interchangeable—and made similar wages to white sailors'. Unlike other parts of the Americas, Boston's enslaved mariners served mostly onboard oceangoing vessels rather than the coastal trade, although slaves did serve on coasting vessels as well, as when Captain Samuel Osborn paid two slaves for three days' work aboard the sloop *Betty*.[57]

Life onboard the ship for enslaved sailors was similar to that of white sailors. Slaves manned and hoisted the sails, worked bilge pumps, made repairs, secured the cargo, responded to the onerous demands of the captain, and, if they were cooks, prepared food for the crew. They also drank, fought, whored, and gambled like their working-class brethren when at port, shamelessly flaunting and spending the wages they received, only to find themselves in trouble with the law.[58] An enslaved sailor's experience at sea oscillated from being horrendously oppressive to effectively free. Slaves who served under their captain-masters were never far from their purview, and even if the slaves were hired, masters sometimes instructed the captain to keep a close eye on them in case they ran away.[59] On the other hand, life on the open sea guaranteed a degree of personal freedom, and many enslaved sailors were removed from the onerous restrictions of the mainland. Likewise, these bondsmen had the opportunity to travel around the Atlantic world and visit exotic and foreign places. All of these experiences can be seen in the story of Jeffrey, an enslaved sailor from Boston belonging to John Mico. Mico instructed the captain to keep a close eye on Jeffrey during his trip from Boston to Barbados and London but also to treat him "as if he were your owne." Once in

London, however, the captain was to give Jeffrey leave to visit Mico's family in London if he desired.[60] The captain would not have kept track of Jeffrey, so he would have had the opportunity to explore the city and take in its vibrant urban life. Work experiences differed greatly for enslaved sailors, sometimes experiencing both autonomy and restriction in the same voyage, but they nevertheless had many opportunities otherwise unavailable to their land-bound comrades.

A famous example of the life of adventure offered to enslaved sailors was Briton Hammon, one of the first African Americans to publish in what was to become the United States. An experienced sailor by the time he wrote his pamphlet, *A Narrative of the Uncommon Sufferings and Surprizing Deliverance of Briton Hammon*, he was supposed to have a relatively quick six-month journey to Jamaica and British Honduras to pick up logwood. Hammon's sojourn quickly turned into a thirteen-year misadventure. On the return journey, his ship ran aground in the Florida Keys. After the captain and crew tried to dislodge themselves, they abandoned the ship and made camp on a nearby landmass. Almost immediately after the sailors set up their temporary shelter, local Indians attacked them, killing everyone but Hammon, who, as an African slave, was a valuable commodity. The Indians, allies of Spain, sold the slave to a Spanish ship captain, who later sold him to the governor of Cuba. He served as a butler for the governor for a year, spent over four years in prison for refusing to serve onboard a Spanish galleon, and carried the bishop of Havana around the countryside in a litter before escaping on an English ship to Jamaica. From there, he sailed to London, working as a sailor to pay for his passage. In London, he worked on the docks and eventually found passage on a vessel to Boston, once again hiring on as a sailor to pay for his passage. That vessel also happened to be carrying his master, a General Winslow, back to New England, and he and Hammon were reunited for the first time in thirteen years. According to Hammon's own narrative, he was an experienced sailor whose skill, despite landing him in a Cuban prison, ultimately enabled him to return home.[61]

Although not all enslaved sailors had adventures like those of Hammon, the relatively high wages they received explain why so many sought work onboard Boston ships. The need for maritime labor meant that, like other professions, Boston merchants and ship captains looked for workers from any source. Unlike work on land, however, sailing and working aboard ships offered slaves good wages, not to mention adventure and freedom from their master's purview—unless their masters were ship captains. John Herrick paid "Sesor" fourteen pounds per month when he served aboard the sloop *Betty*, a substantial sum considering that most white laborers and craftsmen could expect to make between thirty-five and sixty pounds a year.[62] While some of the slaves' wages went to their masters and shipboard work could be dangerous, relatively good pay and autonomy could assuage any fears of taking to the high seas.

Autonomy and good pay also help to explain why so many runaway slaves attempted to hop aboard a vessel leaving Boston. Eager captains were more than happy to negotiate with slaves about serving aboard their ships. Alexander Mitchell, mate of the sloop *Dollahide*, testified to the Massachusetts Superior Court of Judicature that Boston, a slave belonging to John Smith, met with the captain, Robert Boyd. After initial negotiations, Boston invited his friends Pompey and Sharper to meet with Boyd, and when they did, Boyd ordered Mitchell to fetch the slaves a "Dram of Rum." Two days later, when Mitchell was "turned out of Cabbin," he found the three men "stowd away" in the ship's forecastle. Mitchell also noted that when Boyd went onshore one evening, the Africans followed, and "they went up together the wharfe talking," leading Mitchell to conclude that "Boyd intended to carry them off." A sailor onboard the sloop, Cornelius Lamb, also testified that the slaves wanted him to "make [haste] and shut down the Shuttle for fear they should be seen." Boyd, for his part, never denied what Mitchell or Lamb had said and understood the risk he took by illicitly recruiting slaves. Given the absence of depositions from other sailors, it is likely the *Dollahide* was undermanned. Boyd, seeing an opportunity with Sharper, Boston, and Pompey, agreed to hire them to serve aboard the ship, even ordering Mitchell to provide them with provisions until they left port.[63] The need for maritime labor led many slaves to serve as sailors but also pushed the bounds of the law, leaving almost every runaway-slave advertisement to conclude, "All Masters of Vessels and other Persons are hereby cautioned against harboring, concealing or carrying off the said Servant, as they would avoid the Penalty of the Law."[64]

Slaves skilled in an artisanal craft and working for either their masters or on their own made up the final category of enslaved laborer in Boston. Contemporary newspapers testify to the sheer diversity of enslaved artisans. Newspapers brimmed with advertisements for coopers, tailors, blacksmiths, and almost every other skilled trade. Like white craftsmen, slaves began training at an early age as apprentices, usually to their masters.[65] The *Boston Gazette* advertised a fifteen-year-old slave boy who was "very fit for a Tradesman," indicating the subscriber's knowledge of the labor market and the desire of crafts-men to have both apprentices and bound laborers.[66] It made sense to train slaves in a trade, as most white artisans were self-employed and needed extra labor, which slaves provided at a relatively low cost and without the threat of future competition from taking on a white apprentice.[67] Some craftsmen sought these enslaved men—and they were all men—for their labor, and advertisements catered to that desire, one noting that an enslaved sawyer was "very suitable for a Master Builder or Cabinet-Maker."[68] Once the tradesman completed his training, his "master either used him as a journeyman at his own shop or hired him out for stated periods."[69] Even though enslaved artisans could cultivate skills, their race and legally dependent status meant that they could never achieve the rank of master craftsman or own their own shop. Also hard to discern is whether the children of skilled slaves learned their father's trade as the sons of white crafts-men did—although Peter Fleet, an enslaved printer, passed his craft on to his son Pompey—or if they were even considered part of the same trade hierarchy.[70]

Interestingly, many artisanal slaves served with white indentured servants and apprentices. Masters such as Edward Langdon, a Bos-ton tallow chandler (candle maker), received eight-year-old Ebenezar Blancher as a pauper apprentice in June 1764 until Blancher reached his majority at the age of twenty-one. When Langdon died two years later, he had an anonymous "Negroe Man" listed in his probate inven-tory. Although we can only speculate at the relationship between the African and the pauper boy, it is safe to assume that Blancher learned at least some aspects of candle making from the slave. After their master's death, they also suffered a similar fate. The slave would have been sold, possibly tearing him away from his family and commu-nity, while Blancher returned to the almshouse and was reindentured to a man from Plymouth, likewise severing any relationships he had formed in Boston.[71]

The working lives of slave artisans were similar to those of white apprentices and journeymen. Hours were long, and they were always subject to their master's whim—a doubly troubling prospect for slaves who sometimes answered to two masters, one in the workshop and one at home. They also tended to perform the worst parts of their respective trades, usually the dirty, tiresome, menial, tedious, and dangerous jobs.[72] In December 1748, an enslaved caulker, sent high up on the stern of a ship under construction, fell onto the timber lying below and died shortly thereafter.[73] The fact that the newspaper went out of its way to report this story indicates that enslaved artisans were a valuable product and that their death was a considerable loss. While that did not prevent these craftsmen from being commodified for the specialized labor they provided, it did give them certain protections and leverage against their masters and the institution of slavery in general. Masters had to be careful not to trifle with enslaved artisans because their skills could easily be put to use elsewhere, as when Bethia Tucker, a Boston widow, posted a runaway ad for her slave Cato. Cato, Tucker was at pains to acknowledge, was a "Shipwright by Trade." As long as he absconded to another seaport, or even another shipyard in Boston, he could find work.[74] It is safe to assume that despite back-breaking work conditions and long hours, slave artisans possessed a fair degree of autonomy attributable to their skill set and ability to work independently of their master.

Although workplace conditions, day-to-day experiences, and interactions varied by occupation, all jobs had three commonalities. First, work was, as indicated earlier, dangerous and grueling for all laborers, even domestic servants spending most of their time in their master's home. Moreover, despite the risks, Boston's slaves became talented at their jobs and sometimes even proud of their work. Finally, most of this talent and pride stemmed from the independence they experienced, as every job presented opportunities to slip away from an owner's purview and take charge of some aspects of their working lives. All of this is not to say that Boston was different from other parts of the Americas. An Anglican chaplain on the Codrington plantation in Barbados noted that skilled slaves had a "surprising influence over their inferiors, and enjoy several privileges above them." In almost all plantation societies, artisans were allowed to labor for their own wages in their spare time.[75] As these examples of skilled slaves suggests, it was not that the workplace leverage that enslaved Bostonians possessed did not exist elsewhere, but the very nature of the slave system in Boston created a labor regime in which there were more skilled slaves with control over their working lives.

The first of these themes, danger, was ever present in an enslaved Bostonian's workplace. Reports of work-related deaths are ubiquitous throughout published accounts of Boston's slaves and legal records.

Every county coroner in Massachusetts had the power to convene a jury to examine suspicious and/or sudden deaths. These "inquisitions on the body" regularly investigated workplace fatalities. One of these probed the death of James, an enslaved laborer belonging to Samuel Dunkin. Dunkin assigned James to dig into a sand hill, which subsequently collapsed and killed him in early March 1749.[76] Another horrific accident involved the slave Jack, who operated a small boat in Boston Harbor. He used an oar to steer the vessel, and one day in August 1750, it slipped, pulling Jack into the water, where he proceeded to drown.[77] Another slave, Cato, fell from the top of a still in the distillery where he worked, crushing his skull and killing him instantly.[78] An even more macabre scene appeared in an August 1735 issue of the *Boston Evening Post*. The article did not list the name of the slave, but he belonged to the distiller Isaac White, whose property was in Boston's North End. While carrying a pail of "high Wines from the Still," the slave tripped and fell down, spilling the spirits into a fire. The "whole was in a Flame in a Moment," including the slave, as "some of the Liquour . . . fell on the Fellow's Cloaths." Being near the harbor, he "ran into the Sea to quench himself" but was so terribly burned that he died shortly thereafter.[79]

Numerous injuries appear in probate records, where the court attempted to place a value on the recently deceased person's chattel. The clerk recorded that John Rowe's slave Devonshire had "lost several of his fingers," reducing his worth.[80] Even more cold and calculated was the assessment of Adam Winthrop's "old Negro man," who was so "Decrepit" as to be "of no value."[81] No matter how Winthrop regarded this bondsman while alive, there were no thanks, no reparations, no comfort for an enslaved man who labored hard his whole life, eventually ruining himself and being reduced to nothing more than a line in a ledger with "£0" beside his name. Danger was not only death lurking around every corner of the workplace, but even if one survived the rigors of urban slavery, there was still the threat of being completely consumed by an oppressive slave regime.

One way slaves resisted this dehumanization was by embracing their occupation. They became as talented and skilled as they could, using their skills to challenge their slavery. In early October 1741, six "Spanish Negroes"—Spanish sailors of African descent captured by British privateers and sold into slavery—stole a boat and attempted to go to St. Augustine in Florida, the nearest Spanish possession, but they were too poorly equipped to make the journey and were soon captured.[82]

Other slaves challenged their enslavement by taking pride in their work and becoming exceptionally skilled. Peter Fleet, a slave belonging to the printer Thomas Fleet, left a will and used it to prove that he was a good, productive member of society by reassuring his master and "Mistres" that he did not earn his money through "Rogury" or theft of "any thing belong'd to [Fleet] or any body else." Instead, he "got it honestly; by being faithful to people ever since [he] undertook to carry the Newspapers."[83] Peter took pride in his job and wanted to ensure that posterity knew he worked hard and honestly earned his wages. Likewise, Caesar, a slave living in Barnstable County, played an important role in a dispute between competing mills over water rights. The court called Caesar as an expert witness to discuss the argument's finer points, and he began by explaining how "the [flume] of the Old Grist Mill was taken up and the ditch dug deeper." The problem, the slave continued, was that "water [had] been drawn away from the New Grist Mill," which had been "greatly to her damage in grinding eversince." Caesar concluded that the newer mill had "not ground two-thirds so much as he otherwise might have done" had the ditch not been dug. Caesar understood not only how mills operated using waterpower but also the amount of flour created at any given time.[84] Finally, "a remarkably old Negro" named Quashee had his obituary printed in the Boston Gazette. He was "well known in" Boston for "bringing Sauce [liquor] to Market."[85] Quashee, like Peter Fleet and Caesar, became valuable to Bostonians for the service he provided, and he used that skill to claim a space in colonial society and become a well-known fixture of Boston's vibrant working world, even receiving memorialization in the printed record.

The skills and experience acquired by enslaved Bostonians allowed them not only to become valued members of the labor force but to claim a certain degree of independence and autonomy in their everyday lives. Even the most watched-over domestic servant would sometimes leave the house. In fact, many slaves used trips to the market to acquire the goods they and their households needed. A 1728 act forbade "Indian Negro or Mulatto" slaves from buying food for their masters from area farmers and retailers because they had "Inhanced the Price of Provisions."[86] Backed with their master's resources, slaves were able to manipulate the market to better provide for their owners and, by extension, themselves and any other servants living in their homes. Some slaves, like sailors, left their masters' homes for long periods of time, only obligated to complete the tasks they were assigned. During the British occupation of Boston in 1775, Sharper, a slave belonging to the Bostonian in exile Enoch Brown, went on an extensive "trading journey" all throughout southeastern Massachusetts, traveling from Dartmouth to Middleborough and then on to the Continental army's camp in Cambridge. Sharper's journey did not seem to be anything out of the ordinary, and the only reason we know about it is that his wife, a slave belonging to Josiah Quincy of Braintree, inquired after him.[87] Independence—like that enjoyed by Sharper—in the working lives of enslaved Bostonians may have come as part of their various occupations, but slaves eventually learned to use the advantages it brought.

While it is easy to demonstrate the workplace autonomy experienced by Boston's slaves, it had a deeper meaning, one that allowed slaves to shape the terms of their enslavement to their own ends. The vibrant working world of a cosmopolitan seaport like Boston meant that slaves were employed in a variety of different professions, each with its own set of restrictions and freedoms. Slaves manipulated these limitations to capitalize on the autonomy offered by an urban work environment. Important to understanding how this happened is the concept of boundaries—both those of enslavement and the labor regimen and those constructed by slaves in their own working lives. We need to analyze not only how slaves behaved in the workplace but also their relationships with coworkers and, in some cases, coconspirators, bosses, and other enslaved people they encountered. Examining how enslaved Bostonians protested working conditions, contested wrongful claims to their labor and interruptions to their working lives, and, most importantly, created a sense of self and personality built out of their workplace experiences allows us to understand these trends. Interpreting the meaning of labor independence illustrates how slaves challenged boundaries forced on them, while upholding boundaries they created and ameliorating their condition in the absence of a call for emancipation.

Complaints concerning working conditions were quite common among enslaved people, leading many to protest against them. Whether slaves worked in a distillery or in their owner's home, they had plenty to complain about. Hours were long, the work was demanding and unrewarding, and masters and bosses were never completely satisfied. This led to a number of different types of protests that ranged from relatively benign to wildly destructive. Some were simple and straightforward, such as the enslaved boy who burned down his master's barn, killing ten horses and a "Yoke of fat Oxen," because the boy was "tired of tending the Creatures."[88]

Compared to the simple protest in the preceding example, some slaves concocted more elaborate conspiracies to challenge their working conditions. Two examples help to illustrate this subterfuge. The first involved three slaves named Yaw, Caesar, and Betty, Yaw's spouse. They belonged to Humphrey Scarlett and his wife, Mary. Scarlett owned a tavern, where his slaves worked. Although Yaw and Caesar often went on errands and purchased supplies for the tavern, they spent a considerable amount of time at the tavern itself. Mary Scarlett must have also been at the tavern often because both slaves later testified that she "plagued them everyday." While the two men offered conflicting evidence, in spring 1731, they conspired to poison Mary, hoping to silence her annoying demands. Caesar acquired arsenic from another slave, as Yaw claimed he did not have the money to purchase it. Meanwhile, Caesar claimed that Yaw pestered him about the poison for a few months until mid-August, when he finally stole some of the poison from Caesar. Yaw mixed it into water, which was then used to make Mary's drinking chocolate. This is where their plan went awry. Mary was the only person supposed to drink the chocolate, but when Betty served breakfast the following morning, the whole family imbibed. Caesar claimed to have returned home at that point, having taken breakfast elsewhere, and "found his Master's Family in great Confusion," all of them taken ill. Luckily for the Scarletts, nobody died from the poisoning, but Caesar and Yaw both went to trial. Through the use of poison, Caesar and Yaw protested their nagging mistress's onerous workplace demands and hoped to eliminate a burden in their working lives.[89]

Attempts to kill were rare; many more slaves simply absconded. In 1747, George and Richard Hewes, two brothers who owned a tannery in Boston, filed suit against Nathaniel Cunningham, a Cambridge farmer. Eight years earlier, Cunningham, according to the Heweses, "unjustly contrive[ed] to disable" their tannery when he "seduced" the brothers' slaves Cato, Nero, Quaco, and Scipio—all skilled tanners— to leave Boston and work on Cunningham's farm. Although the case took almost seven years to go to trial, there was plenty of evidence given shortly after the slaves departed to support the tanners' claims. Richard Champney, Cunningham's neighbor, encountered one of the farmer's other laborers leaving Cambridge to "fetch up George and

Robert Hewes's Negroes." He later saw three of the four African men hoeing corn in Cunningham's field. Finding the situation peculiar, Champney stopped and spoke with Cato, Nero, and Quaco, who informed him, among other things, that Cunningham had taken them from the Hewes brothers and that Scipio was going to join them soon. Thomas Thwing, another Cunningham neighbor, confirmed what Champney had said and even provided a physical description of the enslaved men. Before Cunningham returned the slaves to the Hewes brothers, both witnesses also testified that Quaco "was there some time and some time gone," meaning he had ran away. George and Richard Hewes eventually won their case, and the court ordered Cunningham to pay them £400 in damages.[90]

Yet it is hard to believe that these four slaves were passive victims, stolen away by a greedy farmer in need of labor. There had to have been some form of consent to go and work for Cunningham and a reason for leaving the Heweses' employment. Nor were they trying to escape work, as both Champney and Thwing witnessed them laboring on Cunningham's farm. Although working may not have been an issue, the type of work may have. Tanning in the early modern era was not pleasant. Tanners worked long hours around putrefying animal skins that required three arduous steps to turn into leather. First, the flesh had to be repeatedly treated with either urine or lime to loosen the hair, so it and the fat could be scraped off the rotting skins. This step also required precision because if a skin did not spend enough time in the lime bath, it was unworkable, but if it was submerged too long, it broke down and had to be discarded. After the tanners removed the hair, they began a process called "bating," in which the hides would be soaked in a solution of water and fecal matter—usually from dogs or birds—which would soften the hides. The final stage, also the least revolting, required soaking the bated skins in oak bark and water for a period of six months to two years, conditioning the hides. The skins were then dried and sold as raw leather.[91] As the process suggests, tanning was hard, potentially dangerous, and absolutely disgusting. The tannery itself would smell horrendous and be full of hazardous lime, feces, and festering flesh. Given these conditions, it should be no surprise that Cunningham could so easily entice Cato, Nero, Quaco, and Scipio to go and work for him. Given that Quaco ran away when he found out they would be returning to the tannery, the slaves may have approached Cunningham in the first place. By absconding to a country farm, the slaves lodged a powerful protest against their working conditions, one that worked for almost a year but ultimately proved futile.

Both of these cases demonstrate that slaves challenged their working conditions, sometimes in violent ways, other times by simply absconding. Interestingly, however, work-related protests were devoid of calls for freedom or even a challenge to being enslaved. These examples suggest that slaves, rather than protest their status as slaves, contested the type of work they had to do and the people they worked for. The actions of these six slaves suggest that they never contemplated a world without masters. Yaw and Ceasar's master would still have owned them, while their mistress would be out of the picture. Nero, Cato, Quaco, and Scipio also traded one set of masters for another and seemed satisfied with working for Cunningham. These protests were not attempts to become free laborers but expressed the desire to work under a more agreeable master and in better conditions. In that sense, these slaves must be understood in the context of other eighteenth-century workplace protests, in which laborers were concerned not with overthrowing the social order but with defending their rights and position in society.[92]

In this vein, slaves not only protested against onerous working conditions; they also fought against those who challenged their workplace prerogatives or made unjust claims to their labor. Unlike the disputes just detailed, most of these were not against masters and/or employers but against other workers, usually whites, or even imperial and military officials. We can see this in the case of Titus, a slave belonging to Edward Durant of Newton. Titus worked on Durant's farm and carted goods from there to market in Boston. On 25 November 1766, Titus crossed paths with Ebenezer Dewing, a farmer from Needham returning home from Cambridge. Both men "had Teams in the Road, the Countryman's empty and the Negroes loaded," and the road was only wide enough for one of the wagons to proceed, leading to a dispute over "which should turn out of the Path-way."[93] Neither the newspaper nor the court recorded the words exchanged between the two men, but we can speculate that Dewing expected the slave to defer and give him right of way. Titus, having a full cart, saw his passage as more pressing. Eventually, the argument escalated, "blows ensued," and Titus went after Dewing with the "Butt End of a Whip."[94] Titus attacked the "Countryman" with the whip handle, leaving a two-inch gash on his head, and repeatedly hit him in the kidneys. After beating the farmer, Titus cleared the path and traveled to Boston. Dewing, beaten so severely that he could not ride home, spent the night in the snowy woods near the path, dying of exposure and his untreated wounds.[95] Titus was later arrested in Boston and transferred to Middlesex County, where the crime occurred. The case went to the Superior Court of Judicature, which found him not guilty for want of evidence.[96] Titus's case demonstrates that slaves were not only subject to the same passions as other colonists but also fiercely protective of their labor and work arrangements.

Many of the cases just evaluated examine individual actions of one slave or a small group of slaves, but enslaved Bostonians also participated in general protests defending workers' rights. A good example was the Impressment Riot of 1747. Also known as the Knowles Riot, after Commodore Charles Knowles, the riot involved a large swath of working-class Bostonians, white and black, free and enslaved, taking control of the town and challenging imperial authority over a three-day period in November 1747. Impressment, the legal authority given to a ship captain to conscript or "press," usually forcefully, laborers into maritime service, had been a point of contention throughout the eighteenth century, as the Royal Navy was in desperate need of sailors to fight against the French and Spanish. The American colonies proved to be easy picking for the navy, especially seaports like Boston, where navy captains, admirals, and commodores were usually some of the most powerful imperial officials around and could use their power to leverage conscripts. Pressing men into service had a long history, and every time it occurred in the colonies, it was met with more and more resistance, culminating in the Knowles Riot. Parliament attempted to respond by decreeing that only royal governors, not naval officials, could issue impressment orders, but this law went unheeded. As most press gangs targeted unskilled laborers, poorer artisans, and dockworkers, they also seized a number of enslaved workers, who, like their white counterparts, eventually grew tired and fearful of impressment.[97]

The particular details of the Knowles Riot are important to understanding why enslaved Bostonians protested. In early November 1747, during the War of Austrian Succession (1740–1748), Commodore Charles Knowles and a Royal Navy fleet took refuge in Boston Harbor to resupply and protect themselves from French depredations. The navy was not an illustrious career, and sailors were subjected to hard work, grueling conditions, and corporal punishment if they challenged authority. Needless to say, a large number of Knowles's crew took the opportunity of being in port to desert from the navy and escape into Boston and the surrounding towns. The fleet suffered a high-enough attrition rate that Knowles barely had the manpower to leave. To combat this shortage, on November 16, the commodore, without the permission of the governor, sent press gangs onto Boston Harbor and into the city itself. They rounded up a number of laborers by stopping skiffs transporting goods and workers into Boston. Not only did this action horrify working-class Bostonians, who thought they were next, but when many of the farmers and small merchants from surrounding towns heard the news, they stopped using the harbor to supply the town, cutting off a large portion of its lifeline. Soon mobs of workers formed, which included "Foreign Seamen, Servants, Negroes, and other Persons of Mean and vile condition,"[98] and in a reversal of fortune, they captured some Royal Navy officers, threatening to return them only if the press gangs released the men they had captured. Tensions ran high over the next three days, while town officials negotiated with Knowles, who at one point threatened to bombard the town. Eventually, however, the sides exchanged prisoners, and the British fleet left.

Slaves, like white workers, participated in the Impressment Riot because they felt their rights had been violated. Working on the docks or in shipyards might have been hard, but life in the Royal Navy was intolerable for them. Such an interruption in their everyday lives, with little or no chance of returning to Boston, was unthinkable. The press gang represented instability, drudgery, and a form of slavery that completely restricted the autonomy that most enslaved Bostonians enjoyed.[99] In fact, by protesting, slaves joined the chorus of working-class voices across the Atlantic world who agreed that no "institution was as much hated in the eighteenth-century, as the press gang."[100] It is unknown, however, if the Knowles Riot was a transformative event in the slaves' understanding of rights. Many radicals, like "A Lover of His Country," who published *An Address to the Inhabitants of the Province of Massachusetts Bay* shortly after the riot, linked the disturbance to both the protection of their customary rights as Englishmen and John Locke's theory of natural rights.[101] Unfortunately, slaves did not leave records indicating their attitudes toward the event, but their participation in the riot does acknowledge that they were staunch defenders of their workplace privileges and independence.

As we have seen, enslaved Bostonians used the autonomy they enjoyed in the workplace to protest and protect their working lives, but this workplace independence was also important to crafting an identity. This identity was not built on a desire for legal freedom or universal emancipation but constructed in the relationship between slaves and their coworkers, by imposing limits on the degradation they were willing to experience as chattel, and in exploiting the terms of their enslavement to best suit themselves. We can see this clearly in a case involving an enslaved sailor. On the night of 2 January 1759, one McCloud was asleep on his boat in Boston Harbor along with his fourteen-year-old son and his slave, whose names do not appear in the newspaper account. After docking for the night, "they kindled up a Charcoal Fire in the Cuddy, shut the Door, and then lay'd themselves down to sleep." They had not been asleep long when the slave woke up, and "finding himself much disorder'd, without knowing the Occasion of it, he opened the Door and got out into the Air, and soon came to himself." Although the slave did not know what was going on, he then looked back into the cabin, where he saw his master, ran in, and pulled him out into the night air, but the owner had been "so much overcome that he could not stand nor speak." The slave hailed a nearby ship for assistance, and when the sailors came onboard, they helped McCloud. It was too late for his son, however, who died from the "steam of the Charcoal," most likely carbon monoxide poisoning.[102] The slave's actions were admirable, but they may well have represented a complex mix of loyalty to his master, solidarity with his fellow workers, a desire not to be sold away from a situation that he may have found suitable, and a basic response to a situation that threatened the life of another human being. Despite the dehumanizing nature of the institution that constrained slaves, they rose above it not just in asserting their own rights but in protecting those of others to whom they were tied.

As the example of this slave implies, identity was not only tied to resistance, and the next two examples show that identity must take into consideration a whole range of factors. We have seen how slaves protected their workplace independence, but they also defended themselves against the insults and depredations of their coworkers and employers. Adam, a slave hired to work on the construction of Castle William in Boston Harbor, got into an altercation with his boss. John Shine and William Lee, two of Adam's coworkers, witnessed the event. One of the managers, Captain Timothy Clark, spoke with Adam and gave him instructions. While the details of these orders are unknown, Adam must have found them unsatisfactory. Adam's response was not one of a docile laborer, and he "Showed himself very surly" and "gave saucy Answers" to all of Clark's inquires. Clark, infuriated with Adam, took a small stick, struck the slave's tobacco pipe out his mouth, shoved him, and "Struck him a blow over the shoulders." Adam, "in a great fury and rage" because his honor had been insulted, shoved Clark, took the stick from him, and broke it. He then picked up a shovel and with the "Iron upward offered a stroke" to Clark, who deflected the blow with his arms. A number of the other workers interfered to stop the fight, fearing Clark would be "grievously" injured. Adam was so "furious" that it took "six or seven" of the workers to "hold and restrain him."[103] Adam was deeply protective of his personhood, resorting to violence to defend against abuses and protect his honor.

Violence characterized a number of encounters between slaves and those who denigrated them in the workplace. London, a slave who worked on the ship *Gideon* sailing out of Boston, was in port in Newbury loading timber. Months earlier, William Kipp, a sailor aboard the ship, had had a dispute with London, calling him a "Black Rouge," with the slave responding that Kipp was "the more black Rogue than himself." Kipp took the words in jest, but another crewman, Ralph Wheeler, interrupted and asked why London talked so "saivoirly to all White Men." The bondsman told Wheeler to "mind his Own Business," while Kipp walked away. The fight escalated when Wheeler, upset at London's attitude and lack of deference to the white crew, picked up a stick and "flung it toward" the slave. The stick missed but rebounded off the side of the ship and "struck [London] some place about the Belly." London lived after that encounter, but once in Newbury, he took ill and died. The ship's doctor, Nathan Hale, had the coroner examine the slave's body and found that he had died of a "break at the bottom of his belly."[104] Defending one's identity and autonomy, especially against rowdy and rambunctious coworkers quick to resort to violence, sometimes proved to be fatal. No matter what the risks, however, slaves found it necessary to confront those who threatened to deride them. Had they not challenged every affront, no matter how dangerous or how violent it could become, enslaved Bostonians would not have had the workplace independence or sense of self they possessed.

Although violence characterized many of the attempts of enslaved Bostonians to craft an identity, they also used ingenuity and cunning to shape the terms of their enslavement and workplace arrangements. Titus, an enslaved sailor belonging to Edward Lyde, who "sent him to sea with Capt. Zachariah Fowle," illustrates this point. In early 1714, Fowle was on a trading voyage to the West Indies, and according to a crewmember, Jonathan Mason, the ship ran aground on an island off the coast of Saint-Domingue (modern Haiti). Eventually, a passing ship rescued Fowle and the crew, transporting them to Danish St. Thomas, and from there, they found passage to the English St. Christopher. Looking to get passage back to Boston and short on cash, Fowle decided he would sell Titus. The captain told the merchant Anthony Fay that Titus was his property, and Fay purchased the slave. When the crew started to drift back into Boston and Titus was nowhere to be found, Lyde became worried, especially when crew members like Mason spoke of Titus's sale. Lyde turned to his acquaintance William Harris, who had a good friend in St. Christopher named William Fenton. Fenton was eventually able to find Titus and send him back to Boston, but it was a process full of tribulation and folly.[105]

According to Fenton, he was able to recover Titus from Fay, but not without significant consternation. Despite Fay demanding the full cost he paid for Titus, the merchant was more than happy to be rid of his charge. Fay did not even want Titus in the first place but was just going to sell him in Martinique to labor-hungry French planters. Every time he attempted to sell Titus, however, the slave "feigned himself sick," and potential buyers demurred. When Fenton bought Titus, he wanted to send him back to Boston as soon as possible, but Titus "plaid several rogue tricks" on him. Most prominently, the enslaved man broke into Fenton's storehouse and "stole a considerable Quantity of wine." In Fenton's last letter to Harris, his frustration was palpable as he explained he could only deal with Titus because he had a "Value for [Harris's] friendship." Fenton was a good friend to deal with Titus's transgressions and eventually secured the slave passage on a ship to Boston. To keep him out of trouble while onboard the ship, Fenton negotiated that Titus would work to pay his passage. Fenton's and Fay's frustrations were Titus's attempts to shape his enslavement. Not wanting to work on a sugar plantation on a foreign island, Titus faked illness, making him less appealing. Once acquired by Fenton, Titus was going to make the most out of his time in the Caribbean, enjoying drink and prolonging his stay there through several clever tricks. Although Titus's case is exceptional, he exploited his unique position through chicanery to create a space where he could protect his independence.

Not all slaves were like Titus, however, and many did not have the opportunity to exercise autonomy in their workplaces. Many slaves, especially females, served at the whim of their master and in their master's home. Nor were all slaves skilled enough to be considered valuable, and they could be easily sold away. The gaze of the master and threat of sale severely circumscribed the ability to protest or craft a workplace identity. It is important to note that three of the four examples in the discussion of identity were enslaved sailors, who had much more autonomy than those who were confined on land. Even the simplest protests by domestic servants could prove disastrous. Bristol, a domestic slave belonging to Jonathan Simpson, suffered numerous abuses from his master's son, Jonathan Simpson Jr. One day in January 1746, the son "punished"—how is not stated—Bristol for some transgression while he was working around the Simpson house, pushing the slave to the breaking point. Bristol pulled a knife and threatened to "Stab or kill any person that should offer to lay Hold on him." The younger Simpson called for the constables of Boston, and three town watchmen, Ebenezer Winbourne, Nathaniel Band, and Patrick Camel, answered his call. When they entered the home, Bristol threatened to kill the watchmen if they tried to arrest him. The three men attempted to subdue Bristol, nevertheless, and he stabbed Camel in the arm. Camel, now enraged, grabbed Bristol's shirt collar, attempting to stop the slave from doing further harm, and later alleged he "accidently" strangled Bristol to death in the process.[106]

While protests could be futile and deadly, sometimes autonomy itself proved to be counterproductive, such as when Godfrey, a bondsman belonging to a Boston ship captain, joined in with other sailors while in Newfoundland and stole some "fowl" to eat. When caught, Godfrey offered compensation for the fowl but paid with stolen money, which ultimately not only led to his being whipped by the authorities in Newfoundland, but most of the crew received whippings as well.[107] Godfrey's desire to create mischief with his crewmates landed not only him in trouble but his coworkers as well, most likely earning their distrust and leaving them all keeping a close eye on him. Workplace autonomy, even for enslaved sailors, could be quite fleeting and impermanent.

The ability to make meaning of even a modicum of workplace independence, while highly restricted for many slaves, allowed some to lodge protests against working conditions, defend their perceived rights as workers, and craft a workplace identity. They were able to do so largely because slave labor in Boston was diversified and important to the town's economy. Enslaved Bostonians were not confined to a plantation and often did not work in the company of large numbers of other enslaved Africans. Instead, they forged workplace connections and conceptions of traditional liberties in response to their masters or in conjunction with their white coworkers. Rarely did they assert claims for freedom, but they did seek to ameliorate their condition, articulate their rights, and secure a greater degree of autonomy than we might expect that a slave would enjoy. In the process, they may not have contributed to the eradication of slavery as an institution, but they did have a role in shaping its terms.

Eighteenth-century Boston contained a large and dynamic slave workforce. These enslaved laborers worked in myriad professions, from dockworkers to sailors and artisans. Constituting an important component of the town's labor force, most slaves were domestic servants, unskilled laborers, maritime workers, and craftsmen. Slaves in each of these occupations fostered their own relationships with masters, employers, and coworkers, both black and white. Despite occupational hazards, slaves became incredibly skilled and gained a certain degree of autonomy by working. The meaning of this independence can be directly linked with their desire to ameliorate their condition. Slaves, especially artisans, used their occupational knowledge—valuable skills in a labor-starved economy—as leverage against the threat of sale or abuse. They also lodged protests against workplace conditions that they found disagreeable or against those who threatened to change their employment arrangements. Finally, enslaved workers created an identity surrounding their occupations. This identity involved not only the aforementioned protests but also the relationships they formed with their employers and coworkers and attempts to protect their autonomy. Much of this was characterized by violent encounters, but slaves also engaged in subterfuge to foster this identity. Nevertheless, the ability to capitalize on workplace autonomy was highly conditional and not available to all slaves.

Peering into the laboring world of enslaved Bostonians allows us to view a world of ever-shifting boundaries. On the one hand, slaves faced numerous restrictions because of their legally established status. On the other, once a slave became integral to the economy, filling a role not easily filled by another, he or she could begin setting limits and manipulating the terms of his or her slavery, in effect redrawing its boundaries. Conceptualizing slavery as a relationship of boundaries allows us to think beyond modern conceptions of liberty.

Emancipation and personal liberty were at best far-off dreams and, more likely, mere abstractions that would not have made sense in slaves' unfree, hierarchical world. In their everyday lives, however, they contemplated how they might escape abuse, find a moment of pleasure, excel at the performance of a chore, or have a meaningful relationship. Those were the attainable goals, and from the small slice of slavery we have been able to glimpse in the lives recounted here, at least some enslaved Bostonians insisted on their inherent humanity.

5 / Appropriating Institutions

In Phillis Wheatley's famous, or rather infamous, poem "On Being Brought from Africa to America," the poet and enslaved Bostonian wrote that it was divine mercy that brought her from her "*Pagan* land."[1] The Holy Spirit, according to Wheatley, "taught [her] benighted soul to understand" the salvation offered by belief in Jesus Christ. While the poem described Wheatley's spiritual transformation from an African heathen into an African American Christian, it also demonstrates that Christianity had more to offer enslaved Bostonians than religion. Wheatley learned or, in her own words, came to "understand" that Protestant Christianity and other European institutions offered valuable tools that aided the poet in adjusting to her new homeland.[2]

Throughout the first three quarters of the eighteenth century, enslaved Bostonians like Wheatley learned an effective way to resist the dehumanization of enslavement by appropriating Euro-American institutions. The two chief ones they learned to navigate were the law and Protestant Christianity. Both offered many skills that slaves could use to change the terms of enslavement. These skills were not used to obtain legal freedom or emancipation until the 1760s. Instead, slaves channeled them into manipulating the terms of enslavement. Some of these skills included knowledge of the law that could be used to obtain legal redress; literacy or at least the ability to read from learning Christian texts; and a powerful legal and religious vocabulary, which allowed slaves to effectively communicate with colonial authorities. Although the acquisition of this knowledge was haphazard, took time—sometimes generations—to hone and learn, and could not always be employed successfully, by the eve of the American Revolution, familiarity with local Euro-American institutions was one of the best skills enslaved Bostonians could draw on.

By examining how enslaved Bostonians appropriated white institutions and the skills they provided, we see not only how slaves were able to successfully decode and navigate the world they were thrust into but how these structures were open to the enslaved. Sometimes just the smallest opening, the chance to appear before a justice of the peace or learning to read a passage of the Bible, opened a whole new realm of possibilities, especially for resistance. Instead of futile acts of violence or taking the risk of running away, appropriation offered a different form of empowerment, one that was subtler, less uncertain, and, in the end, more powerful.

Of the two major Euro-American institutions appropriated by enslaved Bostonians, the law proved to be the most important in the long term. The law allowed slaves to ameliorate and shape the conditions of enslavement. Some of this had to do with the judicial climate and the ambiguous legal status of slaves in eighteenth-century Boston, which lacked a comprehensive slave code, and local justices of the peace adjudicated cases involving slaves with little guidance. These justices drew on popular English legal theory, usually printed in readily available guidebooks, which regulated traditional servitude. Such a devolved understanding of the law also reached slaves, as they acquired an intimate knowledge of the law throughout the provincial period. Slaves channeled this knowledge into redefining the nature of enslavement using the law to better their day-to-day life.

To understand how slaves eventually learned the law and exploited it for their own advantage, we need to examine the nature of slave law in eighteenth-century Boston. In practice, if not in law, magistrates recognized slaves as servants, governed by the same statues concerning white indentures. This is why slaves were often not recognized as such but were considered servants or "servants for life." There was a large corpus of servant law available to justices of the peace in Massachusetts. As many of these men did not have any legal training and tended to be respected members of the community rather than judicial authorities, justices turned to widely published commentaries on English law to effectively adjudicate it. Three of these books, Michael Dalton's *The Countrey Justice* (1618), William Nelson's *The Office and*

Authority of a Justice of the Peace (1704), and William Blackstone's *Commentaries on the Laws of England* (1765–1769), were widely available in Massachusetts, carefully read by justices of the peace, and used in decisions involving slaves.

The first of these books, Dalton's *Countrey Justice*, a manual "containing the practice of the Justice of the Peace," was most popular in the seventeenth century, but Bostonians continued using the book throughout the colonial period. Its significance can be seen in the practices of Justice of the Peace John Clark, who served in that office from 1700 to 1726. He did not even own a copy of Dalton's book, but his record book revealed a "judicial world not far from that depicted in the 1705 edition of . . . *The Countrey Justice*."[3] Even people at the highest echelons of political authority could not escape Dalton's influence and commonly cited him, such as when Governor Joseph Dudley and Chief Justice Samuel Sewall turned to *The Countrey Justice* to figure out how to handle an adulterer's petition.[4] Perhaps it was commonly used because *The Countrey Justice* was readily accessible and easy to navigate for nonlawyers. To help readers more easily understand servitude, Dalton grouped servants, apprentices, and other indentures under the label "Laborer."[5] He explained who could be masters and servants, laws governing the behavior of servants while under indenture, and the punishments for servile transgressions, such as running away, which allowed justices to commit the recalcitrant servant to "Ward [jail], there to remain without Bail."[6] More importantly, however, Dalton explained the legal obligations that masters and servants had to one another. Masters could not discharge bound laborers from their service without servants' consent. Moreover, both the indenture and discharge had to be in writing, as informal agreements could lead to one side cheating the other. Servants were also entitled to payment, although masters could not pay them "excesse wages" and servants forfeited compensation if they ran away.[7] In addition to questions of payment, Dalton elucidated the protections servants had against masters. If masters "misused" their servants or if servants felt they had "just cause to complain," retainers had full legal recourse and access to a justice of the peace who could hear the case. If the abuse was bad enough, a quorum of four justices could discharge a servant from his or her indenture. Of course, had the servant lied to the justice, he or she could be imprisoned.[8] As with abuse, if a master did not provide his or her servant with "Wages, Meat or Drink," the servant could go before a justice and have his or her indenture annulled. While Dalton's text still meant to protect the interest of masters, it laid out a clear set of responsibilities that both parties had and ensured that servants had legal recourse against abusive or neglectful masters.

Another legal guidebook used by Boston's justices was William Nelson's *The Office and Authority of a Justice of the Peace*. Nelson's book could be found in the libraries of Boston's justices of the peace, and some like Anthony Stoddard, a Boston magistrate from 1715 until his death in 1748, owned both Nelson's and Dalton's books.[9] Originally published in 1704, Nelson's guide was a compilation of English common and statutory law and dedicated twenty-four pages to discussing servitude, which he listed under the heading "Apprentices."[10] Echoing Dalton, Nelson explained the duties that masters and servants had to one another, even including a clause concerning the provision of food and drink. Nelson, however, was more concerned with wages. If a master were "Detaining Wages, or not allowing Meat," it constituted a "good Cause" for an apprentice to leave his or her service.[11] Likewise, masters had to pay even if they discharged a servant, and in the case of death, their estate had to pay servants for their time. Justices were to look out for the welfare of servants, and in case of illness, their "Wages ought not to be abated."[12] Once again, Nelson encouraged both servants and masters to resolve their concerns with a justice of the peace. Unlike Dalton, Nelson provided actual cases that readers could use as precedent. One concerned an abusive master who "doth not allow unto his said Apprentice sufficient Meat, Drink, and Apparel, but hath often immoderately corrected him without any just Cause." This master was in direct violation of the contract between him and his apprentice, allowing the servant recourse to the law. If the bondsman or bondswoman approached a justice, the justice first had to try and reconcile master and servant, and failing that, the master was to appear before the next court session and answer for his transgressions. The court would then rule whether to "discharge the Apprentice."[13]

William Blackstone's *Commentaries on the Laws of England* was the final popular law book. First published in 1765, the book was a wildfire success and continues to be used in American and English jurisprudence to this day.[14] Blackstone proved indispensible not only for Boston's justices of the peace but for its burgeoning first generation of professional lawyers. These men, including such luminaries as Robert Treat Paine, John Adams, and Josiah Quincy, all read Blackstone.[15] In doing so, they would have found the author's commentaries on servitude especially enlightening. In a ten-page chapter titled "Of Master and Servant," Blackstone succinctly defined servitude as "founded in convenience, whereby a man is directed to call in the assistance of other, where his own skill and labor will not be sufficient to answer the cares incumbent upon him."[16] Blackstone did not consider servitude to be about oppression and dominance but about the recognition that man is dependent on others to accomplish certain tasks. Such a benevolent definition of servitude led to his abhorrence of slavery, the only one of the three authors to address the institution directly. Slavery, by his estimation, "does not, nay cannot, subsist in England; such I mean, whereby an absolute and unlimited power is given to the master over the life and fortune of the slave." "And indeed it is repugnant to reason, and the principles of natural law," Blackstone disdainfully continued, "that such a state should subsist anywhere."[17]

Despite invoking natural law, Blackstone's abhorrence of slavery was a conservative reaction to an institution that undermined traditional notions of English liberty and servitude. This can be seen when reading his examination of the types of servants and the obligations masters and servants had to one another. Blackstone's version of servitude is not at all different from that of Dalton and Nelson. Servants, except apprentices, were entitled to wages. Likewise, masters could not beat servants excessively, and if a laborer assaulted a master, he or she could be imprisoned for up to one year. Justices and sessions courts were in charge of adjudicating these cases, which could be brought by both masters and servants, and of making decisions about what constituted abuse and absconding.[18] Finally, Blackstone emphasized that the master was ultimately responsible for the behavior of his or her servant, as "the wrong done by the servant is looked upon in law as the wrong of the master himself."[19] Never once did Blackstone condemn servitude in the same way he attacked slavery. Instead, as a traditional institution, servitude was a natural part of English law and life, not a repugnant, exploitative institution. Service and dependence were natural manifestations of a world where no one person could be self-sufficient, but those who were obligated to serve had certain rights, privileges, and protections from abuse.

Dalton, Nelson, and Blackstone all provide important insights into the law of early modern English servitude, a legal definition applied to most unfree Bostonians, including African slaves. All three jurists grant considerable discretion to local justices of the peace. These men, usually untrained in the law, were more concerned about communal tranquility and stability than the concerns of masters or servants. This stability rested on the ability for all, free and unfree, to have legal recourse and access to justices and the courts, a point emphasized by all three authors. Servants could lodge complaints against masters, especially when they were neglected and abused. These protections constituted a set of legal rights available to all dependent classes. Although status was still a factor and justices meted out draconian punishments for servile transgressions, these rights provided a defensible set of principles for slaves and others to rally around. These rights were never enumerated or written down, leading to some confusion, as in 1771, when Thomas Hutchinson wrote to Secretary of the Colonies Lord William Hillsborough, "I do not know that it has been determined that [slaves] may not have a property in goods."[20] Yet this ambiguity favored slaves, who found servitude and its accompanying rights a much more permeable institution than chattel slavery.

The legal definition of slaves as servants most likely occurred because the restrictive legislation against people of color, taxation schemes that classified slaves with other forms of chattel such as livestock, and slavery's legal position was ad hoc and ambiguous at best.[21] There was never a comprehensive slave code enacted, leaving individual acts to govern the institution. However, Boston did pass something like a corpus of slave law in 1723, titled "Articles for the Better Regulating Indians, Negroes and Molattos within This Town . . . ," and included such measures as a sundown-to-sunup curfew, a prohibition on carrying weapons, and restrictions on gathering in groups of more than two.[22] This legislation never gained traction at the provincial level and only served to infuriate a number of slaves, who attempted to burn down the town.[23] Outside of disinterest and potentially destructive blowback from the targets of these acts, the lax enforcement of the legislation guaranteed that only a few slaves received punishments for violating them.[24] Instead, authorities used these statutes to further punish slaves who were already in trouble with the law or slaves who had an "infamous reputation." Moreover, these laws never combined to completely deprive slaves of certain liberties, especially their rights to judicial recourse, to a trial by jury (even if only a commitment to the process), and to testify against whites.[25] While other legal means to control slaves existed, they proved too haphazard and incomplete to effectively govern slavery in Boston in the way that servant law was.

Such legal ambiguity meant that whites and blacks alike needed a deep knowledge of the law to help better navigate and define enslavement. The lack of formal legal training and institutions caused the law to become "simplified and popular," leading to its wide diffusion throughout colonial society.[26] Whites acquired legal knowledge through a number of informal ways such as reading legal treatises and discussing law with others. Given the relatively high literacy rates among Afro-Bostonians (see later in the chapter) and availability of law books in Boston, it was feasible for slaves to learn the law. The intimate contact between slaves and other Bostonians meant they could have shared personal stories of their encounters with the law.

More significantly, slaves commonly ran afoul of white society and appeared before justices and the General Sessions court, giving them experiential knowledge. The relative openness of the court system meant that enslaved Bostonians had nearly constant interaction with legal apparatuses, and they could share that information with their various communities. In early June 1727, a slave named Scipio claimed to have gotten off work early and saw a "Quarol among the Negroes." Two other slaves, Shoro and Roy, were breaking into homes in Boston to steal goods. When they broke into the merchant John Fairweather's home, Fairweather's slave Jersey took a stand. Defending his and his master's home, Jersey confronted the two slaves in the home, only to be stabbed by one of the intruders.[27] After further investigation, however, the courts found that it was Scipio who stabbed Jersey, not Shoro or Roy, and that Scipio had lied in his deposition.[28] Although Scipio stood accused of a crime, he still had a voice in the legal system and used it to save himself, possibly learning important lessons about the law in the process. Slaves were involved in other aspects of the legal process as well. For example, when Richard Dana gathered information to prosecute Cato, a slave accused of setting fire to a cooper's shop, he interviewed not only white witnesses but also "Quawio a negro."[29] Both those who were accused of crimes and those who called to testify would have gone before magistrates, sworn an oath, and recounted events, making them active participants in the legal system. Enslaved Bostonians in turn gained a "legal consciousness" that allowed them to effectively appropriate the law for their own means.[30]

One of the areas in which legal knowledge became important was ownership, which was (and is) an issue of property transfer. While servant law governed the role and occupations of slaves, slaves were still transferable property and thus subject to laws governing the sale and transfer of property. Slaves often sued on grounds of their master lacking clear ownership in writing. Pompey, a slave belonging to

Benjamin Faneuil, brought suit against his master for holding him in "Servitude against his free will" and owing him back wages amounting to £180. There are a few issues beneath the surface of this case. First, it is unclear whether Pompey actually sued his master for his freedom. Rather, Faneuil seemed to have been denying Pompey his right to earn wages and own property, thus denying him "free will," explaining why the case was more concerned with back wages than liberty. Second, Pompey most likely had previously belonged to Benjamin's brother, Peter Faneuil, one of the wealthiest men in eighteenth-century Boston. Peter died intestate in 1743, and the "5 Negroes" along with the rest of his property went to his brother.[31] Benjamin may have inherited Pompey from Peter, but with no will, the transfer of property and the fate of Peter's slaves were not laid out clearly in writing. Pompey must have had a chance at winning, as the attorney Benjamin Kent took his case. Faneuil also found a lawyer, Benjamin Pratt, who argued that Pompey could not even bring suit because he was a slave and Pompey's claim had no bearing or precedent in law. Before the Common Pleas Courts, staffed by justices versed in the law of servitude, Pompey won the case, but on appeal, most likely before more learned judges, the court rejected Pompey's suit. Faneuil also countersued his slave for court costs, which the judges awarded, but Pompey fled before the decision was made final, and the court ordered the sheriff to "cause the said Pompey to be return'd" to Faneuil.[32]

Like Pompey, James, a slave formerly belonging to Samuel Burnell, sued his new master, Burnell's son, in 1735 over an inheritance dispute. According to James, in four different wills, his late master guaranteed him his freedom upon the death of Burnell's widow. When the widow died, all the wills mysteriously disappeared. James took the younger Burnell to court, claiming his master freed him in writing. In a bitterly fought court battle that lasted for two years, Burnell threatened James's life, leading the slave to file a writ of protection with the House of Representatives. The House went above and beyond a writ of protection and declared James a freeman, as long as he could post the requisite fifty-pound bond.[33] Once again, the lack of written documentation confirming a slave's status resulted in a legal conflict.

The question remains, however, as to what slaves recognized as formal ownership. Both James's and Pompey's cases suggest that probate records, especially wills, were important to determining legal status and the future of one's enslavement. Pompey belonged to Peter Faneuil, not his brother Benjamin, and Peter's death and lack of written instructions meant that, at least to the slave, his obligation to serve ended along with Peter's life. James, meanwhile, believed at least one of Samuel Burnell's four wills freed him from service. Lacking documentation and condemning the younger Burnell's violent behavior, the legislature sided with the slave, believing that the wills were real and that James had a right to his freedom. While probate records may have provided some sense of proper ownership for the enslaved, many slaves were not inherited but sold. Bills of sale may have also been a way of tracing ownership. While they were contracts not between masters and slaves but rather between buyers and sellers of a slave, they were still a legal compact. The act of purchasing a slave may have led slaves to believe that masters agreed to certain obligations, such as providing food and lodging to their bondsmen and bondswomen, and that they were entitled to receive certain protections. For slaves, instead of being a simple transferal of property, the obligations insinuated in bills of sale harked back not to property law but to laws governing the behavior of people toward one another. Details concerning this phenomenon are vague, but servant law provides some details. Masters could sell servants or give them to a new master, but law required the permission of the servant and for the bound laborer to be provided with all due wages.[34] Of course, we have to be careful in overstating the importance of these bills, as most masters ignored these provisions, most slaves directly from Africa would not have been familiar with servant law at the time of sale, and these qualms, if they existed, did not stop the commerce in human chattel.

Legal knowledge and contractual obligations aside, slaves learned to use the law in order to better their condition. They knew how to get legal redress, to go before justices of the peace, to file petitions, and eventually to sue for their freedom. The courts remained open to enslaved people, who took full advantage of the ambiguity and permeability in Massachusetts slave law. Unlike other British colonies such as Virginia, Massachusetts did not establish special courts for trying slaves and instead allowed slaves to appear in the same courtrooms as whites.[35] Despite having access, learning how to navigate the law took time, and some slaves learned how to use its institutional manifestations before others did. Titus, an African man whose status is unclear, provides a good example of this learning process. In October 1727, he brought suit against Jeremiah Bills, the master of Titus's wife, Dinah. Earlier that year, in March, Titus and Bills met at the house of a free black woman named Tidec, where the African man paid Bills twenty pounds to procure his wife's freedom. Nevertheless, after Titus procured the money "with great Difficulty" in order to live with his wife, Bell refused to free Dinah, and she was "still his slave." Titus took the appropriate legal steps to rectify the situation. He hired an attorney, who helped him draft a petition. Titus made a fatal error, however, when filing it. Either the lawyer had left Titus's service or Titus could not afford to pay him, as Titus mistakenly sent the petition to the Court of General Sessions of the Peace, Boston's lower criminal court. Unfortunately, financial transactions gone awry were not criminal matters but civil ones, which fell under the jurisdiction of the Common Pleas Court. The General Sessions court had no option but to dismiss the petition because it did not fall "under the cognizance" of that court.[36] Titus might have had some knowledge of the law, but it was ultimately incomplete; and this experience most likely served as a hard-learned lesson in how the law functioned.

Nevertheless, slaves could successfully use the law. We can see this most clearly in the record books of Boston's justices of the peace. Not many of these documents exist, but two that do, those belonging to John Clark and Richard Dana, indicate that enslaved people knew how to receive justice from local magistrates. John Clark, whom we met earlier, served as justice of the peace for the first quarter of the eighteenth century. His record book, a 269-page tome containing nearly fourteen hundred entries, suggests that slaves regularly approached Clark for redress. In five different cases, Clark convicted either a white person or a person of color for assaulting an enslaved African. One of these cases involved a sawyer named John Peak. Clark forced Peak to pay a forty-pound bond to ensure Peak would appear at the next sessions court. In court, Peak would need to explain his "cruel treatment towards his Negroman Primus" to the justices. His recognizance was intended not only to ensure that he would appear before the court but also to ensure "that he shall carry it well toward his said Negro in the meanwhile." Clark seemed legitimately concerned for the welfare of Primus, and although there is no direct evidence, Primus had most likely approached the justice seeking redress.[37]

Of course, this is not to imply that Clark was a champion of the slaves. His business was justice and public order, not ensuring equality. More often than not, Clark punished recalcitrant slaves, especially those who disrupted the peace. He sent Mrs. Moor's slave woman Lucy to jail for fortune telling, although Moor later posted a bond for her slave. Even more interesting was the case of John Endicott, a Boston cooper, who asked Clark to send his recalcitrant slave to jail because of his "ungovernability and stubbornness." Here a master turned to a justice of the peace, an agent of the state, to help govern his unruly property. It is unknown if Clark complied with Endicott's request, but three weeks later, Endicott had to meet with Clark again, this time to post bond for his slave who "published a lie" about a local carpenter.[38] Although Clark disciplined slaves more often than aiding them in legal struggles, his involvement in so many cases involving slaves implies that justices frequently intervened in the relationship between masters and slaves. Mediation was common, possibly teaching slaves how to approach the justices and the types of cases they could hear.

Like John Clark, Richard Dana was a justice of the peace in Suffolk County, although he spent the first two years of his judgeship in Middlesex County, mostly in two towns neighboring Boston, Cambridge and Charlestown. The scion of a prominent New England family, Dana served as a local justice for nearly thirty years from 1746 to 1772. Also like Clark, Dana concerned himself with communal stability, and his records contain cases of slaves seeking redress and being punished. An example of Dana's commitment to order can be found early in his career, when in 1746, he fined Nero, "a negro Slave belonging to Hephzibah Barret of Boston Widow," four shillings for "profane Cursing."[39] Dana did seem, however, more tolerant than other justices. Although he sentenced offenders to be whipped, a common punishment, he often considered fines to be enough. We can see this in the case of Stephen, alternatively described by Dana as "an Indian molatto servant" and "mulatto servant." In May 1764, Stephen pilfered goods worth four pounds from Dorcia Griffis. Stephen's master, Francis Richey, posted bond, and Stephen laid low for a while. While still out on bond on 26 January 1765, he violated it, although Dana does not describe how. By this point, the justice could not have had a good opinion of Stephen, but the worst was yet to come. Less than a month after Stephen's last encounter with Dana, both Stephen and his master had to appear before the magistrate. The two men publicly assaulted James Mortimer's slave named Yarrow, and a number of people testified against them. Even Stephen's third transgression in nine months did not send him to the whipping post. Instead, Dana forced Richey to post a fifty-pound bond for his slave in addition to a twenty-pound one for himself.[40] Although Stephen's understanding of this situation is unknown, it is not hard to imagine the slave knew how Dana adjudicated the law. Again and again, he broke the law, yet somehow he always appeared before Dana, possibly on purpose, knowing the judge would only fine his master, not have him beaten.[41] Not only did slaves gain an understanding of the law, but it is entirely possible they knew which justice would give them the best outcome or mete out the lightest punishment.

Dana also had a commitment to upholding the law that gave slaves a chance of redress when appearing before him. Like Clark, Dana heard a number of cases in which slaves were looking for redress. In May 1758, Fortunate, "a Negro" of unknown status, sued Francis Ackley for assaulting him. Dana reviewed the case and awarded Fortunate forty shillings for his trouble.[42] Plaintiffs such as Fortunate had an advantage because they filed suit, but defendants also received a fair hearing. In 1770, two slaves, Felix and Caesar, appeared before the magistrate, accused of firing a gun in the streets, which scared a horse, causing it to run amok through Boston. After Dana weighed the evidence, Caesar appeared "to be innocent," while Felix went to trial.[43] That same year, Rebecca Edes accused Cloe, a slave, of "converting to her own use" Edes's gold locket and coral necklace. Dana rejected Edes's complaint and, after finding Cloe innocent, was "fully satisfied" with his decision.[44] Dana's actions demonstrate that being a slave or having black skin did not automatically equal guilt. Thus, encounters with the law proved that it was an open institution that allowed the enslaved to approach the courts and justices in order to seek justice and redefine their enslavement.

One of the legal mechanisms most commonly employed by slaves was the petition. As an important tool for seeking legal action, knowing how to create, file, and pursue petitions was vital to legal success. As the aforementioned case of Titus demonstrates, petitions required a certain degree of legal knowledge that he did not possess, but others did. Boston, a slave sitting in prison during the winter of 1723, filed a petition complaining that he had spent a long time in jail for a minor offense. He thought it unfair that the court had sentenced him to three months for "some small Difference with Mr. James Scolley." It was not the jail time that bothered him most, however. He complained most vehemently about having been taken away from his "Lawful Imployment" and having to take on "considerable charges for His subsistence."[45] Whether or not Boston was sincere about his situation and his desire to return to work, we see a slave using his power of petition to further his own agenda—getting out of prison—using a language appealing to his jailers. White Bostonians would have sympathized with Boston's desire to work for himself and not be idle sitting in the town jail. Petitions allowed slaves to appropriate the language of their oppressors, defend their own positions, and lay claim to a legal identity beyond that of property, all of which furthered their own ends in cases of divorce (see later in this chapter), abuse, and, eventually, freedom.

By the time of the American Revolution, Afro-Bostonians had mastered the use of the petition and used it to pursue goals far larger than the slave Boston's attempt to get out of jail. In January 1773, a free black Bostonian named Felix petitioned the royal governor of the Massachusetts Bay Colony and the House of Representatives. The petition implored the leaders of the colony to take the "unhappy State and Condition" of Massachusetts's slaves under consideration. Believing that God had recently "put it into the Hearts of Multitudes on both Sides" of the Atlantic to reexamine the condition and status of slaves in British territories, Felix hoped the Bay Colony's leaders would do the same. The enslaved population, outside of a few "vicious" members, offered positive contributions to civil society and were "discreet, sober, honest, and industrious." More importantly, they were deeply religious and upheld "every moral Virtue except Patience." For their patience had worn thin after generations of being treated as "Beasts that perish." Until they were free, Felix passionately declared, they "have no Property, . . . no Wives, . . . No Children, . . . no City, . . . No Country." All the slaves in Boston and other towns in Massachusetts had was a "Father in Heaven," who commanded them to be obedient to their masters and to "pray and hope for relief" from their bondage.[46] Once again, slaves and free blacks appropriated Euro-American language, this time conceptions of independence and freedom, to further their own ends. They became adroit at filing these petitions and filed no fewer than seven petitions and other requests for freedom between 1773 and 1777, suggesting that slaves believed the petition to be an effective way of achieving their goals.

While Felix and his comrades filed petitions for emancipation, in the decade and a half before the American Revolution, a number of slaves sued their masters for freedom and back wages. These cases, known as "freedom suits," occurred throughout the eighteenth century, as the case of Pompey and Faneuil demonstrates, but did not appear in large numbers until the late 1760s and 1770s. Slaves won their freedom in two cases, both in Essex County. The first involved a slave named Caesar, who in 1773 sued his master, Richard Greenleaf of Newburyport, for fifty pounds for "unlawfully detaining him in slavery." The court awarded Caesar his freedom, eighteen pounds, and court costs for his trouble. A year later, a Beverly, Massachusetts, slave won against his master, Caleb Dodge, and the court held "that no legal justification existed" for Dodge to retain his bondsman for life.[47] Courts were willing to grant slaves their freedom on a case-by-case basis, and knowledge of this part of the law became an effective strategy for winning legal freedom in the late colonial period.

That said, however, we must be careful of overstating the significance and purpose of "freedom suits." These were adjudicated on an individual basis and were nonbinding for similar cases. Not until 1783 was there an attempt to apply the outcome of these trials on a larger scale. Moreover, most of these cases were not really about "freedom" but about back wages. In the 1769 case involving the Cambridge merchant Richard Lechmere and his slave James, the enslaved man sued Lechmere because he "assaulted the said James & him took & imprisoned & restrained him of his Liberty & hold him in Servitude." Yet James—and his counsel, Francis Dana—did not ask for freedom but £100 in back wages and damages. Although Lechmere won in the lower court, James appealed the decision, and his exasperated master freed him and gave him two pounds.[48] To better understand James's case and freedom suits in general, we have to return to Blackstone. The jurist's hatred of slavery did not preclude him from protecting the rights of all those involved. It was not servitude that bothered Blackstone but the inability of the law to protect the slave "in the enjoyment of his person, his liberty, and his property." In his estimation, slaves should enjoy these liberties, but masters still had rights to the "perpetual service" of the freed slave, who would "remain exactly in the same state as before."[49] Thus, when enslaved Africans engaged in these "freedom suits," they were more likely seeking to secure their rights— namely, to be paid for their work. Courts granted them "freedom" to protect those rights, but that liberty did not necessarily remove the obligation to serve.

The law was an important institution that enslaved Bostonians learned to appropriate and use toward their own ends. The town of Boston tended to govern slaves using extant servant law, as the half-hearted measures it passed were ambiguous and next to impossible to enforce. Like white colonials, slaves learned the law through informal channels such as reading law books and discussing legal matters with others, although slaves tended to encounter the law on a regular enough basis to gain a working knowledge of it. They would use this knowledge to their advantage, approaching local justices of the peace for legal redress and filing petitions using the same legal language as white colonials. They even sued for the rights they believed they were entitled to, which eventually won them legal freedom. All of this allowed slaves to actively shape their enslavement on their own terms and challenge the boundaries of slavery using the language and process of Anglo-American law.

Although the law proved to be the most important institution appropriated by slaves in the long term, Protestant Christianity also offered opportunities for them to challenge the boundaries of slavery. In the years preceding the American Revolution, enslaved Bostonians appropriated Christian ideas and institutions in their many forms to ameliorate their condition. Sincerity of conversion does not matter—some were true believers and some were not. What is important is how slaves used what they learned in Boston's many churches to better themselves, their families, and their communities. Most churches offered institutional support to slaves, while Afro-Bostonians in turn adapted their ability to read the Bible and newfound Christian vocabulary to their everyday lives. The latter two skills enabled slaves to make public appeals to white audiences, and the former provided some protections against the abuse and trauma that characterized African slavery in the Americas. By examining these three themes, we see not only how slaves used the literacy and Christian vocabulary made available to them by Protestant Christianity to decode the world in which they lived but also how slaves used these to pursue a variety of objectives, not just the fight for liberty.[50]

Studying the interaction between slaves and churches in Boston presents an additional challenge because despite the state support the Congregational churches enjoyed, there was no monolithic, hegemonic institution like the Catholic Church. Rather, a myriad of different denominations—Congregational, Presbyterian, Anglican, Quaker, Baptist, and French Huguenot, to name a few—proselytized, baptized, and married slaves. Such a dynamic religious panoply created space for slaves, who could pick and choose their church affiliation.[51] Boston's ministers, however, thwarted and stymied such shopping around, enforced standards and norms, and acted as gatekeepers to who could and could not affiliate themselves with a church. The interplay between the desires of slaves and the imperatives of ministers often shaped the interaction and support a slave could receive from any given church.

Examining the career of a Boston cleric, Anglican Timothy Cutler, allows us to better understand the relationship between slaves and Boston's churches. Cutler ministered to enslaved men and women, baptized them and their children, and worked with masters to ensure that their slaves received proper Christian instruction. A native of Charlestown, Massachusetts, Cutler attended Harvard and became a Congregational minister. After serving the town of Stratford, Connecticut, he became rector of Yale College, but the trustees dismissed him three and half years later because of his conversion to Anglicanism during his years in Stratford. After his dismissal, Cutler traveled to England, where he received a doctorate of divinity from both Oxford and Cambridge and became a minister in the Church of England. With his ordination came his first—and only—parish assignment. Cutler became the first minister of Christ Church (now the Old North Church) of Boston. Despite his brilliance, which even his worst enemies acknowledged, Cutler was known for his intransigence and his dislike for Congregationalists, whom he referred to as "dissenters." This distaste is evidenced in his discussion of a Congregational foe, who, he said, "in lying and villainy is a perfect over-match for any Dissenter that I know."[52] Nevertheless, Cutler was heavily involved in the Society for the Propagation of the Gospel to Foreign Parts (SPG), the main Anglican missionary society. The SPG had a number of goals, including the conversion of Native Americans and African slaves in the British North American colonies. Cutler, whose parish duties confined him to the town of Boston, openly proselytized African slaves and invited them into his parish. In his correspondence with the SPG, we see a man concerned with converting Boston's African American population and inviting them into his church.

Most of the information dealing with Cutler's relationship with the SPG and his interaction with slaves comes from a series of his letters to the secretary of the society. These letters covered the years 1725–1751 and mostly recorded slave baptisms. Over this period, Cutler documented baptizing more than fifty infant, children, and adult "Negroes," most of whom were slaves. A majority of these baptisms occurred in the fall of 1740, after George Whitefield's Boston revivals, when Cutler baptized "37 Infants, 30 of which were Negro Slaves."[53] These successes aside, the minister was not impressed with Boston's black population. On one occasion, he noted that slaves "(generally speaking) show very little respect for religion or virtue," and on another, he noted how most slaves were "stupid and unconcerned about religion."[54] When slaves joined Christ Church, however, Cutler's tone completely changed. He noted that one of the male slaves he baptized was "much reformed in his life" and had "a worthy character of seriousness and religion."[55] Cutler described another slave as a man of whom he had "received an excellent Character from his Master, and who has been of much visible Seriousness and good behavior, long before his baptism," indicating that Cutler believed that slaves could be good people even before being received into his flock. Even his old grudge against Congregationalists could be assuaged by a slave conversion. Some time in the fall or winter of 1735–1736, the cleric received into his parish a "negro servant to a Dissenter . . . who, from great irregularities, is become a serious & sober man, & now bears a worthy character from his Master & Mistress, who have encouraged him in these good dispositions and have recommended him to [Cutler]."[56] Dissenters were not such bad people when Cutler received well-behaved, reformed congregants from them. What Cutler's attitude and behavior—frequent baptisms, irreligious Africans, and redeemed congregants—indicates is that once slaves joined his church, they became an integrated part of the parish community. No longer were they irreligious, heathenish, or outside the realm of Christian behavior. Instead, they were part of his flock and the greater Church of England, an institutional affiliation that provided slaves with full spiritual equality or, in Cutler's words, made them "worthy of their standing in the Church of Christ."[57]

The question remains, however, why slaves would want to be affiliated with a religious institution. Outside of the skills that church affiliation brought, there is little evidence as to why a slave joined a church. Many did so because their masters strongly suggested church attendance, as the Congregationalist's slave recommended to Cutler demonstrates. Given the close contact that slaves and masters had in Boston—living in the same household—maybe maintaining domestic tranquility by attending church was important to the enslaved. Other documentation indicates that slaves may have used church affiliation as a way of resisting their masters. Matthias Plant, the Anglican minister in Newbury, Massachusetts, wrote of a bondswoman who was a "woman of wonderful sense & prudent in matters of equal knowledge in Religion with most of her sex, far exceeding any of her own nation that ever yet [he] heard of," but she was denied baptism by her master.[58] Why the master did so is unclear, but it seems that the slave was trying to use Plant as leverage against her master.

Another possibility was the ability of slaves to redeem themselves. Cutler's letters to the secretary of the SPG were full of slaves rectifying unchristian behavior or recovering from a fallen state after their baptism. He wrote of one male slave who after joining Christ Church was "much reformed in his life."[59] A second "Negro man" had "long time discovered to all the impressions of religion in the reformation of his temper and carriage, his fidelity in his business, and abandoning all loose and dangerous conversation."[60] While many slaves found religion spiritually and intellectually fulfilling and this slave's conversion may have been sincere, more importantly, this appropriated framework of sin and forgiveness, possibly alien to newly arrived Africans, put slaves on a level playing field with whites by giving them a shared religious experience.

While Cutler took pride in his ability to reform and save the souls of the Africans he baptized, there may be another reason why slaves received baptism from him. By publicly announcing and recording their redemption, Cutler, a well-respected man in Boston, also helped to change public perception of a particular slave. As the historian John Wood Sweet argues, churches served an important function in New English society, and affiliation with them "may have been particularly useful venues for slaves seeking public recognition as members of the colonial body politic."[61] Slaves understood the role of churches in New English life and the value of using the language of salvation employed by ministers like Cutler in an attempt to better integrate themselves into white society and build or repair their reputation with their masters, with their community, or with the town of Boston.

If the previous three reasons why slaves affiliated themselves with churches are rather abstract, there are two more concrete reasons why slaves would join: marriage and education. Slave marriage was quite common and was actively encouraged by masters and town officials. The Massachusetts legislature, at the behest of Justice Samuel Sewall, legalized slave marriage in 1705. Some masters even fought to preserve their slaves' Christian marriage. John Gyles owned two slaves, Boston Jethro and Hagar, who married in 1731. About six years into the marriage, Hagar gave birth to a "Female Molatto Child," and Gyles believed the father to be one William Kelly, a "Soldier at St. George's River." Despite Hagar's confession of adultery, Gyles tried to reconcile his two slaves, ultimately to "no purpose."[62] Another man,

Thomas Saunders, corroborated the master's testimony, stating that Gyles endeavored to "reconcile . . . Jethro and Hagar but all in vain."[63] Boston Jethro and Hagar's relationship eventually deteriorated to the point that Gyles had to sell Boston Jethro to the merchant Edward Bromfield. This master's pleas aside, some historians have recognized slave marriage as meaningless to some owners, while others, such as Lorenzo Greene, argue that for slaves, "marriage did little more than legalize sexual intimacy" because masters commonly separated married couples.[64]

The evidence strongly suggests that historians have erred. Many slaves married in Boston's churches. Thus, for slaves, marriage had a different meaning and was more than a license to have sex. Evidence of this comes from a petition sent to General Thomas Gage in 1774. Although the petition was immersed in natural rights discourse and a plea for freedom, the authors, "a Grate Number of Blackes," argued that slaves were not allowed to enjoy the "endearing ties of husband and wife," even if they were married. Instead, masters forcibly separated spouses and parents from their children.[65] This petition provides a glimpse into how Afro-Bostonians interpreted marriage. For slaves, formal marriage, often performed by a minister, meant that their relationships received the same protections as marriages of white people. Getting married in a church guaranteed a certain amount of protection and legitimacy to their marriages and families. As a safeguard, Christian matrimony often failed, and marriages tended to be "irregular and unstable."[66] Nevertheless, slaves tried to use the church as a bulwark against the economic interests of their masters and as leverage to protect their own interests.

Perhaps the greatest benefit that religious affiliation provided to enslaved Bostonians was education. The Congregational minister and leading intellectual Cotton Mather set up a reading school catering to blacks and Indians—he was explicit in not teaching them how to write. This school existed for three years from 1718 to 1721. Although the school stopped functioning as an institution, classes presumably lasted longer.[67] Most ministers exhorted slave-owning congregants to educate their charges. In *The Negro Christianized*, Mather advocated masters teaching slaves to read, as it would be "*Wise unto* [their] *Salvation.*" Reading was an "Advantage" for slaves because it offered a path to heaven, not education.[68] Not all masters took Mather's exhortation to heart. According to the freedwoman Chloe Spear's biographer, the slave's mistress felt no obligation to instruct her. The mistress made

Chloe attend church, but she and her fellow slaves "did not understand the preaching, they took no interest in it, and spent the time in playing, eating nuts, &c. and derived no benefit whatever." It was only after meeting a local schoolmistress that Spear became interested in religion and learned to read.[69] As Spear's account demonstrates, the ability of ministers to persuade their congregants to educate their slaves was incomplete at best. Likewise, Timothy Cutler complained that while many masters educated their slaves to read the gospels, there was "too great a remissness upon this article."[70] Despite the ad hoc process, enough slaves learned to read that Boston's slaves may have been one of the most literate enslaved populations in the Atlantic world.[71]

As the willingness of Boston's churches to educate slaves suggests, literacy was an important skill learned in ecclesiastical settings. Protestant Christianity's emphasis on reading the Bible was the driving force behind educating slaves to read. Such opinions were held by both masters and community leaders, and these attitudes extended beyond Boston to leaders like the bishop of London, who desired that masters "encourage and promote the Instruction of their *Negroes* in the Christian Faith."[72] Slave owners in Boston believed that literacy was essential to their slaves' salvation, but slaves had a different interpretation. According to one scholar, slaves believed that "literacy could bring power, that illiteracy was one of the factors that whites exploited in order to maintain their dominance, and that writing was the literacy skill that could aid self-definition."[73] Although slaves learned to read more frequently than they learned to write, they nevertheless put both skills to use.[74] Black Bostonians transformed what began as a religious imperative into a useful and applicable knowledge base and employed this ability to better their everyday lives.

Cotton Mather's slave Onesimus allows us to better understand the process of literacy acquisition and how slaves interpreted that development. Mather acquired Onesimus as a gift from his congregation in 1706. Over the next decade and a half, the men had a tumultuous relationship that resulted in Onesimus leaving Mather's service and becoming free. The turmoil can be traced through Mather's diary. The entries concerning Onesimus are not frequent, but they occur enough to see this process in motion. After Mather acquired his slave, he first mentioned Onesimus five years later, noting that he had to "keep a strict eye on [his] servant Onesimus" because he kept bad "Company" and engaged in some "Actions of a thievish Aspect."[75] Onesimus's behavior seemed to change two years later, when Mather noted that his

"Negro-Servant, is one more Easily govern'd and managed by the Principles of Reason, agreeably offered unto him, than by other methods."[76] Once again, Onesimus misbehaved, but this time Mather was able to control the slave with reason. The minister did not note what exactly constituted "reason," but a later entry noted, "There are several points, relating to the Instruction and Management of my Servant *Onesimus*, which I would now more than ever prosecute. He shall be sure to read every Day. From thence I shall have him go onto writing." Mather's ability to reason with his slave coincided with Onesimus's instruction in reading and writing. These years proved relatively peaceful, and Mather even allowed Onesimus the "conveniences of the Married State."[77] Onesimus's marriage was not entirely a blessing, however. He lost two sons between 1714 and 1716. It was after the death of Onesimus's second son that the relationship between Mather and his slave became unsustainable. In August 1716, Mather noted that Onesimus had grown "useless, Froward [obstinate], and Immorigerous [rude or disobedient]" and had to be replaced with a "better Servant."[78] Shortly thereafter, Mather released Onesimus from his service, giving the slave his liberty and allowing him to live with his wife.[79]

Scholars attribute the growing distance between Onesimus and Mather to the slave's desire for independence, but that is not the whole story.[80] One has to question whether the slave ever wanted to be associated with Mather or whether Onesimus only obeyed to become literate. Onesimus's actions demonstrate his ability to do what he wanted and use his master to his advantage, especially learning to read and write. When Mather was a teacher, Onesimus was obedient and "reasoned," but when Mather became a master who threatened Onesimus's autonomy, the slave became obstinate and incorrigible. Enslaved Bostonians, like Onesimus, knew literacy was an important skill and how to acquire it and were even able to jettison the baggage—obligation, dependence, and deference—that came with such instruction.

The fact that slaves went through such trouble to learn to read and write is not surprising given the opportunities literacy created for them. The ability to read empowered slaves in three key ways. First, Africans were able to spread printed ideas or possibly even teach one another to read and write in order to have better-informed communication networks. Second, reading opened new possibilities for employment. Third, literacy created new possibilities for enslaved Bostonians to shape their own lives and, in a few cases, their freedom.

Of these, the spread of the printed word among slaves is the hardest to discern. One side effect of the high literacy rate, however, was a unique way of selling slaves in Boston. Since so many slaves could read, more than half of all slave-for-sale advertisements were anonymous and requested potential buyers to inquire with the printer. Not only did this make the "printing office the busiest slave mart in town," according to the historian Robert Desrochers, but it also prevented literate slaves—including an educated, enslaved newspaper delivery-man—or slave information networks from reporting "news of imminent sale for local slaves."[81]

Other evidence of these literacy-driven communication networks comes from Timothy Cutler. In his letters to the SPG, he complained about "bad books" that further corrupted already heathenish, unconverted Africans. He claimed the slaves in Boston were "stupid or Infidels in religion," and that there were "too many others, with Heretics, that cover themselves even with the name of Churchmen and privately Jest and oppose Revelation and the sacred Doctrines of the Divinity of our Savior," all assisted by "bad books, continually imported."[82] Although Cutler was not specific about what books the slaves read, given the date of these writings in the late 1730s and his ecclesiastical conservatism, the books were most likely evangelical tracts published on the eve of the Great Awakening. Interestingly, religiously inspired slave literacy created black communication networks that influenced the spread of some forms of Christianity over others.

The ability to read and write also opened up new occupational opportunities, especially in trades usually limited to skilled white workers. Chief among these was printing. Given that Boston was the center of printing in New England, if not the American colonies, it is not surprising that slaves were employed in this trade. At least three enslaved men worked for printers. One slave, Peter Fleet, known as "Black Peter," was a delivery man for Thomas Fleet, a task for which literacy was not required—although Peter left a will written in a "crude and illegible hand," indicating he could read and write—on top of working the press and in the print shop.[83] Peter worked the press, set type, and carved woodcuts for the prints. On this latter task, Isaiah Thomas—the printer, first historian of printing in the American colonies and United States, and friend of most of the printers in Boston—noted that Peter was an "ingenious man, and cut, on wooden blocks, all the pictures which decorated the ballads and small books of his master." He even left his imprint on Fleet's edition of the *Prodigal Daughter*, a story about a fallen daughter redeemed by a journey to the afterlife.[84] Peter's ability to read and write created new professional opportunities and even gained him a certain degree of public recognition.

Another black printer, Primus or "Prime" Fowle, belonged to Daniel Fowle, one half of the printing firm Rogers & Fowle and publisher of the *American Magazine and Historical Chronicle* and the *Independent Advertiser*. Primus deserves special attention because he became embroiled in a controversy over press freedom in Boston. In October 1754, town authorities arrested Primus's master, Daniel. The Massachusetts House of Representatives accused Fowle of printing a pamphlet titled *The Monster of Monsters* and penned by one Tom Thumb, Esquire, which poked fun at members of the legislature. In the course of Fowle's being questioned as to whether he printed the pamphlet or not, he replied that he did not but that he did receive some copies to sell in his shop. When asked whether he helped to print or distribute the text, he stated that he did not but said, "my negro might, as he sometimes worked for my brother." Fowle later confessed that his brother Zechariah did have a hand in printing the pamphlet. Had Primus helped Zechariah print and distribute the text, he would have been a central figure in the controversy. Although not as important or extensive as the John Peter Zenger case in New York, this case did result in Fowle's being held in jail for a week and in the arrest of Royall Tyler, the alleged author. Fowle, disgusted with his treatment, published a damning retort to his imprisonment and moved to Portsmouth, New Hampshire, with Primus and his family. Isaiah Thomas was quite close to Fowle—he apprenticed under his brother Zechariah—and remembered that the event left a "deep impression" on his mind "in favor of liberty of the press." What Primus thought of the affair is, unfortunately, lost to history.[85]

The documents do not reveal if Primus was questioned or arrested during the controversy, but Isaiah Thomas does fill in some biographical details. Primus was black, indicating that he not only learned to read and write but also had to learn English. He was a hard worker, often labored "without an assistant," and worked until "prevented by age." Thomas believed Primus worked as a printer for over fifty years.[86] He worked so long, in fact, that an apocryphal story from Portsmouth claimed that "long service in bending over the press" caused him to remain "bent to an angle of about forty-five degrees."[87] Another early history of Portsmouth noted that Primus was "very illiterate," a near impossibility given that both Thomas and Primus's own master acknowledged that he could work the press and set type alone.[88] This book, published in 1825, reveals how quickly whites were to dismiss skilled, literate slave labor only fifty years after slavery began to erode. Men like Primus Fowle and Peter Fleet demonstrate that the ability to read and write greatly aided slaves in finding occupational security and carving out their own spaces in the workplace.[89]

Literacy also allowed slaves to shape their own lives and resist the commodification that came with enslavement. Peter Fleet in 1743 left his last will and testament. This curious document, one of the only surviving wills belonging to a slave, indicates how literacy could empower a slave. Especially surprising is the money he left to the children of his master, the printer Thomas Fleet. To Thomas Jr., he left ten shillings and a pair of buckles that he "shall not wear" for three years. He also left money for Nathan Bowen Jr. and Thomas Oliver, men who served as witnesses for the will. Moreover, Peter's will allowed him to demonstrate his personhood. He accumulated a certain degree of wealth in his lifetime—especially for a slave—and showed this by opening the will with a statement to Fleet's children. He left them "some thing, that's more than any Richest Master's, Servant would leave to their Master's Children considering what profit [he had] to [his] trade." Fleet's daughter Molley received money because she was "very good to servants," illustrating that Peter rewarded the good treatment and judged that treatment by his own criteria.[90] In leaving a will, Peter was able to meet death on his own terms, reward his owners for their good treatment, and bequeath the rewards of his hard work to his "family"—black and white. By implementing these measures in writing, this enslaved man challenged the notion that he was merely chattel—Peter's last will and testament was, in many ways, the embodiment of his humanity.

Finally, literacy could contribute to slaves becoming free. Religion usually played a role in this newfound literacy-based independence, as it did for Nathaniel Byfield, a wealthy Boston judge and landowner, and his slave Rose, whom he wished to free after his death. While he acknowledged the law that required masters to post bond for manumitted slaves as a "good Law founded upon good Reason," he thought Rose should be exempted. Rose had, over the years Byfield owned her, been a "faithfull servant," gained "Considerable Knowledge in Religion," and "truly fears God." Of special consideration in his discussion of Rose was her literacy. She had, with "Great Pains &

Diligence," learned to read, making her particularly eligible for free-dom.[91] It should be noted, however, that most masters did not believe that literacy or even religious conversion earned a slave the right to freedom. Mather, for one, understood the "vast improvement" that education had brought to some slaves and used this as an argument that all Africans were able to reason, but he did not think that baptism and religious instruction meant that masters had to free slaves. There were no laws that forced masters to free slaves and especially not the "*Law of Christianity*," which "wonderfully Dulcifies, and Mollifies, and Moderates the Circumstances of" slavery.[92] It was only in rare cases that religious instruction and literacy brought freedom. In most cases, however, religious appropriation did expand the opportunities for increased autonomy and allowed Africans to better communicate and to resist the institution of slavery.

While Christianity did not guarantee liberty, exposure to it and church affiliation gave slaves a powerful new vocabulary from which to draw. When dealing with whites, slaves used religious language to make appeals, justify their actions, and even gain fame and recogni-tion. It is in this realm that we see slaves actively appropriating Eng-lish values and ideas in their everyday lives. The use of this language produced ambivalent results. In many cases, it did not have any effect on the slaves' condition, while in other instances, slaves were able to use religious rhetoric to gain autonomy and ameliorate their situation.

As the letters of Timothy Cutler suggest, most whites believed Afri-cans to be heathens. A Boston newspaper also articulated this idea. After describing crimes committed by runaway slaves in New Hamp-shire, the editor of the *Boston Gazette* sarcastically noted that these were the "*blessed* Effects of bringing Negro Slaves into the Country!" "Scarce one in a hundred," the editor continued, proved "good for any Thing." He concluded the article by rhetorically asking, in Latin, what "are [slave owners] doing for God, dealing with such thieves?"[93] Slaves challenged these ingrained attitudes by meeting whites on their terms, using their language.

Afro-Bostonians often used religion in their appeals to civil author-ities. Divorce proceedings involving blacks oftentimes contained these pleas. When Boston Jethro went to divorce his wife, Hagar, for giving birth to a mixed-race child in 1742, he argued that she com-mitted the "Detestable sin of Adultery."[94] The general court eventually granted his divorce. A later case involving a free black woman, Lydia Sharp, and her enslaved husband, Boston, a slave belonging to Joseph

Belknap, also illustrates this trend. Sharp accused Boston of being a philanderer who lived in "constant Violation" of their marriage vows. She even noted that the Reverend Samuel Mather officiated their marriage.[95] While it is not apparent whether Sharp won—Boston twice failed to appear for the hearing—her use of religious language is unmistakable. Both her and Boston Jethro's appeals must have struck a nerve with authorities in New England, who believed, according to one scholar, that the "marital bond, the covenant of husband and wife, and the benevolent exercise of paternal authority lay at the center" of the Puritan mission.[96] The descendants of the Puritans took these obligations seriously, and their slaves, equipped with a Christian vocabulary, understood and exploited those beliefs to achieve their various aspirations.

If religious appeals could aid slaves in achieving their goals, religious justifications, although widely employed, rarely worked. This Christian-based reasoning can be found in the judicial records of Massachusetts. John Codman's slaves Mark and Phillis used biblical justifications for murdering their master. According to Phillis's testimony, Mark was the one who decided to poison Codman. He "had read the Bible through, and [found] that it was no Sin to kill him [Codman] if they did not lay violent Hands on him So as to shed Blood, by sticking or stabbing or cutting his throat," meaning that poisoning was biblically acceptable.[97] Needless to say, the court did not believe Mark's analysis or Phillis's attempt to prove her innocence and sentenced both slaves to death.

The most famous black appropriator of Christian language in Boston—and perhaps in the Atlantic world—was Phillis Wheatley. The African-born poet also illustrates the ability of slaves to adapt the various teachings of Christianity—both religious and secular. A regular church attendee at the Old South Meeting House, Phillis could read and write and eventually became world famous for her poetry. She was brilliant and by the age of twelve was reading Latin and Greek in addition to English. Wheatley began writing prose about the same time. Her poetry reveals a woman adept at using Christian language not only to better her condition but also to challenge the status quo. In one of her unpublished poems, "Deism," Wheatley opened with the line, "Must Ethiopians be imploy'd for you."[98] Her use of the term "Ethiopian" is significant. As Wheatley's biographer Vincent Carretta notes, by referring to Africans as Ethiopians, a term from the Old Testament, "rather than an African or a black in a religious poem, she claims an identity that grants her biblical authority to speak to her readers."[99] By writing in such a fashion, this enslaved woman had the ability to establish equality between herself and her white audience. Carretta argues that Wheatley "repeatedly appropriates the values of Christianity to judge and find wanting hypocritical self-styled Christians of European descent."[100] Shrouding her writing in Christian language allowed Wheatley to subtly criticize slavery and still be palatable to Europeans. After Wheatley published a few of her poems in New England newspapers, eighteen of the "most respectable characters in Boston" scrutinized her to make sure she could produce such high-quality poetry. Wheatley's Christian vocabulary aided her acceptance by the panel, which legitimated her work. She went on to publish her first book of poems in 1773.[101] Nevertheless, Wheatley was an exceptional case. Very few Afro-Bostonians ever gained fame or notoriety, let alone published, before the American Revolution. The fact that she was literate and versed in Christianity, however, was not so abnormal but rather was the norm for many enslaved Bostonians.

When enslaved Bostonians joined Christian churches, it was not a matter of submission to authority but a way of empowering themselves. Even when slaves submitted, they used churches to their advantage. Benefits included a genuine affection for Christianity; the redemption, either real or performative, offered by Christianity; the ability to establish a framework for resistance that made it hard for masters to intervene; the protection of slave families through legal marriage and baptism; and the benefits of literacy. None of this implies that the appropriation of European religion and practice caused slaves to alter an earlier set of African beliefs and values. Rather, it speaks to the incredible resilience and adaptability of Boston's slaves. Instead of being passive, powerless victims, slaves found innovative and effective paths of resisting slavery using Protestantism and its teachings.

Enslaved Bostonians effectively appropriated Euro-American institutions to better their condition. These included legal structures, as slaves exploited the loopholes in existing servant law and the ambiguity of statutes. They gained a deep understanding of the law, using that knowledge to file petitions in a language understood by colonial officials and to bring suit against abusive masters and others who violated the rights they believed they possessed. They eventually used this knowledge to petition and sue for their freedom, although this was not until the eve of the American Revolution, and it is unclear what their expectations were, especially in the so-called freedom suits. Meanwhile, slaves used Protestant Christianity and local churches to learn a number of valuable skills, such as literacy and a Christian vocabulary that allowed them to better communicate with other Bostonians. They had the ability to join churches, to be redeemed both for their own salvation and to save face in the public, and to build networks with other churchgoers. Churches and the law offered plenty of opportunities for bondsmen and bondswomen to empower themselves and challenge the institution of slavery.

Neither of these institutions offered a direct path to freedom, although slaves eventually learned to use them to that end. That said, this was never the primary goal. The knowledge and skills gained through careful appropriation allowed slaves to use these institutions to better their everyday lives. Slaves could confront abusive masters and receive legal redress, while learning to read and write offered better job opportunities and the chance for their voices to be heard in public forums. It also ingrained them into the colonial body politic, where they carved out a space for themselves. As contributing members of society, enslaved Bostonians, using white institutions, proved their worth and challenged any belief that they were property and not people. Freedom and emancipation grew out of this desire to be part of a larger society, one in which everyone had a voice and control over his or her own affairs.

Afterword: The Fall of the House
of Unfreedom

Ezekiel Price's career as a notary in Boston spanned nearly five decades from the late 1740s until the 1790s. He specialized in maritime affairs, recording depositions of lost cargo, damaged and scuttled ships, and encounters with pirates, enemy vessels, and some of the most savage tempests in the early modern Atlantic. Some of this may have been self-interested, given that Price sold maritime insurance. Nevertheless, he also recorded bills of sale from across the Americas and Europe, and there are no fewer than six languages in the seven volumes of his extant notary records. In between stories of storms and Dutch receipts, Price also recorded slave manumissions. These were often recorded at the behest of slaves, as when Price recorded the manumission of an enslaved boy named James at the "desire of Lettice, Negrowoman belonging to Mr. David Burnett," the boy's mother.[1] These manumissions often noted why masters freed slaves, such as being trustworthy or being loyal and hard workers. In 1770, William and Margaret Hall freed their slave Prince (the famed Prince Hall) for his twenty-five years of serving them "faithfully."[2] Just nine years later, however, the nature of Price's manumissions changed. Ralph and Elizabeth Inman freed their slave William not only for his "long and Faithful Services" but in "Consideration of the Rights of Humanity."[3] Nine short years—a complete change in attitude.

In the years leading to and during the American Revolution, white and enslaved Bostonians began to believe in the "Rights of Humanity." As white Bostonians began protesting what they saw as British tyranny following the Seven Years' War, they deployed a language of natural rights and desired "freedom" from the yoke of British "slavery."[4] Most white Bostonians, many at the epicenter of revolutionary foment, did not recognize the irony of asking for political emancipation while owning African slaves. The irony, however, was not lost on slaves and a number of white observers.

Just as enslaved Bostonians used local institutions, they appropriated the language of natural rights and other forms of resistance in order to protest their enslavement. Unlike earlier attempts to change the conditions of their servitude or gain autonomy from the master class, this strategy led to a demand for universal freedom and emancipation, one that was hard fought and eventually won. In order to better understand this phenomenon, we need to look at how slaves participated in the revolutionary movement and how they deployed and used the language of natural rights. Especially important are a series of petitions circulated by Afro-Bostonians, both free and enslaved, in the mid-1770s, asking for an end to slavery. They appealed to a variety of political authorities, including the British military governor Thomas Gage, but they always insisted on freedom as an outcome. The struggle for freedom culminated in an enslaved man suing his master for freedom. When the case, *Commonwealth v. Jennison*, appeared before the Massachusetts Supreme Court, the court ruled that slavery was incompatible with the Massachusetts Constitution of 1780.

While most histories of slavery in Massachusetts end with the *Jennison* decision, the actual end of slavery in the Bay State is much less clear. For one, the decision applied only to the case before the court and was never enforced. Freedom was uncertain, and there is evidence that slavery persisted into the 1790s. Nevertheless, enslaved Bostonians came to believe that natural rights were the ultimate way to guarantee the protection of their families and community from abuse and to bring an end to slavery.

The path to emancipation began when slaves became embroiled in the imperial crisis that precipitated the American Revolution. As early as 1764, when James Otis delivered a speech asserting the rights of the colonists against the alleged tyranny of the British, he also called for the abolition of slavery.[5] Otis's call seemed not only odd but misplaced, given the topic of his speech, yet during the Stamp Act Crisis a year later, slavery became politicized in ways it had never been before. Writers referenced African slavery when discussing the rights of Englishmen. When Governor Francis Bernard made a speech concerning the act in October 1765, one rebuttal in the *Boston Gazette* declared that Parliament had forced the colonists into a state of servitude, but they would not be Parliament's "negroes." The writer said, "Providence never designed us for negroes," as the colonists did not have the same physical attributes, and since Bostonians were "as handsome as old England folks," they "should be as free."[6] In his critique of imperial policy, this author made a stark distinction between white colonists and African slaves. Slaves were meant to be enslaved, while Englishmen deserved to be free. Although abstractions in this author's writing and that of many others, slavery and the slaves became woven into the heated political discussions of the 1760s.

Not all colonists denigrated Africans as incapable of freedom while holding aloft the rights of Englishmen. Some even saw the hypocrisy of fighting for freedom while owning slaves. In a 1768 letter to the editor of the *Boston Chronicle*, an author writing under the pseudonym Homogeneon recalled an encounter he had with an "old gentleman" who was "an idle spectator of the times." The author inquired about the man's opinions about recent political developments, to which the gentleman replied with a simple question for Homogeneon: do you own "a Negro?" The author replied in the affirmative, stating he owned two slaves. "Pray then," the old gentleman chided, "with what face can you pretend talk of burthen and encroachments, when you yourself have encroached upon every thing that is held dear by mankind!" He dismissed Homogeneon, claiming that as a slaveholder, he "cannot argue upon the subject of liberty" and could "be never zealous in the cause of liberty" until denouncing slavery. The conversation with the old man thoroughly shamed the author, who offered an apology at the end of his letter, stating he was sorry that he was "the owner of any slaves" and promising to free them.[7] Whether Homogeneon's encounter with the old man actually occurred is irrelevant. What matters is that a number of commentators began to critique the existence of chattel slavery in a land of contested freedom. In this politicized landscape, anything could be sacrificed in the name of liberty, even the institution of slavery. The abolition of slavery was not only politically expedient for white Bostonians fighting to be free but, for the first time, a real possibility.

Slaves took full advantage of the opportunities presented by this new political landscape. They were both observers and participants in the larger protests, demonstrations, and movements that characterized the lead-up to the American Revolution in Boston. They were present in the public demonstrations against British policy, even if they were not allowed to participate. During the height of the Stamp Act Crisis in early November 1765, Bostonians gathered for their annual celebration of Pope's Day, the commemoration of Guy Fawkes's 1605 attempt to blow up the House of Parliament and a day of riot, revelry, and drunken fun for town dwellers. It could be quite tumultuous. Groups of "Servants and Negroes" would wait until sundown to attack one another with clubs and other weapons. Eventually, two groups emerged out of this nighttime ritual, one representing the North End neighborhood and the other the South End. Every November 5, townspeople could expect these two groups to meet in a rowdy battle to destroy each other's parade float—containing effigies of Guy Fawkes, the Pope, the Devil, and "other Effigies signifying Tyranny." In the charged political environment of the Stamp Act Crisis, however, the celebration took a different turn. The two sides came together to form a "UNION." There was no battle, no beating, but a mutual burning of each side's float. More importantly, however, no "Negro [was] allowed to approach near" the effigies. Although Pope's Day in 1765 may have been the most peaceful of a generation—leaving the *Boston Post-Boy* to comment that the event "may be look'd upon as the (perhaps the only) happy Effect arising from the S[tam]p A[c]t"— for the first time, slaves were explicitly excluded from the celebration, relegated to mere observers.[8] The message was clear. Colonists need to overcome their differences to effectively resist British authority and tyranny, but that unity explicitly excluded those who were deemed too disorderly.

To think slaves stood idly by while being relegated and marginalized in the political movements of the 1760s and 1770s is to misunderstand the level of organization slaves possessed and their increasing commitment to the natural rights expounded on by white colonists. By the late 1760s, reports began appearing in the newspapers of slaves and other blacks forming organizations and having other public gatherings. Unlike earlier generations, when slaves participated in roving gangs of malcontents, these organizations seemed to serve a larger purpose. In 1770, the *Massachusetts Spy* reported a number of "Negro Grenadiers" gathered on the town common complete with commanders—"flushed with a military spirit"—who began patrolling Boston's streets. They had a drum and fife and paraded around until some white inhabitants broke the drum and quickly dispersed the crowd, telling them to "go peaceably home to their masters." The newspaper blamed such behavior on masters giving their slaves "too much liberty."[9] Like other white Bostonians, these slaves thought they had the right to organize and show a united, martial front.

There is further evidence to suggest these groups had political affiliations. A year after the first report of "Negro *Grenadiers*," another article appeared in the *Boston News-Letter* describing how the town's black population divided itself into "Companies" that met together for "Entertainment." These groups, however, began quarrelling with one another, arming themselves, and threatening to fight in the streets.[10] While we can never know why these various groups came to violence, it is safe to assume political issues were at the heart of the conflicts, especially given the context in which the groups formed. What these "companies" and their duels suggest is a latent black politics with its own struggles and divisions that also fed into the American revolutionary movement.

Although enslaved Bostonians may have had their own politics that unfolded with the imperial crisis as a backdrop and were excluded from many white protests, some whites saw slaves as allies. This was especially true of British soldiers, who in the aftermath of the Stamp Act and Townshend Acts crises occupied Boston. In November 1768, Captain John Wilson of the Fifty-Ninth Regiment of Foot encountered a group of slaves and encouraged them to "beat, insult, and otherwise ill treat their said Masters, asserting that now the Soldiers are come, the Negroes shall be free." For the British soldiers, Boston's slaves were potential allies in a struggle against a hostile population. A few days after Wilson's indictment, a rumor started that a group of British officers were heard saying "that if the Negroes could be made Freemen, they should be sufficient to subdue these damn'd Rascals," referring to the colonists.[11] It is unknown how the slaves felt about the prospects of joining the British soldiers, although the actions of African Americans in other colonies during the American Revolution suggest that if slaves joined the British, they might have represented a fifth column for the colonists.[12] They were potential allies to those who were looking to steal the liberty of white Bostonians, an especially troubling prospect as they began forming politicized gangs.

Nevertheless, participation in political protests does not demonstrate how slaves appropriated natural rights discourse and used it to argue for emancipation; instead, we need to look at the writings of enslaved and free blacks in Massachusetts on the eve of the American

Revolution. The first of these was an editorial written by Cæsar Sarter of Newburyport. Not much is known about Sarter's background outside of the details he provided in his article. He seems to have been born in Africa, brought to Massachusetts at a young age, enslaved for twenty years, and then "by the blessing of God" freed. How he acquired the ability to write or was allowed to publish is unknown, although his article was meant to get the attention of the reading public. Comprising nearly three-quarters of the front page of the *Essex Journal and Merrimack Packet*, Sarter's essay is important for a number of reasons. First, he separated the colonists' struggle against the British from the slaves' struggle for freedom, opening the essay by noting, "this is a time of great anxiety and distress among you, on account of the infringement not only of your Charter rights; but of the natural rights and privileges of freeborn men." While the white colonists' rights were under attack and the slaves had no place in that fight, African slavery was an obstacle to whites finding true freedom. Sarter begged readers to "consider the evil consequences, and gross heinousness of reducing to, and retaining in slavery" Africans who were just as deserving of liberty as whites. The first step to colonial freedom was to "let the oppressed Africans be liberated." Then, and "not till then," he told the colonists, "may you . . . look to Heaven for a blessing on your endeavors to knock the shackles with which your task masters are hampering you."[13]

Most important, however, Sarter wrote his essay fully immersed in the language of natural rights and universal liberty. His opening salvo declared, "Slavery is the greatest and consequently most to be dreaded of all temporal calamities; so its opposite, Liberty, is the greatest temporal good." His use of slavery and freedom as analytical categories would have been appealing to white readers, themselves exposed to the same language in hundreds of contemporary political pamphlets and newspaper articles. Yet Sarter pushed his argument even further. Not only was freedom a universal good, but all human beings were "entitled to the same natural rights of mankind." These rights were also individual, and every "man is the best judge of his happiness, and every heart best knows its own bitterness."[14] Sarter's appeal to individual rights was a recent development and a reflection of a growing commitment to universal freedom among enslaved and free blacks in Massachusetts.

While Sarter made a direct public appeal for the end of slavery through a newspaper article, Afro-Bostonians took their fight directly to the colonial government. In a series of petitions filed between 1773 and 1777, they asked for the emancipation of the colony's slaves. The target of these petitions varied over the years, including the House of Representatives; the royal governor, Thomas Hutchinson; and the military governor, General Thomas Gage. Slaves understood the colonial government, its institutional structures, and how best to appeal to and communicate with those structures by petition. They also understood the rapidly changing political climate leading to the American Revolution. At least one of the petitions, if not all of them, was created by one of the "committees" described earlier, providing further evidence of Afro-Bostonians' politicization.

These petitions also deployed the language of natural rights. In the April 1773 appeal addressed to Thomas Hutchinson, the committee of blacks, including Peter Bestes, Sambo Freeman, Felix Holbrook, and Chester Joie, invoked the "divine spirit of freedom," which "seems to fire every humane breast on this continent."[15] A subsequent petition by a "Grate Number of Blacks" to General Gage informed him, "we have in common with all other men a naturel right to our freedoms with Being depriv'd of them by our fellow men." African slaves were, according to this petition, a "freeborn Pepel and have never forfeited this Blessing by aney compact or agreement whatever."[16] An even more forceful appeal to natural rights appeared in the final 1777 petition to the Massachusetts legislature—the only one filed after independence—in which the petitioners claimed to be "detained in a state of Slavery in the Bowels of a free and Christian Country." Once again, they claimed to "have, in common with all other Men, a natural and unalienable right to that freedom" and deserved "freedom, . . . the natural right of all Men." Taking the argument a step further, the 1777 petition claimed that a "Life of Slavery, like that of [the] petitioners, deprived of every social privilege, of every thing requisite to render Life even tolerable, is far worse than Non-Existence."[17] In short, slavery was a fate worse than death. Over four years, the petitioners' desire for freedom and claim to having natural rights only grew stronger and more forceful. They grew to believe that they shared the same rights as white colonists. Freedom and the elimination of slavery became ingrained in protests of Boston's black population and replaced the subtle demands and ameliorative measures of earlier generations of slaves.

As slaves became more politicized and forceful in their demands, their willingness to use violence to achieve freedom and emancipation also grew. After Boston's slaves petitioned Thomas Gage for their freedom in May 1774, Abigail Adams wrote her husband, John, then in Philadelphia attending the First Continental Congress, the following September, concerned about a "conspiracy of the Negroes" in Boston. According to Abigail, the slaves had sent a second petition to Gage, this time pledging their assistance in his struggles against the colonists in exchange for their liberty. Gage seriously considered the matter and consulted with Hugh Percy, 2nd Duke of Northumberland and commander of the British soldiers in Boston, but Abigail knew little of "what Steps they will take in consequence of it."[18] While Gage never conscripted black Bostonians to fight against the Patriot scourge, Abigail's fears were not unfounded. After having three petitions ignored by various royal governors and the Massachusetts legislature, slaves were ready and willing to turn to violence to achieve their ends.

Little is known about the 1774 conspiracy. Indeed, the editor of the Adams family correspondence noted sardonically that everything "about this rumored 'conspiracy of the Negroes' was kept so 'private' that the editors cannot further elucidate it."[19] There are not any newspapers articles describing the event either. How Abigail obtained this information is lost to history, but she contended that the plot "was discovered by one who endeavourd to diswaid them from it." Even more problematic, Abigail provides few details and instead uses the opportunity to opine on slavery, adding, "I wish most sincerely there was not a Slave in the province."[20] To better understand this conspiracy, then, we have to parse the information Abigail does provide and combine it with what we know about enslaved Bostonians in this given moment, especially their earlier May 1774 petition to Thomas Gage.

A nonslave actor was instrumental to the 1774 conspiracy, as the slaves found an "Irishman" to write the petition to Gage. This piece of information is important to understanding the plot. When looking at the petitions sent to the Massachusetts government, they were all written by, most likely, free black or enslaved authors. The unsteady hand, phonetic spellings, and frequent corrections suggest that while the person creating the petition had the ability to write, it was either recently learned or self-taught. Nevertheless, the petitioners wrote them. Contrast that with the information provided by Abigail. An anonymous Irishman wrote for these slaves, suggesting that they were a distinct group from earlier petitioners. Even more telling for this point was the "one" who attempted to dissuade the other slaves from submitting the document to Gage. Most likely another slave, "one" had his or her life threatened by the conspirators and appealed to Justice Edmund Quincy for protection. Once again, there seems to be a division in the black community and a black politics that has thus far eluded historians.

But political differences did not mean the objectives were different. It seems to be a case of same end, different means. Whereas the group involved in the 1774 conspiracy advocated violence and desired to ally with the British government, others were content to petition, go through the legal channels, and work with whoever was willing to answer their petition. Yet the end result was still the same. The 1774 conspirators offered to help Gage in exchange for their liberty, not far off from the petitioners who begged Gage earlier in the year to honor their natural right to their freedoms.[21]

The question remains, however, why blacks began using natural rights discourse. Quite simply, slaves continued doing what they had been doing for the previous seventy-five years. As white Bostonians began appealing to natural rights, enslaved Bostonians appropriated that same language. While the methods may have been the same, the stakes were much higher. Throughout the imperial crisis and the early years of the Revolution, the world of dependence unraveled, hierarchy collapsed, and the house of unfreedom fell. Sons defied their fathers, women disobeyed their husbands, and slaves challenged their masters' authority. Prerevolutionary society, with its strict, patriarchal social order, began to come undone at the seams, presenting opportunities to defy that order and, for Afro-Bostonians, an opportunity to make a claim for freedom. Personal liberty, in this context and really for the first time, was a real option, the ultimate safeguard for property and families, and an avenue to becoming full members of American society.

Both Sarter and the petitions address these issues. Sarter asked his readers to imagine being "trappanned" (taken) away from the "dear wife of his bosom," the "wife from her affectionate husband," or the "parents from their tender and loved offspring."[22] The petition to Gage noted how enslaved spouses lacked the "endearing ties" because their masters and mistress controlled slave marriages. Children, the petitioners exclaimed, were "taken from us by force" and "sent maney miles from us," never to be seen by their parents again. More importantly, however, being a slave did not allow them to "perform the duties of a husband to a wife or parent to his child." Their obligations were to their masters, not their families, leaving wives unable to "submit" to husbands and children unable to "obey" their parents.[23] Beyond the family, slavery prevented the enslaved from being responsible citizens. In the earliest petition, filed in January 1773, Felix, the author of the text and most likely the free black Felix Holbrook, promised that if made free, ex-slaves "would soon be able as well as willing to bear a Part in the Public Charges." Most slaves were "discreet, sober, honest, and industrious" and would only make positive contributions to society.[24] Slavery degraded slaves and did not allow those shouldering its burden to effectively protect their families or to be full members of a rapidly changing society, leaving only universal freedom to safeguard a place in Boston.[25]

At odds with this desire for universal freedom, however, was the language of dependence in which some of these appeals were couched. Some of this can be dismissed as merely a rhetorical appeal to their audience, such as referring to the colonial legislature's "Humanity and justice" or Sarter's wish that his article "not be less noticed for coming from an African."[26] Other uses of deferential language suggest something deeper. In the petition to Gage, the authors posed a number of questions. One of those questions concerned how slaves could fulfill their "parte of duty" to their masters while enslaved.[27] Likewise, the earliest petition argued that the best form of freedom would be one that caused the "least Wrong or Injury" to masters, meaning that owners would not be immediately deprived of their slaves' labor.[28] The deference inherent in these petitions suggests that slaves still had an older picture of their place in Euro-American society, where they were consigned to serve; but instead of destroying all constraints, liberty made slaves free to better serve their masters.

Similarly problematic are the slaves' descriptions of what they would do after being freed. On the one hand, they wanted to be part of white society, as suggested earlier, but on the other, they desired to be removed from white society. Sarter recommended after freeing the slaves to give them "grants in some back part of the country."[29] The 1773 petition to Hutchinson suggested an even more radical solution. As soon as the "joint labours" of the newly freed black population earned enough money, they would "transport" themselves to "some part of the coast of Africa," where they proposed "a settlement."[30] We could dismiss these ideas as attempts to soften fears of emancipation, but they can be interpreted in another way. Both suggest that after nearly three generations of slaves attempting to integrate themselves in colonial society, they had simply given up on Euro-Americans and were willing to sacrifice all material comfort in order to have freedom and to provide for their families. While Sarter's proposition meant that the frontier settlement of ex-slaves would still be under the jurisdiction of Massachusetts, removing to Africa meant eschewing white political authority altogether in order to secure their freedom and all the benefits that came with it.

Slaves' willingness to remain dependent on the master class or to remove themselves from the United States altogether was the ultimate tragedy of their attempts to gain their freedom. It does not suggest any hesitancy or fear of liberty, however. Instead, personal freedom and natural rights were the newest mode of challenging their enslavement and were to be attained at any cost, no matter how steep. Yet even while blacks were willing to leave their homeland, white authorities never acknowledged the petitions outside of a few tertiary debates, and it is unknown if Sarter's article gained any traction. Slavery persisted even in the midst of the struggle for independence and freedom from Great Britain.

Despite the failure of the petition campaign and the ambiguity of Sarter's message, emancipation eventually came to the Bay State. Coinciding with the imperial crisis, the rise of natural rights discourse, and the continued use of individual strategies to challenge slavery were a number of court cases called "freedom suits," in which slaves sued their masters for freedom. Between 1760 and 1779, there were around twenty of these cases, although none of them were filed in Boston. Most used preexisting legal mechanisms to challenge an individual's enslavement rather than slavery as an institution.[31] Like freedom suits, the Massachusetts Constitution of 1780 provided slaves with a powerful tool to aid them in the struggle for freedom. Article 1, section 1, baldly stated, "All men are born free and equal, and have certain natural, essential, and unalienable rights." Jeremy Belknap, founder of the Massachusetts Historical Society and the first historian of slavery in the Bay State, argued in 1795 in a series of letters to St. George Tucker that this clause was meant to "establish the liberation of the negroes on a general principle, and so it was understood by the people at large."[32] Samuel Dexter, one of the men Belknap corresponded with to write his study, acknowledged that after ratification of the constitution, many slaves did not even bother taking their masters to court, instead deserting "from the service of those who had been their owners."[33] Between the freedom suits and the powerful message (real or imagined) of the constitution, the end of slavery became more of a reality by the early 1780s.

These gains, however, were based primarily on individual deci-sions, and slavery persisted for those slaves lacking the will or means to abscond or bring suit. A series of court cases involving an enslaved man from central Massachusetts named Quok Walker and his owner, Nathaniel Jennison, finally dealt a serious blow to slavery as an insti-tution. In 1781, Walker fled to the home of Seth and John Caldwell, two men who employed Walker to work on their farm. Walker told the farmers that Jennison had allegedly promised to free him but refused. When an enraged Jennison appeared at the Caldwell farm, retrieved Walker, beat him, and locked him in a barn, Walker filed suit against Jennison for assault and his freedom. Meanwhile, Jen-nison filed suit against the Caldwells for harboring and profiting from Walker's labors. These two cases took two years to resolve themselves in the court, eventually reaching the Massachusetts Supreme Court as *Commonwealth v. Jennison*. Chief Justice William Cushing presided over the case, and in his instructions to the jury, he told them slavery was "wholly incompatible and repugnant" to the spirit of the Mas-sachusetts Constitution. "Servitude," the judge passionately declared, "can no longer be tolerated in our government."[34] The jury, inflamed by Cushing's impassioned instructions, freed Walker and allegedly ended slavery in Massachusetts once and for all.[35]

Yet we have to question whether this was in fact the end of slavery in Massachusetts. Cushing's arguments against slavery were not included in the actual decision. They were only instructions to the jury and were never published until the late nineteenth century. Moreover, the case received little attention in the press, a far cry from the near obsession with slavery during the imperial crisis. One wonders how masters and slaves even knew about the *Jennison* decision, let alone its implica-tions. Likewise, no one was sure what the larger ramifications of the case were, even for the parties involved.[36] Cushing's brother Charles, the clerk of the court during the trial, acknowledged fifteen years after *Jennison*, "the question [of slavery] has never come directly before our Supreme court," and he described it as a simple case of "common assault & Battery."[37] Likewise, the case was never cited as precedent in any case involving slavery until 1808, a generation after the original decision.[38] All of this suggests that *Commonwealth v. Jennison* was not a watershed moment in the abolition of slavery but just one of many individual cases leading to the end of slavery in Massachusetts.

Even more insidious than the continued ownership of slaves in Massachusetts was the sale of slaves out of New England during the

1770s, 1780s, and 1790s. During these decades, many masters knew that slavery was coming to an end. As slaves became increasingly locked out of the labor market and rendered useless by a growing surplus of unskilled white labor moving to Boston from the countryside, slaveholders sold their bondsmen and bondswomen to the southern states and the West Indies, where they still had value. Numbers on how many slaves were sold out of New England during the revolutionary period are hard to find and even more difficult for an individual place like Boston. The ever-shrinking black population in both Boston and elsewhere during this period, which cannot be explained by declining birthrates or high mortality, however, suggests that a large number of slaves were sold south.[39] Ezekiel Price's notary books offer some evidence for this practice in Boston. In September 1769, Price recorded a bill of sale in which the tobacconist Simon Elliot sold his slave Peggy to Archimedes George, who lived in Jamaica.[40] More circumstantial evidence also appears in the notary records, including a manumission recorded by Price on 25 February 1789. In the document, John Soley freed Charleston after the slave purchased his freedom from Soley. Interestingly, however, is that Charleston, according to the original date of the manumission, gained his freedom on 7 May 1777. What this suggests is that Charleston, possibly fearful of being captured and sold back into slavery, had Price create a legal copy of his manumission that he could use in any future court battles.[41] Twelve years after Charleston had gained his freedom, he had legitimate concerns about being kidnapped and sold away from his home.

Given the ambiguity of the *Jennison* decision and the robust traffic in slaves and free blacks out of Boston, the question remains as to when slavery actually ended there. Even the 1790 census, in which there were not any slaves enumerated in Massachusetts, is not a good date to use, as there is circumstantial evidence to suggest that census takers deliberately avoided counting slaves.[42] Instead of looking for a particular date or event, it might be better to envision emancipation as a process, one that occurred haphazardly during the revolutionary era.[43] Slaves sued for freedom, absconded, joined the Continental and British armies, and found other creative ways of gaining liberty.[44] Emancipation was not bestowed from on high but was something slaves fought for. In this new world of unlimited individual freedom, slaves and free blacks were the foot soldiers fighting against unfreedom in all its nefarious forms. Nevertheless, the concept of freedom remained problematic and fraught with difficulty. Rather than being treated as equal citizens of a new republic, freed men and women experienced for the first time scientific racism, systematic discrimination, and segregation from the American body politic.[45] The fight for legal freedom may have been come to an end, but the struggle for equality and acceptance was just beginning.

Despite the great strides made in destroying slavery in Boston and the rest of Massachusetts during the American Revolution, emancipation was fraught with its own set of problems, especially the rise of racism and racially exclusive restrictive legislation that was much worse than that of the colonial period. Given the ultimate failure and ambiguity of this first attempt for freedom and equality, it is not surprising that older attempts at amelioration, ones crafted in a world of bondage and unfreedom, persisted after the American Revolution. In the middle of this emancipatory moment, a lone voice spoke up using the language of dependence. We can see this in the petition of Belinda, a free African woman who had no surname, when she petitioned the Massachusetts General Court for relief in 1783, demanding to be paid out from her Loyalist master's confiscated estate after he failed to uphold his side of a dependent relationship. Even in an era of unbound freedom, an older language, one created in the house of unfreedom, persisted and produced results similar to those of an earlier generation.

Belinda was the slave of Isaac Royall, a wealthy merchant and slave owner who lived in Medford, Massachusetts. Royall was also one of the few people who could be called a planter in the traditional sense. Like his brethren in the southern colonies and the Caribbean—Royall's father had moved to Medford from Antigua—he owned a six-hundred-acre farm and over twenty slaves, and he even built separate slave quarters for them.[46] When revolution came to Massachusetts, however, Royall, a Loyalist, fled the colony, abandoning all of his slaves. Belinda, now a free woman, moved to Boston with her handicapped daughter, Prine. Belinda was elderly, was unable to care for herself and her daughter, and lived in abject poverty. She eventually petitioned the Commonwealth of Massachusetts, which had seized her former master's property after he fled, asking it to pay her an annual "allowance" from the Royall estate.[47]

The petition itself is a personal testament to a new world of unlimited freedom. Comprising six paragraphs, the document opens with a long (longer than all the other paragraphs), idyllic description of Belinda's childhood in Africa. She vividly recounts her experience of the Middle Passage—"a floating World"—and its horrors, including being bound with "three hundred Affricans in chains, suffering the most excruciating torments," where "death came like a balm to their wounds." She was then subjected to the "doom" of slavery, "from which death alone was to emancipate her." Despite being a "free moral agent," Belinda spent fifty years working for the Royall family, until the American Revolution, when the "world convulsed for the preservation of that freedom which the Almighty Father intended for all the human Race." While freedom triumphed in America, Royall fled to England, where "Lawless domination sits enthroned"—perhaps an appropriate ending for Belinda's former owner. What she asked for next, however, was incredible. For five decades, Royall had robbed Belinda of the fruits of her labor, and now she believed she was entitled to "one morsel of that immense wealth, apart whereof hath been accumulated by her own industry." This small amount, Belinda argued, would prevent her and her daughter from living in miserable poverty. The House of Representatives granted her request and ordered the executors of Royall's estate to pay her a small indemnity each year.

While it is quite clear that Belinda was asking for reparations for her past service using the language of revolution and natural rights, there is another way of reading her petition, this one in the context of a world with which Belinda would have been more familiar, one built on the foundation of dependence and unfreedom.[48] First, Belinda did not write her petition. She signed the document and subsequent requests for funds with an X. Instead, another Afro-Bostonian, most likely Prince Hall, crafted the petition with its appeals.[49] Hall and his compatriots understood the petition as a rhetorical form, knowing how to appeal to white audiences using the language of freedom and Christianity. Below this rhetoric, however, we can hear Belinda's voice. By her own admission, she had been enslaved for fifty years, arriving in the colony when she was twelve years old. She would have inhabited an unfree world in which material comfort was often preferable to freedom. There are undertones that Royall violated the contract between master and slave. Proper masters took care of their bondsmen and bondswomen in their old age, but when the war "compeeled her master to fly," Royall had abandoned that obligation. Moreover, true independence and liberty would have meant that Belinda would not have had to rely on anyone for her support, let alone the estate of her former master.

Belinda was the product of an era quickly being eclipsed. A woman born in Africa and taken to the colonies as an adolescent, she spent most of her life living in a world built on the ties of dependence. She deployed the skills she and fellow slaves had learned over the previous two generations to ameliorate her condition. Her subtle protest was to better her and her daughter's material comfort. Freedom was abstract and unknowable; feeding herself was more immediate, even if it meant entering into a new dependent relationship, this time with the state.

Jack escaped slavery in Barbados only to willingly enter indentured servitude in Boston. Quaco poisoned a fellow slave, using a strategy he had learned during his time in Suriname. Mark, Phillis, and Phoebe murdered their master, believing he violated their rights. Dick helped another slave and two indentured servants rob his master. Cato, Nero, Quaco, and Scipio absconded from their master's tannery to find better work on a farm in Cambridge. Chloe stood accused of stealing a gold necklace but received a fair hearing, and the judge acquitted her. Belinda drew on the language of dependence to receive reparations from her former master.

The chains of dependence bound all of these slaves to a larger world of unfreedom in eighteenth-century Boston. Part of a divinely inspired hierarchy but at the bottom of it, slavery was one of many forms of dependence that layered and structured the social order. Yet the bottom was still part of this order, giving Boston's slaves a place in society. Using various weapons of the weak—work stoppages, running away, and even crowd action—slaves rarely challenged the social order or the institution of slavery, opting instead to push for autonomy, to protect their families and communities, and to demand a place in society. While certainly at a disadvantage given their lowly status and skin color, bondsmen and bondswomen proved capable of working within the hierarchy to ameliorate their condition and create a tenuous yet functional independence. They lived in a place that steadfastly refused to recognize black freedom, often imposed draconian sanctions on free blacks, and did not offer people of African descent the same opportunities as formerly bound whites. Rather than struggling for a restrictive liberty and jeopardizing their ties to the community, many slaves opted to fight for what they saw as their customary rights, an action completely in line with those of other early modern Euro-Americans. Decoding slavery and how it functioned in one particular eighteenth-century society is the purpose of this study. Of paramount importance is context. Without understanding the continuum of unfreedom that characterized life for slaves, their actions make little sense to modern observers. Without understanding the chains of dependence, we risk misinterpreting and caricaturing their lived experiences.

To understand slavery in this context, we had to begin by examining the origins of enslaved Bostonians. They came from across the Atlantic world, reflecting a diversity of experiences and circumstances. Many were creoles born in the West Indies and sold to Boston as children. Others were adults who spent years in the Caribbean. In both cases, those who spent time in the Caribbean learned to speak English and familiarized themselves with Anglo-American institutions, including slavery. Slaves also came from West Africa, where slavery was deeply ingrained in society and culture. Even if born free, these Africans would have encountered slaves and slavery every day and would have had an African understanding of the institution. Instead of fighting for freedom, slaves in Africa worked their way into their masters' society. In this sense, many enslaved Bostonians fought to incorporate themselves into their new homeland, hoping to achieve a place in the body politic. African slavery may have provided a key resource for decoding the institution in Boston, but the town itself was convulsed with change throughout the eighteenth century.

When relatively large numbers of slaves began arriving in Boston during the early 1700s, they would have encountered an inherently unfree society. African slaves labored beside Indian slaves, pauper apprentices, craft apprentices, and other bound workers. Colonial elites saw themselves as presiding over a social hierarchy with God and king at the top and African slaves assigned to the lowest rung on this ladder. Nevertheless, everyone in this order had a set of customary rights and privileges, and slaves argued for their own to better navigate slavery. Important to this argument were the reciprocal obligations that masters and slaves had to one another, which often became points of conflict and which help to explain slaves' running away and violence in the absence of modern notions of freedom.

Slaves were fully ensconced in this unfree world. They inhabited a social world that was multiracial and where people interacted across social class and with people from all walks of life. Forced to live in close quarters, masters and slaves often had fraught relationships, which could have pathological and often violent consequences. In addition, many slaves grew up in households where they shared space with pauper apprentices and indentured servants. Others, both inside and outside the master's house, built long-standing friendships with other dependent classes. Slaves also formed families, and marriages, because of a 1705 law, were legal. Some slaves even married Native Americans, finding a loved one and building a cross-racial alliance all at the same time. Participating in communal activities—legal, illegal, multiracial, or racially exclusive—characterized the social lives of Boston's slaves. Given the instability of master-slave relations, many slaves used their social worlds to form powerful cross-status communities to better resist the degradation of being enslaved and to carve out a certain degree of autonomy.

One of the most important—and successful—sites where slaves found this independence was in the workplace. Given the chronic labor shortages experienced in a bustling port city like Boston, slaves were an important and valued component of the workforce. Even female domestic laborers were integral to household production. Enslaved men served as menial laborers, sailors, and skilled artisans. They could have been found in every sector of the economy, working as blacksmiths, bakers, and braziers. The labor provided by all slaves gave them leverage against some of slavery's worst abuses, and the wages they often earned working helped to secure a degree of autonomy. Slaves regularly protested working conditions, sometimes violently, other times by absconding. They forged relationships with fellow workers, white and black, and participated in riots and other public demonstrations against unfair working conditions or violations of their rights as workers, most famously demonstrated by their participation in the Impressment Riot of 1747. Labor allowed slaves to shape the terms of their enslavement, and formed a central part of their identities.

At the same time that slaves became valued workers, they appropriated local institutions in order to better their condition. Understanding that there was no comprehensive slave law and that most jurists in Massachusetts treated slaves as servants, allowing slaves to claim a set of rights and have an expectation of legal recourse, they took full advantage of the relative ambiguity of their legal status. They also knew they could expect a fair hearing before any number of justices of the peace in eighteenth-century Boston. Doing so allowed them to receive protection from abuse and to exonerate themselves of criminal accusations, thus protecting their communal standing. Having access to Massachusetts's judicial system also allowed slaves to file petitions in an attempt to address their grievances. Likewise, slaves used Boston's many Protestant churches to these same ends and more. Many slaves were certainly true believers, but others used association with a certain church, domination, or minster for their own gain. Religion offered redemption not only for their souls but also for their reputations. Moreover, religious affiliation offered other skills such as literacy and taught slaves a powerful Christian vocabulary they could use when making public declarations. In short, through the use of institutions, slaves learned how Euro-American society functioned.

Like the many slaves who lived in Boston, this study navigates an unfree society. Using Boston as a case study, it reconceptualizes slavery and freedom in the Atlantic world. Instead of understanding slave action and motivation through a prism of freedom, it eschews modern conceptions of liberty to better understand the lives of the enslaved. The early modern Atlantic was a realm of unfreedom where universal notions of human freedom and dignity would have been alien. Applying those principles to the past is not only ahistorical but ultimately wrong. While we certainly cannot know what enslaved Bostonians thought, existing records demonstrate a profound concern with their material condition and the protection of themselves, their families, and their social networks. The desire to protect those interests suggests that it was these factors that motivated slaves' actions, not abstract, modern notions of freedom. They were staunch defenders of a set of customary rights they believed they possessed and used any opportunity to reshape and redefine the terms of enslavement. In a world where freedom could be just as fraught as slavery, the enslaved became masters of their status. They learned and employed notions of deference and dependence to better their own lives. With the coming of the American Revolution, slaves challenged their enslavement and sought universal emancipation. Slaves drew on the skills they had learned over generations of enslavement to become free, and by the last decade of the eighteenth century, slavery was becoming history in Massachusetts. Ex-slaves found freedom only to confront the systematic racism and discrimination of the early American republic, once again pushing many African Americans into a dependent state. The chains of dependence may have been broken, but its vestiges lived on, not in an unfree Atlantic world but in a new nation dedicated to liberty.

Notes

Notes to the Introduction

1. For Jack's story, see "Case of Jack, Alias Venture, a Negro, Who Broke into the House of David Gwin," *Suffolk Files* #7710, Massachusetts State Archives, Boston, MA (hereafter MSA).

2. Other works that examine unfreedom and the interaction between bound white laborers, poor white workers, and slaves include Seth Rockman, *Scraping By: Wage Labor, Slavery, and Survival in Early Baltimore* (Baltimore: Johns Hopkins University Press, 2009); Simon Newman, *A New World of Labor: The Development of Plantation Slavery in the British Atlantic* (Philadelphia: University of Pennsylvania Press, 2013); and Max Grivno, *Gleanings of Freedom: Free and Slave Labor along the Mason-Dixon Line, 1790–1860* (Urbana: University of Illinois Press, 2011).

3. In this vein, this book echoes the sentiments of Justin Roberts, who argues that the "early modern Atlantic was an unfree world. Most workers were dependent, bound, or coerced in some way, denied specific bundles of rights and freedoms. The difference between slavery and other forced labor systems is more a matter of degree than kind." Justin Roberts, *Slavery and the Enlightenment in the British Atlantic, 1750–1807* (New York: Cambridge University Press, 2013), 4.

4. See, for example, Theodore W. Allen, *The Invention of the White Race*, vol. 2, *The Origins of Racial Oppression in the United States* (New York: Verso, 1997); and Eugene Genovese, *Slavery in White and Black: Class and Race in the Southern Slaveholders' New World Order* (New York: Cambridge, 2008).

5. David Eltis, *The Rise of African Slavery in the Americas* (New York: Cambridge University Press, 1998), 22.

6. The standard account of slaves appropriating Euro-Americans ideas and values and using them for their own purposes is James Sidbury, *Ploughshares into Swords: Race, Rebellion, and Identity in Gabriel's Virginia, 1730–1810* (New York: Cambridge University Press, 1997).

7. Benjamin Franklin, *The Autobiography of Benjamin Franklin and Other Writings* (New York: Oxford University Press, 1993), 20–21. For more on Franklin, his experience as a runaway, and how that affected his attitudes toward slavery, see David Waldstreicher, *Runaway America: Benjamin Franklin, Slavery, and the American Revolution* (New York: Hill and Wang, 2005).

8. According to Justin Roberts, treating slavery as exceptional and outside customary labor relations because of race during the eighteenth century threatens to transform our understanding of slavery into a "simple contest between heroically resisting bondsmen and their evil oppressors." Roberts, *Slavery and the Enlightenment*, 4–5.

9. These attitudes conform to early modern understandings of poverty and the poor, where it was mostly a "problem of public order." Robert Jütte, *Poverty and Deviance in Early Modern Europe* (New York: Cambridge University Press, 1994), 195. Thomas Hutchinson used "mean and vile condition" to describe the lower-class and multiracial participants in the Impressment Riot of 1747. For an exploration of this phrase, see Gary Nash, *The Urban Crucible: Social Change, Political Consciousness, and the Origins of the American Revolution* (Cambridge, MA: Harvard University Press, 1979), 222–223.

10. Scholarship on slavery in New England dates back to the 1860s and has had something of a renaissance in recent years. The earliest work is George H. Moore, *Notes on the History of Slavery in Massachusetts* (New York: D. Appleton, 1866). The first modern study of slavery in New England and still a standard work is Lorenzo Johnston Greene, *The Negro in Colonial New England* (New York: Columbia University Press, 1942). More recent scholarship includes William D. Piersen, *Black Yankees: The Development of an Afro-American Subculture in Eighteenth-Century New England* (Amherst: University of Massachusetts Press, 1988); Joanne Pope Melish, *Disowning Slavery: Gradual Emancipation and "Race" in New England, 1780–1860* (Ithaca, NY: Cornell University Press, 1998); Robert K. Fitts, *Inventing New England's Slave Paradise: Master/Slave Relations in Eighteenth-Century Narragansett, Rhode Island* (New York: Garland, 1998); John Wood Sweet, *Bodies Politic: Negotiating Race in the American North, 1730–1830* (Baltimore: Johns Hopkins University Press, 2003); Catherine Adams and Elizabeth H. Pleck, *Love of Freedom: Black Women in Colonial New England* (New York: Oxford University Press, 2010); C. S. Manegold, *Ten Hills Farm: The Forgotten History of Slavery in the North* (Princeton, NJ: Princeton University Press, 2010); Margot Minardi, *Making Slavery History: Abolitionism and the Politics of Memory in Massachusetts* (New York: Oxford University Press, 2010); Richard Bailey, *Race and Redemption in Puritan New England* (New York: Oxford University Press, 2011); Allegra di Bonaventura, *For Adam's Sake: A Family Saga in Colonial New England* (New York: Norton, 2013); Wendy Anne Warren, "Enslaved Africans in New England, 1638–1700" (PhD diss., Yale University, 2008).

11. See Roberts, *Slavery and Enlightenment*, 2–5, for a discussion of how historians have "fetishized" slavery and transformed it into something "uniquely different from other forms of coerced labor." Two recent studies have similarly collapsed the boundaries between bound laborers. These studies contend that labor, in whatever form, was necessary to economic development and that demand for workers led to new and unique forms of exploitation, be it of free laborers working beside slaves in

early republic Baltimore or white Irish indentured servants being treated as chattel slaves in early Barbados. Likewise, those oppressed workers devised strategies and ways of challenging their condition. See Rockman, *Scraping By*; and Newman, *New World of Labor*. For examples of other Atlantic entrepôts with mixed labor systems, see Linda Rupert, *Creolization and Contraband: Curaçao in the Early Modern Atlantic World* (Athens: University of Georgia Press, 2012); and Michael Jarvis, *In the Eye of All Trade: Bermuda, Bermudians, and the Maritime Atlantic World, 1680–1783* (Chapel Hill: University of North Carolina Press, 2010).

12. A discussion of the problems and limitations of "resistance" and "agency" as categories of analysis can be found in Jared Ross Hardesty, "Slavery, Freedom, and Dependence in Pre-Revolutionary Boston, 1700–1775" (PhD diss., Boston College, 2014), 10–13. An explanation of the liberal-republican ideology and its relationship to slavery and slave resistance can be found in François Furstenberg, "Beyond Freedom and Slavery: Autonomy, Virtue, and Resistance in Early American Political Discourse," *Journal of American History* 89, no. 4 (2003): 1295–1330, esp. 1316–1326.

13. Eugene Genovese makes the distinction between pre- and postrevolutionary slave action by classifying the former as "rebellion" that did not look to destroy slavery as an institution and the latter as "revolution," which sought universal emancipation. See Eugene D. Genovese, *From Rebellion to Revolution: Afro-American Slave Revolts in the Making of the New World* (Baton Rouge: Louisiana State University Press, 1979).

14. For more on popular protest in early modern Europe, see Julius R. Ruff, *Violence in Early Modern Europe, 1500–1800* (New York: Cambridge University Press, 2001), esp. chap. 6, "Popular Protest"; and E. P. Thompson, "The Moral Economy of the English Crowd in the Eighteenth Century," *Past and Present* 50 (1971): 77–136. Scholars of early America have examined popular protest in this era. See, for example, William Pencak, Matthew Dennis, and Simon P. Newman, eds., *Riot and Revelry in Early America* (University Park: Pennsylvania State University Press, 2002). Some scholars of slavery in New England have also acknowledged this phenomenon. William Piersen argues that "until the late eighteenth century [slaves] never organized social revolutions against the institution of slavery itself." Piersen, *Black Yankees*, 144.

15. This idea conforms nicely with James Scott's notion of everyday resistance. When examining why peasants never fought whole-scale revolutions against their oppressors, Scott found that these were oftentimes futile and actually only empowered state apparatuses. Instead, Scott argues that peasant resistance took "*everyday* forms: foot dragging, dissimulation, false compliance, pilfering, feigned ignorance, slander, arson, sabotage, and so forth." These are incredibly devolved and individual acts of resistance requiring little coordination to help the peasantry "defend its interest as best it can." James C. Scott, *Weapons of the Weak: Everyday Forms of Peasant Resistance* (New Haven, CT: Yale University Press, 1985), 29 (emphasis in original). In a study of slavery in colonial Mexico, Frank Proctor notes how slaves oftentimes resisted and rebelled for material benefits or defense of customary arrangements, not, in the words of one of the slave owners under study, "damned notions of liberty:" Instead of shoving slaves into preconceived notions of freedom, Proctor attempts to understand the enslaved on their own terms. See Frank T. Proctor III, *"Damned Notions of Liberty": Slavery, Culture, and Power in Colonial Mexico, 1640–1769* (Albuquerque: University of New Mexico Press, 2010).

16. John Wood Sweet examines how slaves and Indians became incorporated and integrated themselves into colonial society. Despite being about "the North," Sweet's study focuses on New England, especially Rhode Island. See Sweet, *Bodies Politic*.

17. This trope was common in the early literature on slavery in New England, culminating in Lorenzo Greene's *The Negro in Colonial New England* (see Greene, *Negro in Colonial New England*, 218-219). Given the context in which Greene was writing in the 1930s and 1940s when many American historians did not believe African Americans worthy of study, it is hard to pass judgment on him for relying upon earlier and mostly white historians for this point. Many later writers tried to reverse this trend, but tend to go too far in the other direction, over emphasizing instances of horrific violence. For an example, see Manegold, *Ten Hills Farm*.

18. David Armitage, "Three Concepts of Atlantic History," in David Armitage and Michael J. Braddick, eds., *The British Atlantic World, 1500–1800*, 2nd ed. (New York: Palgrave Macmillan, 2009), 13.

19. For the Caribbean, the work of Richard Dunn still proves invaluable, especially given Boston's close ties to Barbados. See Richard Dunn, *Sugar and Slaves: The Rise of the Planter Class in the West Indies* (1972; repr., Chapel Hill: University of North Carolina Press, 2000). For Africa, John Thornton, *Africa and Africans in the Making of the Atlantic World*, 2nd ed. (New York: Cambridge University Press, 1998), is an important starting point for all nonspecialists dealing with African history. As for European notions of unfreedom, I am more concerned with how American colonials interpreted those ideas. To better understand this, I engaged the rich literature on the "Anglicization" of the British North American colonies, starting with John Murrin, "Anglicizing an American Colony: The Transformation of Provincial Massachusetts" (PhD diss., Yale University, 1966). Other works dealing with this are Gordon Wood, *The Radicalism of the American Revolution* (New York: Knopf, 1992), esp. part 1; T. H. Breen, *The Marketplace of Revolution: How Consumer Politics Shaped American Independence* (New York: Oxford University Press, 2004); and Brendan McConville, *The King's Three Faces: The Rise and Fall of Royal America, 1688–1776* (Chapel Hill: University of North Carolina Press, 2006). Most recently, Christopher Tomlins has examined how Anglo-American law was used to take possession of American land and create categories of bound labor. See Christopher Tomlins, *Freedom Bound: Law, Labor, and Civic Identity in Colonizing English America, 1580–1865* (New York: Cambridge University Press, 2010).

20. See, for example, R. Douglas Cope, *The Limits of Racial Domination: Plebian Society in Colonial Mexico City, 1600–1720* (Madison: University of Wisconsin Press, 1994); and Herman Bennett, *Colonial Blackness: A History of Afro-Mexico* (Bloomington: Indiana University Press, 2009). While there are studies of other types of bound labor in British North America, such as David A. Galenson, *White Servitude in Colonial America: An Economic Analysis* (New York: Cambridge University Press, 1984); Abbott Emerson Smith, *Colonists in Bondage: White Servitude and Convict Labor in America, 1607–1776* (1947; repr., Chapel Hill: University of North Carolina Press, 2012); and Richard B. Morris, *Government and Labor in Early America* (New York: Columbia University Press, 1946), these studies are more concerned with economics, law, and labor policy than the lived experience

of the unfree. One work, Lawrence William Towner, *A Good Master Well Served: Masters and Servants in Colonial Massachusetts, 1620–1775* (New York: Garland, 1998), captures the lives of servants and slaves but does not examine their interactions in any systematic way. A good exception to this trend is Ruth Wallis Herndon, *Unwelcome Americans: Living on the Margin in Early New England* (Philadelphia: University of Pennsylvania Press, 2001).

21. For more on the use of criminal records in history, see Edward Muir and Guido Ruggiero, eds., *History from Crime* (Baltimore: Johns Hopkins University Press, 1994), introduction (quotations on vii, viii). Other historians who have used court documents to reconstruct the social world of enslaved Africans are James H. Sweet, *Recreating Africa: Culture, Kinship, and Religion in the African-Portuguese World, 1441–1770* (Chapel Hill: University of North Carolina Press, 2003); and Sidbury, *Ploughshares into Swords.*

Notes to Chapter 1

1. For Quaco, see "Case of Quaco (a Negro)," February 1762, *Suffolk Files* #82628, and "Case of Quaco (Negro)," 13 September 1762, *Suffolk Files* #83313, Massachusetts State Archives, Boston, MA (hereafter MSA).

2. The ethnic origins of the earliest Afro-Bostonians can be found in Linda M. Heywood and John K. Thornton, *Central Africans, Atlantic Creoles, and the Foundation of the Americas, 1585–1660* (New York: Cambridge University Press, 2007), chap. 5. For New England specifically, see Linda M. Heywood and John K. Thornton, "'Cannibal Negroes,' Atlantic Creoles, and the Identity of New England's Charter Generation" *African Diaspora* 4 (2001): 76–94.

3. The one thousand estimate comes from Wendy Anne Warren, "Enslaved Africans in New England, 1638–1700" (PhD diss., Yale University, 2008).

4. United States Bureau of the Census, *The Statistical History of the United States from Colonial Times to the Present; Historical Statistics of the United States, Colonial Times to 1970* (New York: Basic Books, 1976), 1168.

5. For a discussion of slave societies versus societies with slaves, see Ira Berlin, *Many Thousands Gone: The First Two Centuries of Slavery in the United States* (Cambridge, MA: Harvard University Press, 1998), 7–13.

6. For these statutes and an interpretation of them, see Jonathan A. Bush, "The British Constitution and the Creation of American Slavery," in Paul Finkelman, ed., *Slavery and the Law* (Lanham, MD: Rowman and Littlefield, 2002), 392.

7. Warren, "Enslaved Africans," 6.

8. The entire *Body of Liberties* can be found in William H. Whitmore, ed., *The Colonial Laws of Massachusetts* (Boston: Rockwell and Churchill, 1890). For Article 91, see p. 53.

9. For Boyse's will, see *Suffolk County Wills: Abstracts of the Earliest Wills upon Record in the County of Suffolk, Massachusetts* (Baltimore: Genealogical Publishing, 2005), 338.

10. Ibid., 3.

11. Quoted in Warren, "Enslaved Africans," 135.

12. *Suffolk County Wills*, 3.

13. Lorenzo Johnston Greene, *The Negro in Colonial New England* (1942; repr., New York: Atheneum, 1969), 126.

14. Boston Record Commissioners, *A Report of the Record Commissioners of the City of Boston, Containing the Boston Records from 1660 to 1701*, vol. 7 (Boston: Rockwell and Churchill, 1881), 5. For more on the slave labor in eighteenth-century Boston, see chapter 4.

15. See Warren "Enslaved Africans."

16. Greene, *Negro in Colonial New England*, 73.

17. Samuel Sewall, *The Diary of Samuel Sewall, 1674-1729*, ed. M. Halsey Thomas (New York: Farrar, Straus, and Giroux, 1973), 425.

18. Warren, "Enslaved Africans," 151.

19. Boston Record Commissioners, *A Report of the Record Commissioners of the City of Boston, Containing Boston Births, Baptisms, Marriages, and Deaths, 1630-1699*, vol. 9 (Boston: Rockwell and Churchill, 1883), 158, 238.

20. Quoted in Warren, "Enslaved Africans," 152.

21. "Records of the Suffolk County Court, 1672-1680," in *Publications of the Colonial Society of Massachusetts*, vols. 29-30 (Boston: Colonial Society of Massachusetts, 1933), 29:185.

22. Ibid., 30:1164. The fine was later remitted to twenty shillings, suggesting the court did have some sympathy for Kathalina. For more on this case, see Greene, *Negro in Colonial New England*, 204; and Warren, "Enslaved Africans," 156-157.

23. "Records of the Suffolk County Court," 29:233.

24. Hannah's case can be found in ibid., 30:1153-1157. It is possible that Hannah received help and coaching from whites knowledgeable in the law. Even if she did, however, this case still speaks to the openness of Massachusetts's courts and possibilities for slaves to be educated in legal matters.

25. For more on the Royal African Company, see William Pettigrew, *Freedom's Debt: The Royal African Company and the Politics of the Atlantic Slave Trade, 1672-1752* (Chapel Hill: University of North Carolina Press, 2013); and Kenneth G. Davies, *The Royal African Company* (London: Longman and Green, 1957).

26. "Governor Bradstreet to the Committee of Trade and Plantations, 1680," in Elizabeth Donnan, ed., *Documents Illustrative of the History of the Slave Trade to America*, vol. 3 (Washington, DC: Carnegie Institution of Washington, 1932), 14-15.

27. The buccaneer turned royal governor of Jamaica Henry Morgan noted the presence of New England interlopers in the slave trade in 1680. They had been on the coast of Africa buying slaves, and instead of selling them to English colonies, the ship captain attempted a French Caribbean island, where their cargo was seized, leaving the smugglers to seek Morgan for redress. See "Sir Henry Morgan to Lord Sunderland, 1680," in Donnan, *Documents*, 15.

28. An overview of the Massachusetts slave trade can be found in James A. Rawley, *The Transatlantic Slave Trade: A History*, rev. ed. (Lincoln: University of Nebraska Press, 2005), chap. 14.

29. Peter Faneuil to Peter Buckley, 3 February 1738, in *Proceedings of the Massachusetts Historical Society*, vol. 7 (Boston: Massachusetts Historical Society, 1865), 418.

30. For more on the Rhode Island slave trade, see Jay Coughtry, *The Notorious Triangle: Rhode Island and the African Slave Trade, 1700-1807* (Philadelphia: Temple University Press, 1981).

31. "Byfield's Will, 1733," Docket #6391, Suffolk County Probate Records (hereafter SCPR), 31:425, MSA.

32. "Hugh Hall Account Book, 1728–1733," Hugh Hall Papers, Box 1, Ms. N-1352, Massachusetts Historical Society, Boston, MA (hereafter MHS).

33. The 1776 population and 1.8 percent figures are from Greene, *Negro in Colonial New England*, 74.

34. Ibid., 84.

35. The total population of Boston in 1752 can be found in Gary Nash, *The Urban Crucible: Social Change, Political Consciousness, and the Origins of the American Revolution* (Cambridge, MA: Harvard University Press, 1979), 408.

36. "Warning [Out] Book from January 4, 1745 to 1770," in Boston Overseers of the Poor Records, 1733–1925, Ms. N-1879, Microfilm P-368, Reel 1, MHS.

37. *Boston News-Letter*, 10 November 1712.

38. *The Last & Dying Words of Mark, Aged about 30 Years, a Negro Man Who Belonged to the Late Captain John Codman, of Charlestown; Who Was Executed at Cambridge, the 18th of September, 1755, for Poysoning His Abovesaid Master* (Boston, 1755), MHS Broadsides Collection, MHS.

39. Richard Dunn's *Sugar and Slaves: The Rise of the Planter Class in the West Indies* (1972; repr., Chapel Hill: University of North Carolina Press, 2000), despite its age, still provides a great introduction to the early Caribbean and the rise of sugar plantations.

40. For the population statistics, see Russell R. Menard, *Sweet Negotiations: Sugar, Slavery, and Plantation Agriculture in Barbados* (Charlottesville: University of Virginia Press, 2006), 25.

41. Jennifer Morgan, *Laboring Women: Reproduction and Gender in New World Slavery* (Philadelphia: University of Pennsylvania Press, 2004), 96.

42. Ibid.

43. For more on Mark's mobility and autonomy, see chapter 2.

44. Menard, *Sweet Negotiations*, 83.

45. Quoted in ibid., 84. Historians used to argue—and some like Menard still do—that across the board, masters did not want slaves to reproduce and preferred replacing them to providing for their welfare, but the work of Jennifer Morgan suggests that we have to take a more nuanced approach and that many slave owners actively encouraged reproduction among their bondsmen and bondswomen. For more, see the introduction to Morgan, *Laboring Women*.

46. Griffith Hughes, *The Natural History of Barbados in Ten Books* (London, 1750), 14–16.

47. Ibid., 16n21.

48. For the early history of Suriname, see Cornelius C. Goslinga, *The Dutch in the Caribbean and on the Wild Coast, 1580–1680* (Gainesville: University Press of Florida, 1971). In the Treaty of Breda in 1667, the English traded Suriname for Dutch New Amsterdam, modern New York.

49. Natalie Zemon Davis, "Judges, Masters, Diviners: Slaves' Experience of Criminal Justice in Colonial Suriname," *Law and History Review* 29, no. 4 (November 2011): 929–930.

50. Edward Bancroft, *An Essay on the Natural History of Guiana in South America* (London: T. Becket and P. A. De Hondt, 1769), 9–10.

51. Davis, "Judges, Masters, Diviners," 926.

52. The commercial connections between Boston and Suriname are explored in Johannes Postma, "Suriname and Its Atlantic Connections, 1667–1795," in Johannes Postma and Victor Enthoven, eds., *Riches from Atlantic Commerce: Dutch Transatlantic Trade and Shipping, 1585–1817* (Leiden, Netherlands: Brill, 2003). Bancroft also noted that rum, "until the late Act of the *British* Parliament [Molasses Act], for prohibiting the entry of foreign rum into her *American* Colonies, was usually sold to *New-England* traders, in payment for their commodities, but has since been sent to the coast of *Africa*, for the purchase of slaves." Bancroft, *Essay*, 12.

53. Davis, "Judges, Masters, Diviners," 930.

54. John Gabriel Stedman, *Stedman's Suriname: Life in an Eighteenth-Century Slave Society: An Abridged, Modernized Edition of "Narrative of a Five Years Expedition against the Revolted Negroes of Suriname,"* ed. Richard Price and Sally Price (Baltimore: Johns Hopkins University Press, 1992), 15–16.

55. Davis, "Judges, Masters, Diviners," 947–953. For more on the power of Obeah from the same region, but in a different time period, see Randy M. Browne, "The 'Bad Business' of Obeah: Power, Authority, and the Politics of Slave Culture in the British Caribbean," *William and Mary Quarterly* 68, no. 3 (2011): 451–480.

56. Davis, "Judges, Masters, Diviners," 953.

57. Ibid., 959.

58. Ibid., 956.

59. "Deposition of James and Sarah Gardner," 18 September 1761, *Suffolk Files* #83313, MSA.

60. Davis, "Judges, Masters, Diviners," 960.

61. Ibid., 949.

62. Stedman, *Stedman's Suriname*, 20.

63. Ibid., 35.

64. A 1704 advertisement, noted that a "well set middle sized Maddagascar Negro Woman, called Penelope" had run away from her master, Nathaniel Cary. See *Boston News-Letter*, 26 June 1704.

65. This is the same sloop that brought Phillis Wheatley to Boston and that the Wheatleys named her after. See Vincent Carretta, *Phillis Wheatley: Biography of a Genius in Bondage* (Athens: University of Georgia Press, 2011), 4.

66. Timothy Fitch to Peter Gwinn, 12 January 1760, in *The Medford Slave Trade Letters—1759–1765*, Medford Historical Society, http://www.medfordhistorical.org/collections/slave-trade-letters/peter-gwinns-first-voyage-record-behalf-timothy-fitch/ (accessed 6 September 2015).

67. All of Fitch's letters have been accumulated and digitized by the Medford Historical Society. See *The Medford Slave Trade Letters—1759–1765*, Medford Historical Society, http://www.medfordhistorical.org/collections/slave-trade-letters/.

68. Robert E. Desrochers, Jr., "Slave-for-Sale Advertisements and Slavery in Massachusetts, 1704–1781," *William and Mary Quarterly* 59, no. 3 (2002): 646, table 6. For an example of the "lately Arrived" label, see *Boston Gazette*, 18 July 1726.

69. *Boston News-Letter*, 23 August 1744.

70. *Boston News-Letter*, 10 June 1762. It is possible that this advertisement was for Gwinn's leftover cargo from one of his voyages on the *Phillis*.

71. James F. Searing, *West African Slavery and Atlantic Commerce: The Senegal River Valley, 1700–1860* (New York: Cambridge University Press, 1993), 29–30, 35–36, 39–40.

72. John Thornton, *Africa and Africans in Making of the Atlantic World, 1400–1800*, 2nd ed. (New York: Cambridge University Press, 1998), 186–189. Thornton's point is not without its detractors and disagreement. He is writing in response to an earlier generation of scholars who argued that the Atlantic slave trade destroyed African culture and that Africa was too ethnically diverse for any particular cultural traditions to survive in the Americas. For an example of this school of thought, see Sydney Mintz and Richard Price, *The Birth of African-American Culture: An Anthropological Perspective* (Boston: Beacon, 1992).

73. John Matthews, *A Voyage to the River Sierra-Leone on the Coast of Africa . . .* (London: B. White and Son, 1791), 68.

74. William Smith, *A New Voyage to Guinea . . .*, 2nd ed. (London: John Nourse, 1745), 26.

75. Michael A. Gomez, *Black Crescent: The Experience and Legacy of African Muslims in the Americas* (New York: Cambridge University Press, 2005), 136.

76. *Pasmore v. Mahomet*, Suffolk County Court of Common Pleas Record Books, 1743–1744, p. 118, MSA.

77. Boston Record Commissioners, *A Report of the Record Commissioners of the City of Boston, Containing the Records of Boston Selectmen, 1736 to 1742*, vol. 15 (Boston: Rockwell and Churchill, 1886), 258–259. It is unclear whether he was working or just a passenger onboard the vessel as the selectmen keep calling him a "Passenger."

78. Ibid., 48, 133.

79. Boston Record Commissioners, *A Report of the Record Commissioners of the City of Boston, Containing Boston Marriages from 1700 to 1751*, vol. 28 (Boston: Rockwell and Churchill, 1898), 198.

80. Quoted in Sylviane A. Diouf, *Servants of Allah: African Muslims Enslaved in the Americas* (New York: NYU Press, 1998), 49–50.

81. Large concentrations of Muslim slaves could cause problems for Europeans in New World slave societies. In 1835, Muslim slaves in Salvador, Brazil, rebelled against colonial authorities. See João José Reis, *Slave Rebellion in Brazil: The Muslim Uprising of 1835 in Bahia*, trans. Arthur Brakel (Baltimore: Johns Hopkins University Press, 1993).

82. For more on education and literacy in early Massachusetts, see E. Jennifer Monaghan, *Learning to Read and Write in Colonial America* (Amherst: University of Massachusetts Press, 2005). Monaghan specifically examines slavery in chapter 9. For my assessment of slave literacy, see chapter 5 of this book.

83. Matthews, *Voyage to the River Sierra-Leone*, 68–69.

84. Carretta, *Phillis Wheatley*, 4–9.

85. Thornton, *Africa and Africans*, 75–76.

86. Ibid., 85–86.

87. Venture Smith, *A Narrative of the Life and Adventures of Venture, a Native of Africa, but Resident above Sixty Years in the United States of America, Related by Himself* (New London, CT: C. Holt, 1798), 5–7. For more on Venture's African past, see Paul E. Lovejoy, "The African Background of Venture Smith," in James Brewer

Stewart, ed., *Venture Smith and the Business of Slavery and Freedom* (Amherst: University of Massachusetts Press, 2010), 35–55. This volume also contains a copy of the original 1798 edition of Smith's narrative.

88. Smith, *Narrative of the Life and Adventures*, 6–7.

89. Thornton, *Africa and Africans*, 86–87, 89.

90. Matthews, *Voyage to the River Sierra-Leone*, 169.

91. Philip D. Curtin, *Economic Change in Precolonial Africa: Senegambia in the Era of the Slave Trade* (Madison: University of Wisconsin Press, 1975), 36.

92. Thornton, *Africa and Africans*, 91.

93. Ibid., 88; Matthews, *Voyage to the River Sierra-Leone*, 150.

94. Paul E. Lovejoy, *Transformations in Slavery: A History of Slavery in Africa*, 3rd ed. (New York: Cambridge University Press, 2012), 13.

95. Smith, *Voyage to Guinea*, 221.

96. Matthews, *Voyage to the River Sierra-Leone*, 150–151.

97. Walter Rodney, *A History of the Upper Guinea Coast, 1545–1800* (Oxford: Oxford University Press, 1970), 261.

Notes to Chapter 2

1. Abner Cheney Goodell Jr., *The Trial and Execution for Petit Treason of Mark and Phillis, Slaves of Captain John Codman* (Cambridge, MA: John Wilson and Son, 1883), 3–4.

2. Michael Dalton, a seventeenth-century English jurist, defined petit treason as "when willful murder is committed . . . upon any subject, by one that is in subjection, and oweth faith, duty, and obedience, to the party murdered." Michael Dalton, *The Countrey Justice: Containing the Practise of the Justices of the Peace Out of Their Sessions* (London: Societie of Stationers, 1622), 213–215; *Boston Gazette*, 22 September 1755.

3. *Boston Evening Post*, 22 September 1755.

4. "Warrant against Mark (a Negro) for Refusing to Leave Boston," [1752], *Suffolk Files* #28037, Massachusetts State Archives, Boston MA (hereafter MSA). The document is badly damaged and undated but notes it was the twenty-fifth year of George II's reign. George II assumed the throne in 1727, meaning the court made the document in 1752; *Boston Gazette*, 7 July 1755.

5. Cotton Mather, *Tremenda: The Dreadful Sound with Which the Wicked Are to Be Thunderstruck* (Boston: B. Green, 1721), 27.

6. Deference and dependence in the American colonies has been debated for over two decades. Gordon Wood began this debate by arguing that the American Revolution destroyed an old, deferential society and replaced it with a modern, republican one. See Gordon Wood, *The Radicalism of the American Revolution* (New York: Knopf, 1991). Others, such as Brendan McConville, have added to Wood's thesis by showing the persistence of royalism throughout the eighteenth century. See Brendan McConville, *King's Three Faces: The Rise and Fall of Royal America, 1688–1776* (Chapel Hill: University of North Carolina Press, 2006). Others, such as Jon Butler, have argued the exact opposite, that the characteristics that made the United States—pluralism, materialism, free-market economics— existed before the American Revolution and that American society was relatively unaffected by the political structures of the Old World. See Jon Butler, *Becoming*

America: The Revolution before 1776 (Cambridge, MA: Harvard University Press, 2001). McConville and others have criticized Butler for a teleological reading of American history. Michael Zuckerman dismisses deference altogether on two grounds. First, most discussions of deference focus on electoral behavior, without acknowledging the wider realm of politics. Second, by making colonial American society deferential, historians have added "a rhetorical gloss of radicalism on the American Revolution" and "mistaken interpretations of the colonial character." Michael Zuckerman, "Tocqueville, Turner, and Turds: Four Stories of Manners in Early America," *Journal of American History* 85, no. 1 (1998): 15–16. While Zuckerman makes a powerful argument, most of his evidence concerns only bound white male laborers, leaving Kathleen Brown to conclude that "we see an American antipathy to deference arising from the unfree lives of white male immigrant laborers." Kathleen Brown, "Antiauthoritarianism and Freedom in Early America," *Journal of American History* 85, no. 1 (1998): 85.

7. Gordon Wood postulates a similar argument to mine regarding unfreedom, noting that all people in colonial American society were part of a "hierarchy of ranks and degrees of dependency." Further, Wood argues that slavery "could be regarded . . . as merely the most base and degraded status in a society of several degrees of unfreedom." Wood, *Radicalism*, 6, 52. Aaron Fogleman adds to Wood's argument, acknowledging the American colonies as a "complex world of free and unfree, occupying different conditions of liberty and bondage, some tied to masters for brief periods, others viewed as criminal outcasts rightly condemned to forced labor, and many more branded by race and doomed to servitude for life with no rights of their own." All of these peoples were interwoven into both a hierarchical society and "simultaneously a pluralistic world of peoples from Europe, Africa, and the Americas." Aaron Fogleman, "From Slaves, Convicts, and Servants to Free Passengers: The Transformation of Immigration in the Era of the American Revolution," *Journal of American History* 85, no. 1 (1998): 43. In these works, however, neither author spends much time examining how slaves regarded their place in the hierarchy.

8. For Puritan conceptions of hierarchy and patriarchy, see Edmund S. Morgan, *The Puritan Family: Religion and Domestic Relations in Seventeenth-Century New England* (New York: Harper and Row, 1966); and John Demos, *A Little Commonwealth: Family Life in Plymouth Colony* (New York: Oxford University Press, 1971). Especially important to understanding Puritan society is the notion of equity. While the leading historian of this idea, David Hall, acknowledges that the meaning of "equal" or "equity" in Puritan society is "something of a puzzle," it was an important cultural value that shaped economic and political life. Many towns, when giving land to settlers, made sure everyone received "equal proportion for quality and goodness." Likewise, political institutions adopted notions of equity. In this case, it was the expectation that "fairness and reason" would prevail over the "customs or entrenched privilege" built into English political culture. Puritans in New England, in short, still believed in hierarchy and patriarchy but conceived of societal structure differently from their fellow Englishmen and defined their society against what they saw as a corrupt, fallen English culture. While this description of early New English society is broad, outside of greater wealth inequality and a larger, more cosmopolitan, and more transient population, early Boston was part

of this trend. See David D. Hall, *A Reforming People: Puritanism and the Transformation of Public Life in New England* (New York: Knopf, 2011), 64, 146–147. For the classic work about the "dilemma" the Puritans faced in how to both engage this corrupt world and yet remain apart from it, see Edmund S. Morgan, *The Puritan Dilemma: The Story of John Winthrop* (Boston: Little, Brown, 1958). For a less rosy picture of Puritan society, especially the existence of economic elites, see Stephen Innes, *Creating the Commonwealth: Economic Culture of Puritan New England* (New York: Norton, 1998).

9. McConville, *King's Three Faces*, 15. For the American colonies and the Glorious Revolution, see Owen Stanwood, *The Empire Reformed: English America in the Age of the Glorious Revolution* (Philadelphia: University of Pennsylvania Press, 2011).

10. McConville provides the entertaining and enlightening example of Samuel Sewall, a Bostonian, diarist, and justice in the Massachusetts Superior Court of Judicature, and his gradual adoption of imperial norms. See McConville, *King's Three Faces*, 50–56. Also important to understanding how colonists gradually adopted to English imperial norms is Richard Johnson, *Adjustment to Empire: The New England Colonies, 1675–1715* (New Brunswick, NJ: Rutgers University Press, 1981), chap. 6.

11. Alan Taylor, *American Colonies: The Settling of North America* (New York: Penguin, 2001), 177.

12. William Blackstone, *Commentaries on the Laws of England*, vol. 4 (Oxford, UK: Clarendon, 1769), 127.

13. Wood, *Radicalism*, 19.

14. Browne is quoted in Carl Bridenbaugh, *Cities in Revolt: Urban Life in America, 1743–1776* (New York: Oxford University Press, 1971), 137.

15. Richard Lucas, *Rules Relating to Success in Trade* (Boston: B. McCom, 1760), 6.

16. John Adams, *Diary and Autobiography of John Adams*, vol. 1, *Diary, 1755–1770*, ed. L. H. Butterfield (Cambridge, MA: Harvard University Press, 1961), 198.

17. Ibid., 207–208.

18. Wood, *Radicalism*, 22.

19. For more on Hancock, see Herbert Stanford Allen, *John Hancock, Patriot in Purple* (New York: Beechhurst, 1953).

20. For more on the Atlantic economy and the rise of the middle class and how elites used their political authority to control the poor across the Atlantic world, see Simon Middleton and Billy G. Smith, *Class Matters: Early North America and the Atlantic World* (Philadelphia: University of Pennsylvania Press, 2008); and Richard Bushman, *The Refinement of America: Persons, Houses, Cities* (New York: Vintage, 1993).

21. Adams, *Diary*, 294; quoted in T. H. Breen, "'Baubles of Britain': The American and Consumer Revolutions of the Eighteenth Century," *Past and Present* 119 (May 1998): 79.

22. *Boston News-Letter*, 1 December 1707.

23. See Breen, "Baubles"; and T. H. Breen, "An Empire of Goods: The Anglicization of Colonial America, 1690–1776," *Journal of British Studies* 25, no. 4 (1986): 467–499.

24. "Bennett's History of New England," *Proceedings of the Massachusetts Historical Society* 5 (1860–1862): 124–125.

25. *Boston News-Letter*, 28 December 1732.

26. Allen, *John Hancock*, 67.

27. These statistics come from the Suffolk County Probate Records, vols. 14–74, at the Massachusetts State Archives. My study examined 2,570 probate inventories, of which 601, or 23.4 percent, contained slaves. For the erratic exchange rates and monetary values of the colonial period, see John J. McCusker, *Money and Exchange in Europe and America, 1600–1775: A Handbook* (Chapel Hill: University of North Carolina Press, 1978); for Massachusetts in particular, see pages 146–150.

28. "Estate of Newark Jackson, 1744," Docket #7944, Suffolk County Probate Records (hereafter SCPR), 37:52, MSA.

29. "Estate of Philip Audebert Jr.," Docket #8810, SCPR, 40:98, MSA. Audebert had an estate worth £8,958 Old Tenor, and his real estate constituted £7,100 of that. The appraiser counted Prince and Guinea together, and they were worth £610.

30. Thomas Moore to John Carteret, 16 May 1723, in Cecil Headlam, ed., *Calendar of State Papers: Colonial Series, America and West Indies, 1722–1723* (London: HMSO, 1934), 258.

31. A few other scholars have written on middling slave ownership in early America. Shane White, for example, discusses artisan slaveholding in late eighteenth-century New York, while Simon Middleton looks at middling slave ownership as a whole in an earlier period. See Shane White, *Somewhat More Independent: The End of Slavery in New York City, 1770–1810* (Athens: University of Georgia Press, 1991), 10–12; and Simon Middleton, *From Privileges to Rights: Work and Politics in Colonial New York City* (Philadelphia: University of Pennsylvania Press, 2006), 101.

32. *The Charters and General Laws of the Colony and Province of Massachusetts Bay* (Boston: T. B. Wait, 1814), 533.

33. Ibid., 313.

34. A. Leon Higginbotham Jr., *In the Matter of Color: Race and the American Legal Process: The Colonial Period* (New York: Oxford University Press, 1978), 78.

35. Boston Record Commissioners, *A Report of the Record Commissioners of the City of Boston, Containing the Boston Records from 1700 to 1728*, vol. 8 (Boston: Rockwell and Churchill, 1883), 173–174.

36. *Charters and General Laws*, 386.

37. Gary Nash, *The Urban Crucible: Social Change, Political Consciousness, and the Origins of the American Revolution* (Cambridge, MA: Harvard University Press, 1979), 396.

38. Allan Kulikoff, "The Progress of Inequality in Revolutionary Boston," *William and Mary Quarterly* 28, no. 3 (1971): 383–384.

39. Boston Record Commissioners, *A Report of the Record Commissioners of the City of Boston, Containing the Records of Boston Selectmen, 1736 to 1742*, vol. 15 (Boston: Rockwell and Churchill, 1886), 369–370.

40. Laurel Ulrich, "Sheep in the Parlor, Wheels on the Common: Pastoralism and Poverty in Eighteenth-Century Boston," in Carla Gardina Pestana and Sharon V. Salinger, eds., *Inequality in Early America* (Hanover, NH: University Press of New England, 1999), 184–185. Gary Nash has also written on the female factory in

colonial Boston, and Ulrich draws heavily on his work. See Gary Nash, "The Failure of Female Factory Labor in Colonial Boston," *Labor History* 20 (1970): 165–188.

41. Kulikoff, "Progress of Inequality," 383–384.

42. Douglas Lamar Jones, "The Strolling Poor: Transiency in Eighteenth-Century Massachusetts," *Journal of Social History* 8, no. 3 (1975): 44. A detailed account of the Boston Overseers of the Poor and their eighteenth-century records can be found in Eric G. Nellis and Anne Decker Cecere, *The Eighteenth Century Records of the Boston Overseers of the Poor* (Boston: Colonial Society of Massachusetts, 2001).

43. Two recent examinations of poverty in early New England are Ruth Wallis Herndon, *Unwelcome Americans: Living on the Margin in Early New England* (Philadelphia: University of Pennsylvania Press, 2001); and Pestana and Salinger, *Inequality in Early America*.

44. Elaine Forman Crane, *Ebb Tide in New England: Women, Seaports, and Social Change, 1630–1800* (Boston: Northeastern University Press, 1998), 107.

45. "Complaint of Christopher Minot," in "Case of Jeffs (Negro) and Parthenia (Negro), Slaves of Mary Minott," n.d., *Suffolk Files* #101791, MSA.

46. "Indictment," in ibid.

47. "Deposition of Mary Minott," in ibid.

48. "The King v. Jeoffs," in Superior Court of Judicature Records, 1771, Microfilm Reel #15, p. 35, MSA.

49. Sally Hadden, "The Fragmented Laws of Slavery in the Colonial and Revolutionary Eras," in Christopher Tomlins and Michael Grossberg, eds., *The Cambridge History of Law in America*, vol. 1, *Early America (1580–1815)* (New York: Cambridge University Press, 2008), 266–267.

50. Lorenzo Johnston Greene, *The Negro in Colonial New England* (1942; repr., New York: Atheneum, 1969), 298–299.

51. "Robert Love Diary, 1765–1766," in *Pre-Revolutionary War Diaries*, Microfilm P-363, Reel 6, Massachusetts Historical Society, Boston, MA (hereafter MHS). For more on Robert Love and his world, see Cornelia Dayton and Sharon Salinger, *Robert Love's Warnings: Searching for Strangers in Colonial Boston* (Philadelphia: University of Pennsylvania Press, 2014).

52. "Warning [Out] Book from January 4, 1745 to 1770," in *Boston Overseers of the Poor Records, 1733–1925*, M. N-1879, Microfilm P-368, Reel 1, MHS.

53. "Account of Money Received and Distributed to the Poore of King's Chapel May 6, 1753 to April 11, 1757," King's Chapel's Records, Box IV.1, Folder 26, MHS.

54. "Poor Accounts, 1733–1759," Old North Church (Christ Church in the City of Boston) Records, 1569–1997, vol. 33, MHS.

55. Lyndon's diary can be found at the Rhode Island Historical Society. See Cesar Lyndon, "Journal," Rhode Island Manuscripts, 10:81–85, Rhode Island Historical Society, Providence, RI.

56. John Wood Sweet, *Bodies Politic: Negotiating Race in the American North, 1730–1830* (Baltimore: Johns Hopkins University Press, 2003), 81–83.

57. Ira Berlin explores this theme in the antebellum era in his classic *Slaves without Masters: The Free Negro in the Antebellum South* (New York: New Press, 1974). Berlin focuses more on racial categorizations and legal constrictions than on the culture in which emancipated slaves lived.

58. *Sarah Negro and Peter Saveton, a Free Negro, Their Sentence*, Court of General Sessions of the Peace Record Books, 1719–1725, Microfilm Reel #2, p. 113, MSA.

59. *Turner and Wife, Their Sentence*, ibid., 114.

60. *Cuffy Negro and Jane His Wife Their Indictment*, ibid., 167.

61. *Bristol and Hector Negroe's Sentence* and *Holt's Indictment Crushed*, ibid., 276–277.

62. All of the information for Robbin's case can be found in "Case of Robbin, Negro Servant of John Jenkins," February 1735, *Suffolk Files* #38798, MSA. The narrative I constructed consists of the depositions of all the shop owners listed, Samuel Greenwood, Joseph Greenwood, and Joseph Snelling. The verdict can be found in "Dom Rex v. Robbin Negro," Superior Court of Judicature Records, 1733–1736, Microfilm Reel #5, p. 189, MSA.

63. Crane, *Ebb Tide*, 107, 120, 128.

64. Daniel Allen Hearn found eleven people executed for theft, usually burglary, in colonial New England. See Daniel Allen Hearn, *Legal Execution in New England: A Comprehensive Reference, 1623–1960* (Jefferson, NC: McFarland, 1999), 44, 45, 113, 116, 123, 126, 128, 130, 146, 151.

65. *American Weekly Mercury*, 27 March 1735.

66. *Weekly Rehearsal*, 2 September 1735.

67. *Weekly Rehearsal*, 14 July 1735.

68. "Deposition of Mary Whitmore," 28 February 1735, *Suffolk Files* #166001, MSA.

69. *Weekly Rehearsal*, 23 September 1734.

70. Thomas Moore to John Carteret, 16 May 1723, in Headlam, *Calendar of State Papers*, 258.

71. Wood, *Radicalism*, 33–34.

72. Robert J. Steinfeld, *The Invention of Free Labor: The Employment Relation in English and American Law and Culture, 1350–1870* (Chapel Hill: University of North Carolina Press, 1991), 13–14. Christopher Tomlins disagrees with Steinfeld. Tomlins argues that historians must understand regional legal variations and that there was not a uniform legal order like the one Steinfeld describes. While Tomlin's attempt to refute the broad brushstrokes of Steinfeld is commendable, he is too focused in his study of regional variations. While looking at labor law in New England, he uses only Essex County, Massachusetts, as his case study and even then barely examines its urban center, Salem. Urban ports like Boston, Salem, or Newport, Rhode Island, were much more reliant on bound labor, especially slave labor, than were the rural areas Tomlins examines, as their labor needs were much greater. In the urban centers, colonial officials readily adopted oppressive statutes from England or created their own that regulated the behavior of bound laborers, such as a 1728 Boston ordinance that prevented "young People, Servants & Negroes" from "Playing in the Streets." See Christopher Tomlins, *Freedom Bound: Law, Labor, and Civic Identity in Colonizing English America, 1580–1865* (New York: Cambridge University Press, 2010), 246–258, 307–321. For the statute, see Boston Record Commissioners, *Report of the Record Commissioners*, vol. 8, 224.

73. Christopher Tomlins notes these phenomena as well. See Tomlins, *Freedom Bound*, 258, 321.

74. Samuel Sewall, *The Selling of Joseph: A Memorial* (Boston: B. Green and John Allen, 1701), 2.

75. John Adams to Jeremy Belknap, 21 March 1795, "Letters and Documents Relating to Slavery in Massachusetts," in *Collections of the Massachusetts Historical Society*, vol. 3 (Boston: Massachusetts Historical Society, 1877), 402.

76. "Act for the Better Preventing of a Spurious and Mixt Issue, 1705," in Elizabeth Donnan, ed., *Documents Illustrative of the History of the Slave Trade to America*, vol. 3 (Washington, DC: Carnegie Institute of Washington, 1932), 20.

77. "An Act to Encourage the Importation of White Servants," in *The Acts and Resolves, Public and Private, of the Province of Massachusetts Bay*, vol. 1 (Boston: Wright and Potter, 1869), 634.

78. Moore to Carteret, 16 May 1723 in Headlam, *Calendar of State Papers*, 258.

79. See Robert E. Desrochers Jr., "Slave-for-Sale Advertisements and Slavery in Massachusetts, 1704–1781," *William and Mary Quarterly* 59, no. 2 (2002): 623–664.

80. Newspapers include the *Boston Evening-Post, Boston Gazette, Boston News-Letter, Boston Post-Boy, New-England Courant, New-England Weekly Journal*, and *Weekly Rehearsal*.

81. Some masters ran multiple advertisements for a missing servant, while some masters and ship captains from as far away as Maryland and New York advertised for runaways. A May 1754 advertisement from the *Boston News-Letter* is from Annapolis, Maryland, and describes three men, two "Convict Servants" and an African slave, who stole a sloop and were thought to be sailing toward Boston. See *Boston News-Letter*, 25 March 1754. This study concerns only those ads posted by masters in Boston and surrounding towns, including Charlestown, Cambridge, Roxbury, Dorchester, Dedham, Newton, and Watertown. Some advertisements also listed more than one runaway, such as a November 1749 ad in the *Boston News-Letter* describing two Irish servants who ran away from their master, Walter Logan. See *Boston News-Letter*, 9 November 1749.

82. For more on Irish servitude in the West Indies, see Hilary McD. Beckles, "A 'Riotous and Unruly Lot': Irish Indentured Servants and Freedmen in the West Indies, 1644–1713," *William and Mary Quarterly* 47, no. 4 (1990): 503–522.

83. Carl Bridenbaugh, *The Colonial Craftsman* (New York: NYU Press, 1950), 130–134.

84. Herndon documents over twenty-one hundred cases of pauper apprenticeship in southern New England between 1720 and 1820. Ruth Wallis Herndon, "'Proper' Magistrates and Masters: Binding Out Poor Children in Southern New England, 1720–1820," in Ruth Wallis Herndon and John E. Murray, eds., *Children Bound to Labor: The Pauper Apprentice System in Early America* (Ithaca, NY: Cornell University Press, 2009), 39–40.

85. The status of bound Indians was ambiguous at best and usually changed depending on the current laws in effect.

86. Margaret Ellen Newell, "Indian Slavery in Colonial New England," in Alan Gallay, ed., *Indian Slavery in Colonial America* (Lincoln: University of Nebraska Press, 2009), 33, 48–49, 50–51, 59–60.

87. "Case of Titus, an Indian Servant," March 1723, *Suffolk Files* #16568, MSA.

88. The classic work on ideological and intellectual conceptions of Africans in early America is Winthrop Jordan, *White over Black: American Attitudes towards*

the Negro, 1550–1812 (1968; repr., Chapel Hill: University of North Carolina Press, 2012).

89. John Saffin, *A Brief and Candid Answer to a Late Printed Sheet, Entituled, "The Selling of Joseph"* (Boston, 1700), reprinted in Louis Ruchames, ed., *Racial Thought in America: A Documentary History*, vol. 1, *From the Puritans to Abraham Lincoln* (Amherst: University of Massachusetts Press, 1969), 56–57.

90. Ibid., 58.

91. Ibid., 55.

92. Goodell, *Trial and Execution*, 14. Mark claimed that Phoebe burned down the barn and that he could not have been involved because he was ill. He was, however, able to muster enough strength to get out of bed and save some of Codman's horses, "which would have been burnt." Throughout all the trial documents and published material, Phillis and Phoebe blame Mark, while he blames Phoebe. See *The Last & Dying Words of Mark, Aged about 30 Years, a Negro Man Who Belonged to the Late Captain John Codman, of Charlestown; Who Was Executed at Cambridge, the 18th of September, 1755, for Poysoning His Abovesaid Master* (Boston, 1755), MHS Broadsides Collection, MHS. Mark was also the only slave to sign his confession, indicating that Salter taught him to read and write.

93. Goodell, *Trial and Execution*, 14. Phillis claimed that Mark got the idea of using arsenic from slaves belonging to John Salmon, who allegedly poisoned their master and "got good masters" without ever being prosecuted. Ibid., 10. See also Elise Lemire, *Black Walden: Slavery and Its Aftermath in Concord, Massachusetts* (Philadelphia: University of Pennsylvania Press, 2009), 48.

94. Oliver Wendell Holmes, *The Common Law* (Boston: Little, Brown, 1881), 219.

95. Goodell, *Trial and Execution*, 10.

96. Ibid., 21. Although Mark claimed to have no animosity towards Codman, his actions suggest otherwise.

97. Ibid., 10–11.

98. Ibid., 4–5.

99. *Last & Dying Words of Mark.*

100. Lemire, *Black Walden*, 49.

101. Goodell, *Trial and Execution*, 21. Phoebe also tended to Tom's wound.

102. *Last & Dying Words of Mark.*

103. Goodell, *Trial and Execution*, 14. It is unclear whether Phoebe was Codman's formal concubine, but it would not be out of the ordinary for a wealthy gentleman of the eighteenth century to have an enslaved mistress. In that sense, he would not be that different from southern and Caribbean slave owners like William Byrd or Thomas Thistlewood. For an Atlantic perspective on slave concubinage, see Brenda E. Stevenson, "What's Love Got to Do with It? Concubinage and Enslaved Black Women and Girls in the Antebellum South," *Journal of African American History* 98, no. 1 (2013): 99–125.

104. This argument echoes that made by Edmund Morgan in his classic *American Slavery, American Freedom* (New York: Norton, 1976). For an Atlantic perspective on the creation of this social order, especially through the law, see Edward B. Rugemer, "The Development of Mastery and Race in the Comprehensive Slave Codes of the Greater Caribbean during the Seventeenth Century," *William and Mary Quarterly* 70, no. 3 (2013): 429–458.

Notes to Chapter 3

1. "Case of William Heley and Robin (servant of Henry Vassall)," May 1752, *Suffolk Files* #69278, Massachusetts State Archives, Boston, MA (hereafter MSA).

2. Most of the literature concerning slave communities concerns the antebellum South. Some of the major works include John Blassingame, *The Slave Community: Plantation Life in the Antebellum South* (New York: Oxford University Press, 1972); Eugene Genovese, *Roll, Jordan, Roll: The World the Slaves Made* (1972; repr., New York: Vintage, 1976), 443–556; and Charles Joyner, *Down by the Riverside: A South Carolina Slave Community* (Urbana: University of Illinois Press, 1986). Historians of the colonial South have also written on slave communities; see, for example, Lorena Walsh, *From Calabar to Carter's Grove: The History of a Virginia Slave Community* (Charlottesville: University of Virginia Press, 1997). All these works divide white-slave interactions from those between people of color, indicating the degree to which historians have envisioned slave communities as being racially exclusive. More recently, Anthony Kaye, a scholar of the antebellum South, argues against monolithic slave communities and instead contends we need to see multiple slave "neighborhoods" that include many slaves from different plantations and towns, poor whites, and even some of the master class. See Anthony Kaye, *Joining Places: Slave Neighborhoods in the Old South* (Chapel Hill: University of North Carolina Press, 2009). Some scholars of slavery in the North, such as Jill Lepore, also argue for the existence of racially exclusive slave communities, despite the evidence, in her case at least, that poor whites and blacks cooperated during the 1741 slave conspiracy in New York. See Jill Lepore, *New York Burning: Liberty, Slavery, and Conspiracy in Eighteenth-Century Manhattan* (New York: Knopf, 2003). More in line with my argument in this book is Joanne Melish, who argues that New England slaves participated in "two linked communities of families." One of these was the master's family, while the other was the family created by the slaves themselves; and both of these translated into larger forms of communal organization. Poor whites, free blacks, and other people of color, so important to the social worlds of Boston's slaves, could fit into either "family" depending on the situation. See Joanne Pope Melish, *Disowning Slavery: Gradual Emancipation and "Race" in New England, 1780–1860* (Ithaca, NY: Cornell University Press, 1998), 45.

3. For more on the institution of marriage, see chapter 5.

4. For more on Royall, his son, the slaves, and Ten Hills Farm in general, see C. S. Manegold, *Ten Hills Farm: The Forgotten History of Slavery in the North* (Princeton, NJ: Princeton University Press, 2010); and Alexandra A. Chan, *Slavery in the Age of Reason: Archaeology at a New England Farm* (Knoxville: University of Tennessee Press, 2007).

5. Samuel Francis Batchelder, *Notes on Colonel Henry Vassall, 1721–1769: His Wife Penelope Royall, His House at Cambridge and His Slaves Tony and Darby* (Cambridge, MA, 1917), 63.

6. "Case of Quaco (a Negro)," February 1762, *Suffolk Files* #82628, MSA. Different facets of this case are threaded throughout this chapter, illustrating various parts of the social world inhabited by enslaved Bostonians.

7. Papers of John Usher, 1653–1723, Jeffries Family Papers, vol. 15, Ms.-2067 (XT), Massachusetts Historical Society, Boston, MA (hereafter MHS).

8. Carl Bridenbaugh, *Cities in the Wilderness: The First Century of Urban Life in America, 1625–1742* (1938; repr., New York: Oxford University Press, 1971), 196–197, 353–354. The worst of these shortages occurred in 1713, when around two hundred poor Bostonians rioted on the Common after finding out there was not grain available for sale. It is unclear if slaves were involved in this action, but the provincial and town governments learned an important lesson and attempted to at least regulate the price and availability of food, especially grain, throughout the eighteenth century. Nevertheless, prices continued to rise, and war, recession, revolution, and economic upheavals exacerbated an already bad trend. See Carl Bridenbaugh, *Cities in Revolt: Urban Life in America* (1955; repr., New York: Oxford University Press, 1971), 280. For an interesting perspective on meat consumption and availability in colonial Boston, see David B. Landon, "Colonial Boston: A Zooarchaeological Study," *Historical Archaeology* 30, no. 1 (1996): i–vii, 1–153.

9. "Elisha Story Account Books, 1766–1803, Vol. 1: Boston 1766–1776," Ms. N-2171, MHS.

10. *Boston News-Letter*, 7 January 1717.

11. All of these records can be found in Richard Dana, "Justice of the Peace Records," vol. 18, Microfilm P-646 Reel 2, MHS. Dana broke his book down by year and gave each entry for that year a number. For John Knight's Cato, see 1761–1762, entry 24; for John Lamb's Cato, see 1764, entry 12; and for Tom, see 1761–1762, entry 144.

12. For more on this trope, see the introduction.

13. Other historians have applied the notion of patriarchalism to slave-owning households in Virginia, South Carolina, and Jamaica. For the former two places, see Philip D. Morgan, *Slave Counterpoint: Black Culture in the Eighteenth-Century Chesapeake and Lowcountry* (Chapel Hill: University of North Carolina Press, 1998), 273–284; for Jamaica, see Trevor Burnard, *Mastery, Tyranny, and Desire: Thomas Thistlewood and His Slaves in the Anglo-Jamaican World* (Chapel Hill: University of North Carolina Press, 2004), 83–84.

14. Quoted in Greene, *Negro in Colonial New England*, 219.

15. The classic work on the patriarchal family in colonial New England is John Demos, *A Little Commonwealth: Family Life in Plymouth Colony* (New York: Oxford University Press, 1970).

16. *New England Courant*, 15 June 1724.

17. See Sewall's diary for many references to Boston as both a slave and a freed man. Samuel Sewall, *The Diary of Samuel Sewall, 1624–1729*, ed. Milton Thomas (New York: Farrar, Straus, and Giroux, 1973).

18. Manumission, 4 July 1763, in Ezekiel Price Notarial Records, vol. 2, Boston Athenæum, Boston, MA.

19. Manumission, 17 August 1768, in ibid., vol. 4.

20. Manumission, 20 November 1766, in ibid., vol. 3.

21. Historians of southern slavery have argued that masters oftentimes used delayed manumission as a way of preventing slaves from running away. See Eva Sheppard Wolf, *Race and Liberty in the New Nation: Emancipation in Virginia from the Revolution to Nat Turner's Rebellion* (Baton Rouge: Louisiana State University Press, 2009). There are of course exceptions to this. Cotton Mather's slave Onesimus

was so troublesome that Mather eventually freed him to rid himself of Onesimus. See chapter 5 for more about Onesimus and Mather's fraught relationship.

22. Vincent Carretta, *Phillis Wheatley: Biography of a Genius in Bondage* (Athens: University of Georgia Press, 2011), 14–23.

23. "Case of Toney, a Negroman of Samuel Johnson," June 1756, *Suffolk Files* #75761, MSA.

24. "Inquisition on the Body of a Negro Man Called 'James,'" 18 November 1733, *Suffolk Files* #36165, MSA.

25. "Inquisition on the Body of Maria Negro Servant to Roger Hardcastle," 3 October 1736, *Suffolk Files* #42822, MSA.

26. *Boston Evening Post*, 16 February 1741.

27. The documents surrounding Phillis are numerous but do not provide much information beyond the basics. See "Case of Phillis, Negro Servant of John Greenleaf," February 1751, *Suffolk Files* #67676, MSA; Daniel Allen Hearn, *Legal Execution in New England: A Comprehensive Reference, 1623–1960* (Jefferson, NC: McFarland, 1999), 140. Phillis's case can also be tracked in the newspapers; see *Boston Post Boy*, 21 January 1751; and *Boston Evening Post*, 21 January 1751, 4 March 1751, 20 May 1751. The story reached as far as New York, where that city's newspapers noted how Phillis poisoned the other child "some Time before." When the court sentenced Phillis to death, allegedly her mother "died with Excess of Grief." See *Boston Evening Post*, 22 April 1751.

28. *New England Weekly Journal*, 27 October 1729.

29. "Jacobs, Primus (Colored), Dinah," Record #W.21446, Massachusetts, Revolutionary War Pension Records, National Archives and Records Administration, Washington, DC.

30. For pauper apprentices, see "Children Bound Out 1756–1790," in *The Eighteenth-Century Records of the Boston Overseers of the Poor*, ed. Eric Nellis and Anne Decker Cecere, *Publications of the Colonial Society of Massachusetts*, vol. 69 (Boston: Colonial Society of Massachusetts, 2007), 645–667; and Lawrence W. Towner, "The Indentures of Boston's Poor Apprentices: 1734–1805," in *Publications of the Colonial Society of Massachusetts*, vol. 43, *Transactions 1956–1963* (Boston: Colonial Society of Massachusetts, 1966), 417–469. Slaves can be found in Bettye Hobbs Pruitt, ed., *The Massachusetts Tax Valuation List of 1771* (Boston: G. K. Hall, 1978); and Suffolk County Probate Records, MSA. I discuss other facets of the relationship between pauper apprenticeship and slavery in chapters 2 and 4.

31. *Boston Evening Post*, 8 September 1735.

32. For Melvin, see "Children Bound Out 1756–1790," in Nellis and Cecere, *Eighteenth-Century Records of the Boston Overseers of the Poor*, 650, 660 (for Carpenter).

33. "Deposition of Sarah Bartlett," 1 September 1735, *Suffolk Files* #166505, MSA.

34. *Boston Gazette*, 10 October 1737.

35. "Deposition of Hopestill Stone," November 1720, *Suffolk Files* #163629, MSA.

36. For the case of Bristol, see Sylvanus Conant, *The Blood of Abel and the Blood of Jesus Considered and Improved* (Boston: Edes and Gill, 1764), a sermon about Bristol's case. Robert Treat Paine wrote the appendix detailing the facts of case and his opinion on the matter; Alan Rogers, *Murder and the Death Penalty in Massachusetts*

(Amherst: University of Massachusetts Press, 2008), 26–28; *Boston Evening Post*, 13 June 1763. T. H. Breen has also written about the case, seeing it as a turning point in the history of slavery in Massachusetts. Both Paine's indictment of slaveholders and Conant's sermon voice strong doubts about slavery as an institution. See T. H. Breen, "Making History: The Force of Public Opinion and the Last Years of Slavery in Revolutionary Massachusetts," in Ronald Hoffman, Mechal Sobel, and Fredrika J. Teute, eds., *Through a Glass Darkly: Reflections on Personal Identity in Early America* (Chapel Hill: University of North Carolina Press, 1997), 74–77.

37. *Boston Evening Post*, 13 June 1763.

38. "Deposition of James and Sarah Gardner," in "Case of Quaco (Negro)," 13 September 1762, *Suffolk Files* #83313, MSA.

39. *Boston Post Boy*, 3 May 1742.

40. *Boston Evening Post*, 8 December 1746.

41. Marriages can be found in Boston Record Commissioners, *A Report of the Record Commissioners of the City of Boston, Containing Boston Marriages from 1700 to 1751*, vol. 28 (Boston: Rockwell and Churchill, 1898); and Boston Record Commissioners, *A Report of the Record Commissioners of the City of Boston, Containing Boston Marriages from 1752 to 1809*, vol. 30 (Boston: Rockwell and Churchill, 1903). These numbers do not include marriage intentions except from 1752 and 1761, as these are the only records that exist concerning slave marriage. Native American–black marriages have interested scholars for over a century. Lorenzo Greene discusses this at length, although most of his examples concern other parts of New England, not Boston, possibly explaining the low figure in this study. See Greene, *Negro in Colonial New England*, 198–201.

42. William D. Piersen, *Black Yankees: The Development of an Afro-American Subculture in Eighteenth-Century New England* (Amherst: University of Massachusetts Press, 1988), 90.

43. "Case of Flora (a Negro Woman Servant of John Clough) (with Depositions)," February 1758, *Suffolk Files* #78078, MSA.

44. "Flora's Indictment," in Superior Court of Judicature Records, 1757–1759, Microfilm Reel #10, p. 295, MSA; Catherine Adams and Elizabeth H. Pleck, *Love of Freedom: Black Women in Colonial New England* (New York: Oxford University Press, 2010), 111.

45. Quoted in Adams and Pleck, *Love of Freedom*, 113.

46. *A Faithful Narrative of the Wicked Life . . . of Patience Boston* (Boston: Kneeland and Green, 1738), 3.

47. This information has been extrapolated from the difference between the marriage intention, in which Thatcher owned Jenny, and the marriage certificate, in which Gee owned both slaves. See Boston Record Commissioners, *Report of the Record Commissioners*, vol. 28, 188.

48. *The Acts and Resolves, Public and Private, of the Province of Massachusetts Bay, 1692–1714* (Boston: Wright and Potter, 1869), 535.

49. For more on profit motive and the slave family, see Greene, *Negro in Colonial New England*, 210–217.

50. *Faithful Narrative . . . of Patience Boston*, 3–6.

51. The marriage certificate and petition are in "Slavery at Groton in Provincial Times," *Proceedings of the Massachusetts Historical Society* 42 (1909): 196–197.

52. "Lydia Sharp v. Boston (a Black Man)," 5 June 1773, *Suffolk Files* #129775, MSA.

53. "Case of Jeffs (Negro) and Parthenia (Negro), Slaves of Mary Minott," February 1771, *Suffolk Files* #101791, MSA.

54. "Deposition of Jenny," 13 September 1761, in "Case of Quaco (Negro)," 13 September 1762, *Suffolk Files* #83313, MSA.

55. "Deposition of Flora," 15 September 1761, in ibid.

56. Piersen, *Black Yankees*, 94.

57. Ibid., 92.

58. *Boston News Letter*, 25 August 1718.

59. *Boston Weekly News Letter*, 26 June 1760. Despite using the word "breed" in advertisements, Boston masters did not deliberately force slaves to procreate in order to profit from the increase, although there is an apocryphal story from the nineteenth century that a Mr. T who lived in eighteenth-century Hanover, Massachusetts, deliberately bred slaves for the market. See John S. Barry, *A Historical Sketch of the Town of Hanover, Mass., with Family Genealogies* (Boston: Samuel G. Drake, 1853), 175.

60. Transcription of "African-American Baptisms, 1725–1775," Old North Church Records, Box 18, Folder 30, MHS.

61. Quoted in Piersen, *Black Yankees*, 94.

62. For more on Boston taverns, see David W. Conroy, *In Public Houses: Drink and the Revolution of Authority in Colonial Massachusetts* (Chapel Hill: University of North Carolina Press, 1995).

63. *Boston Evening Post*, 14 January 1740.

64. All of this information can be found in Conroy, *In Public Houses*, 125–126.

65. "Oliver Acquitted," Court of the General Sessions of the Peace Record Books (hereafter CGSP), 1719–1725, 193, MSA; "Ned Negroe's Sentence," CGSP, 1719–1725, 197–198, MSA.

66. "Newman Fined," CGSP, 1719–1725, 284, MSA.

67. Richard Dana, "Justice of the Peace Records," vol. 17, March 1746–August 1748, Middlesex County, entry 5, Microfilm P-646 Reel 2, MHS.

68. Ibid., vol. 18, April 1760–December 1767, Suffolk County, entries 150 and 151.

69. *Boston News Letter*, 14 April 1738.

70. Thomas A. Foster, *Sex and the Eighteenth-Century Man: Massachusetts and the History of Sexuality in America* (Boston: Beacon, 2006), 146. For white conceptions of black sexuality in eighteenth-century Massachusetts, see ibid., 147–153. The literature dealing with eighteenth-century male honor culture is quite robust; see Joanne B. Freeman, *Affairs of Honor: National Politics in the New Republic* (New Haven, CT: Yale University Press, 2001); Anne S. Lombard, *Making Manhood: Growing Up Male in Colonial New England* (Cambridge, MA: Harvard University Press, 2003); Ann M. Little, *Abraham in Arms: War and Gender in Colonial New England* (Philadelphia: University of Pennsylvania Press, 2007); and Matthew James Reardon, "The Bonds of Manhood: Public Life, Homosociality, and Hegemonic Masculinity in Massachusetts, 1630–1787" (PhD diss., University of Iowa, 2012).

71. *New England Weekly Journal*, 2 December 1728.

72. "Deposition of Hugh Kennedy that Boston, Negro Servant of Thomas Parker had Recovered from His Wounds Received from Caesar, a Negro," 23 July 1724,

Suffolk Files #37631, MSA; "Case of Cesar (Negro)," August 1734, *Suffolk Files* #37774, MSA; "Petition of Richard Billings for His Negro Cesar's Release, and the Bond for the Same," 1 August 1734, *Suffolk Files* #37851, MSA

73. "Case of Cesar (Negro)," August 1742, *Suffolk Files* #55818, MSA.

74. For more on wrestling and martial arts in the African diaspora, see T. J Desch Obi, *Fighting for Honor: The History of African Martial Art Traditions in the Atlantic World* (Columbia: University of South Carolina Press, 2008).

75. "Deposition of Boston (a Negro), as to Minto (a Negro), Wrestling with Pompey (a Negro)," 28 September 1731, *Suffolk Files* #32611, MSA.

76. "Boston Negro's Case," CGSP, 1725-1732, 367, MSA.

77. *New England Courant*, 11 May 1724.

78. "Case of Eleazer Newall, Harry, Negro Servant of Skinner Russell, Dover, Negro Servant of Thomas Stoddard, Parthenia, Negro Servant of Mrs. Elizabeth Waldron," April 1744, *Suffolk Files* #58549, MSA.

79. "Case of Titus an Indian Servant," March 1723, *Suffolk Files* #16568, MSA.

80. *Boston News Letter*, 23 July 1741.

81. "Record of Those Born in the Alms House" and "Account of Children Born in the Alms House," in Nellis and Cecere, *Eighteenth-Century Records of the Boston Overseers of the Poor*, 628-630.

82. Daniel R. Mandell, *Behind the Frontier: Indians in Eighteenth-Century Eastern Massachusetts* (Lincoln: University of Nebraska Press, 1996), 182-183.

83. "Robert Love Diary, 1765-1766," in Pre-Revolutionary War Diaries, Microfilm P-363 Reel 6, MHS.

84. *Boston Evening Post*, 30 January 1738.

85. This story can be found in Greene, *Negro in Colonial New England*, 206-207.

86. Bowdoin is quoted in Foster, *Sex and the Eighteenth-Century Man*, 148.

87. See Greene, *Negro in Colonial New England*, 205.

88. The stories of Cesar and Goslin can be found in Foster, *Sex and the Eighteenth-Century Man*, 145-146.

89. The literature on Negro Election Day is quite large. See Piersen, *Black Yankees*, 117-142; Joseph P. Reidy, "'Negro Election Day' and Black Community Life in New England, 1750-1860," *Marxist Perspectives* 1 (1978): 102-117; Shane White, "'It Was a Proud Day': African Americans, Festivals, and Parades in the North, 1741-1834," *Journal of American History* 81 (1994): 13-50; Ira Berlin, *Many Thousands Gone: The First Two Centuries of Slavery in North America* (Cambridge, MA: Harvard University Press, 1998), 191-192.

90. For more on "Africanization" in the American North, see Berlin, *Many Thousands Gone*, 190-191.

91. Information on the Lynn ceremony can be found in Piersen, *Black Yankees*, 118, 139.

92. *New England Courant*, 22 July 1723.

93. Quoted in Robert C. Twombly, "Black Resistance to Slavery in Massachusetts," in William L. O'Neill, ed., *Insights and Parallels: Problems and Issues of American Social History* (Minneapolis, MN: Burgess, 1973), 55.

94. For more on the West African origins and nature of black funerals in New England, see John Wood Sweet, *Bodies Politic: Negotiating Race in the American North, 1730-1830* (Baltimore: Johns Hopkins University Press, 2003), 333-335. The

act can be found in Sweet's discussion and in Boston Record Commissioners, *A Report of the Record Commissioners of the City of Boston, Containing the Records of Boston Selectmen, 1716 to 1736*, vol. 13 (Boston: Rockwell and Churchill, 1885), 283.

95. *Boston Post Boy*, 1 July 1765.

96. Both laws can be found in A. Leon Higginbotham, *In the Matter of Color: Race and the American Legal Process: The Colonial Period* (New York: Oxford University Press, 1978), 77, 81.

97. "By Law of Boston Approved," CGSP, 1725–1732, 165, MSA.

98. Quoted in Luke Tyerman, *The Life of the Rev. George Whitefield* (New York: Anson D. F. Randolph, 1877), 411.

99. This argument draws from E. P. Thompson's notion of the "crowd" in the grain riots that occurred in eighteenth-century England. Like the slaves who used communal forms of resistance by reaching across racial and class divides, the crowd was "informed by the belief that they were defending traditional rights or customs; and, in general, that they were supported by the general consensus of the community." E. P. Thompson, "The Moral Economy of the Crowd in the Eighteenth Century," in *Customs in Common: Studies in Traditional Popular Culture* (New York: New Press, 1993), 188.

Notes to Chapter 4

1. A version of this chapter appeared as Jared Ross Hardesty, "'The Negro at the Gate': Enslaved Labor in Colonial Boston," *New England Quarterly* 87, no. 1 (2014): 72–98.

2. Ira Berlin and Philip Morgan argue that slave societies "involved two interrelated and overlapping economies: one organized by and for the master, although contested and constrained by the slaves; the other by and for the slaves, although contested and constrained by the master. Both entailed struggle over the slaves' labor, but they affected slave life in different ways." Ira Berlin and Philip D. Morgan, *Cultivation and Culture: Labor and the Shaping of Slave Life in the Americas* (Charlottesville: University of Virginia Press, 1993), 2. While this may be true for the plantations of the American South and the Caribbean, Boston's economy and slaves' participation and role within it allowed them to transcend this dichotomy. Their labor contributed to the master's economy, but so many of them earned their own wages that they could also participate in ways other than as laborers and producers. The situation in Boston also meant that slaves' resistance to the labor regimen was more robust and complicated than merely creating their own economy beside that controlled by the master class. In many ways, engaging in the master's economy, through the refusal to produce and other forms of participation, was a more invasive form of resistance that allowed slaves to shape the terms of their employment.

3. Scholars of slavery in New England have similarly noted these key factors; see Lorenzo Johnston Greene, *The Negro in Colonial New England* (1942; repr., New York: Atheneum, 1969), 100–101, 102–103, 123; Joanne Pope Melish, *Disowning Slavery: Gradual Emancipation and "Race" in New England, 1780–1860* (Ithaca, NY: Cornell University Press, 1998), chap. 1; William D. Piersen, *Black Yankees: The Development of an Afro-American Subculture in Eighteenth-Century New England* (Amherst: University of Massachusetts Press, 1988), 37–38.

4. Lawrence William Towner, *A Good Master Well Served: Masters and Servants in Colonial Massachusetts, 1620–1750* (New York: Garland, 1998), 88.

5. For trades within shipbuilding, see ibid.,122. These trades included ship join-ers, sailmakers, rope makers, carpenters, mast makers, and shipwrights.

6. "Inventory for John Butler," Docket #9028, Suffolk County Probate Records (hereafter SCPR), 41:436, MSA. Butler's slave Boston was valued at £500, an unprec-edented sum.

7. Indenture, dated 12 October 1760, recorded 9 August 1769, in Ezekiel Price Notarial Records, vol. 5, Boston Athenæum, Boston, MA.

8. "Burrell's Will," Docket #5220, SCPR, 24:407, Massachusetts State Archives, Boston, MA (hereafter MSA).

9. "Forland's Will," Docket #6303, SCPR, 31:150, MSA.

10. "Quaco a Negro, Sold by Waterman to Coleman," 22 September 1730, *Suffolk Files* #30085, MSA.

11. Philip D. Curtin, *Economic Change in Precolonial Africa: Senegambia in the Era of the Slave Trade* (Madison: University of Wisconsin Press, 1975), 30–31, 98. For more on African labor knowledge in the American colonies, see Frederick C. Knight, *Working the Diaspora: The Impact of African Labor on the Anglo-American World, 1650–1850* (New York: NYU Press, 2012). Artisanal knowledge like that val-ued in Boston is discussed in chapter 5.

12. *Boston News-Letter*, 10 August 1747.

13. *Supplement to the Massachusetts-Gazette and Boston News-Letter*, 4 October 1770.

14. *Boston Gazette*, 22 January 1754.

15. Black fiddlers were quite common in colonial New England. According to Robert Desrochers, enslaved fiddle players were the second-most-common type of runaway slave, behind only sailors. See Robert Ernest Desrochers Jr., "Every Pic-ture Tells a Story: Slavery and Print in Eighteenth-Century New England" (PhD diss., Johns Hopkins University, 2001), 85.

16. *Massachusetts Spy*, 9 January 1772.

17. *Boston News-Letter*, 10 March 1718; *Boston Chronicle*, 25 July 1768.

18. *Boston Gazette*, 22 January 1754.

19. *Boston Post Boy*, 20 July 1741. For more on the importance of skilled trades to advertising, selling slaves, and to purchasers looking to buy slaves, see Towner, *Good Master*, 113.

20. All quotations regarding Quaco's case are from "Quaco a Negro," 22 Sep-tember 1730, *Suffolk Files* #30085, MSA.

21. William Townsend to Col. Benjamin Payton, 8 April 1745, in William Blair Townsend letter and receipt books, Mss:766 1743–1805 T752, Baker Library His-torical Collections, Harvard Business School, Cambridge, MA (hereafter BLHC).

22. William Townsend to Col. Benjamin Payton, 24 November 1745, in ibid.

23. For Townsend's correspondence with Payton, see Townsend to Payton, 8 April 1745 and 24 November 1745.

24. Robert E. Desrochers Jr., "Slave-for-Sale Advertisements in Massachusetts, 1704–1781," *William and Mary Quarterly* 59, no. 3 (2002): 633, table 2.

25. London's occupation is revealed in the course of his being investigated and charged with raping Sarah Clark, a white woman. See "Case of London (a Negro), and an Order for a Special Court of Assize," 26 August 1734, *Suffolk Files*

#37890, MSA; and "Case of London (a Negro)," 23 October 1734, *Suffolk Files* #38267, MSA.

26. Desrochers, "Slave-for-Sale Advertisements," 631–632, table 1.

27. For hiring out in the American South, see Jonathan D. Martin, *Divided Mastery: Slave Hiring in the American South* (Cambridge, MA: Harvard University Press, 2004); and John J. Zaborney, *Slaves for Hire: Renting Enslaved Laborers in Antebellum Virginia* (Baton Rouge: Louisiana State University Press, 2012).

28. *Massachusetts Spy*, 31 October 1771.

29. *Massachusetts Spy*, 30 April 1772.

30. *Boston News-Letter*, 4 October 1770. For an example of slaves being hired out for a year, see *Boston Post Boy*, 1 February 1748.

31. *Boston Evening-Post*, 10 August 1747.

32. *Boston News-Letter*, 16 September 1762.

33. "Hopestill Foster Account Book, 1759–1772," Mss:47 1759–1772 F755, BLHC, p. 80.

34. The full contract between Halsey and Lynde is reprinted in Greene, *Negro in Colonial New England*, 121; see also Towner, *Good Master*, 112. The original is in *Massachusetts Archives Collection*, 9:149–150, MSA.

35. Greene, *Negro in Colonial New England*, 120. Despite Greene asserting that when "a slave was rented, master and renter entered into a formal contract specifying" the terms of service, the documentary record does not support this belief. Further evidence of this trend comes from the lack of court cases arising from disputes over slave hiring, whether over payment or usage. There are a couple of cases from the seventeenth century (see ibid., 122, for an example) but few from the eighteenth. More common are cases involving the misuse or outright theft of slaves. See the text later in this chapter for an example.

36. Briton Hammon, *A Narrative of the Uncommon Sufferings and Surprizing Deliverance of Briton Hammon* (Boston: Green and Russell, 1760), 3.

37. Quoted in Kathryn S. Koo, "Strangers in the House of God: Cotton Mather, Onesimus, and an Experiment in Christian Slaveholding," *Proceedings of the American Antiquarian Society* 17, no. 1 (2007): 163. I explore the relationship between Mather and Onesimus further in chapter 5.

38. *The Last & Dying Words of Mark, Aged about 30 Years, a Negro Man Who Belonged to the Late Captain John Codman, of Charlestown; Who Was Executed at Cambridge, the 18th of September, 1755, for Poysoning His Abovesaid Master* (Boston, 1755), MHS Broadsides Collection, Massachusetts Historical Society, Boston, MA (hereafter MHS); "Warrant Against Mark (a Negro) for Refusing to Leave Boston," n.d., *Suffolk Files* #28037, MSA. More evidence for Mark's being a brazier comes from his own testimony, in which both he and the court note a blacksmith shop and a forge on Codman's property. See Abner Cheney Goodell Jr., *The Trial and Execution for Petit Treason of Mark and Phillis, Slaves of Captain John Codman* (Cambridge, MA: John Wilson and Son, 1883), 21.

39. Christopher Tomlins, *Freedom Bound: Law, Labor, and Civic Identity in Colonizing English America, 1580–1865* (New York: Cambridge University Press, 2010), 481.

40. Towner, *Good Master*, 109. For an examination of the more traditional form of domestic servitude, see Ann Kussmaul, *Servants in Husbandry in Early Modern*

England (New York: Cambridge University Press, 1981); R. C. Richardson, *Household Servants in Early Modern England* (Manchester, UK: Manchester University Press, 2010).

41. Thatcher's will can be found in Docket #15261, SCPR, MSA. Mary Guillion's indenture can be found in the Overseers of the Poor Taking Books, 2:28, Boston Public Library, Boston, MA.

42. Andrew Belcher to David Jeffries IV, 23 September 1763, in Papers of David Jeffries IV, Jeffries Family Papers, vol. 14, Ms. N-2067 (XT), MHS.

43. A Lady of Boston [Rebecca Warren Brown], *Memoir of Mrs. Chloe Spear, a Native of Africa, Who Was Enslaved in Childhood and Died in Boston January 3, 1815 . . . Aged 65 Years* (Boston: James Loring, 1832), 24, 32–33.

44. All of the probate inventories are in the SCPR, MSA. There were 2,570 inventories taken between 1700 and 1775, of which 601, or 23.3 percent, included slaves. For more on domestic production and consumption in British homes in England and America, see Carole Shammas, "The Domestic Environment in Early Modern England and America," *Journal of Social History* 14, no. 1 (1980): 3–24.

45. Lady of Boston, *Memoir*, 25.

46. "Deposition of Preserved Williams as to Royall Striking a Negro Servant Called Violet," 6 February 1735, *Suffolk Files* #38864, MSA.

47. Data compiled from Desrochers, "Slave-for-Sale Advertisements," 631–633, tables 1 and 2.

48. Edward Holyoke, "Diary of Rev. Edward Holyoke, of Marblehead and Cambridge, 1709–1768," in George Francis Dow, ed., *The Holyoke Diaries, 1709–1856* (Salem, MA: Essex Institute, 1911), 43.

49. "John Briggs Account Book, 1710–1727," Ms. N-1931, Manuscripts Collection, MHS.

50. "Benjamin Eustis Account Book, 1749–1757," Manuscripts Collection, MHS.

51. David W. Conroy, *In Public Houses: Drink and the Revolution of Authority in Colonial Massachusetts* (Chapel Hill: University of North Carolina Press, 1995), 125. For the Crown Coffee House, see pp. 88–95.

52. Gary Nash, *The Urban Crucible: Social Change, Political Consciousness, and the Origins of the American Revolution* (Cambridge, MA: Harvard University Press, 1979), 16.

53. Berlin and Morgan recognized that the "processes of production were as much a source of working-class culture for slave workers as free ones." Berlin and Morgan, *Cultivation and Culture*, 2. As slaves worked beside free white workers involved in the same types of production as proletarian laborers, unskilled laborers may have forged a working-class culture that transcended race.

54. W. Jeffrey Bolster, *Black Jacks: African American Seamen in the Age of Sail* (Cambridge, MA: Harvard University Press, 1997), 7.

55. *Boston Gazette*, 15 January 1754.

56. Of the 601 Bostonians with slaves in their probate inventories, 82, or 13.6 percent, were mariners. See chapter 2, table 1, for a full breakdown of slave owners by occupation.

57. Bolster, *Black Jacks*, 27; Nathaniel Holmes, "Ships Papers, Sloop *Betty*," orders to pay, 1746, Box 14, folder 29, Melatiah Bourne Record Papers, 1728–1803, Mss:733 1728–1803 B775, BLHC.

58. For more on the life of sailors in general, see Marcus Rediker, *Between the Devil and the Deep Blue Sea: Merchant Seamen, Pirates and the Anglo-American Maritime World, 1700–1750* (New York: Cambridge University Press, 1987).

59. Bolster, *Black Jacks*, 30.

60. *Massachusetts Archives Collection*, 9:151, MSA. Bolster also discusses this case; see *Black Jacks*, 12.

61. Hammon, *Narrative*. For more on Hammon, see Robert Ernest Desrochers Jr., "Every Picture Tells a Story," chap. 6. For a general study of black sailors in the Atlantic world, see Bolster, *Black Jacks*.

62. Nathaniel Holmes, "Ships Papers, Sloop *Betty*," 1747, 1759, Box 14, folder 15, Melatiah Bourne Record Papers, 1728–1803, Mss:733 1728–1803 B775, BLHC; Nash, *Urban Crucible*, 12.

63. "As to Boston, Sharper, Pompey, Negroes on Sloop *Dollahide*, Robert Boyd, Master," 14 January 1738, *Suffolk Files* #45472, MSA.

64. See, for example, *Boston Evening Post*, 16 June 1740.

65. Greene, *Negro in Colonial New England*, 113–114. For more on apprenticeship, see W. J. Rorabaugh, *The Craft Apprentice: From Franklin to the Machine Age in America* (New York: Oxford University Press, 1986).

66. *Boston Gazette*, 12 February 1754.

67. Nash, *Urban Crucible*, 16.

68. *Boston Gazette*, 14 September 1767.

69. Carl Bridenbaugh, *The Colonial Craftsmen* (New York: NYU Press, 1950), 139.

70. Nash, *Urban Crucible*, 17. It is interesting to note, however, that next to none of the defendants in criminal cases were enslaved artisans. While the occupation is not always listed, most male slaves convicted of a crime were usually laborers. We can also safely assume, given the importance of slave artisans, that their occupation would be listed had they committed a crime. For more on Peter and Pompey Fleet, see Isaiah Thomas, *The History of Printing in America, with a Biography of Printers*, vol. 1, 2nd ed. (New York: Burt Franklin, 1874), 99.

71. For Blancher, see "Children Bound Out 1756–1790," in *The Eighteenth-Century Records of the Boston Overseers of the Poor*, ed. Eric Nellis and Anne Decker Cecere, *Publications of the Colonial Society of Massachusetts* 69 (Boston: Colonial Society of Massachusetts, 2007), 653. After Langdon's death, Blancher returned to the almshouse and was later bound out to Abraham Hammatt of Plymouth; Langdon's probate inventory is in the SCPR, Docket #13857, MSA.

72. Towner, *Good Master*, 115.

73. *Boston Evening-Post*, 19 December 1748.

74. *Boston Evening-Post*, 16 June 1740.

75. For the rise and treatment of skilled slaves in British American slave societies, see Philip Morgan, "British Encounters with Africans and African-Americans, circa 1600–1780," in Philip Morgan and Bernard Bailyn, eds., *Strangers within the Realm: Cultural Margins of the First British Empire* (Chapel Hill: University of North Carolina Press, 1991), 177–178 (quote on 177).

76. "Inquisition on the Body of James, Negro Servant of Samuel Dunkin," 4 March 1749, *Suffolk Files* #65001, MSA.

77. "Inquisition on the Body of Jack, Negro Servant of F. Marshall," 7 August 1750, *Suffolk Files* #67044, MSA.

78. "Inquisition on the Body of Cato Negro Servant," n.d., *Suffolk Files* #100199, MSA.

79. *Boston Evening Post,* 25 August 1735. For more descriptions of workplace deaths, see *Boston News-Letter,* 3 April 1729 and 6 June 1765; *New England Weekly Journal,* 21 April 1729 and 20 July 1736.

80. Docket # 6691, SCPR, MSA.

81. Docket #7979, SCPR, MSA.

82. *New England Weekly Journal,* 6 October 1741. Philadelphia newspapers also picked up the story; see *American Weekly Mercury,* 15 October 1741. More information on "Spanish Negroes" can be found in Charles R. Foy, "Ports of Slavery, Ports of Freedom: How Slaves Used Northern Seaports' Maritime Industry to Escape and Create Trans-Atlantic Identities" (PhD diss., Rutgers University, 2008), chap. 4.

83. "Will of a Boston Slave, 1743," in *Publications of the Colonial Society of Massachusetts,* vol. 25, ed. Samuel Elliot Morison (Boston: Colonial Society of Massachusetts, 1924), 253–254. For more on Fleet and his will, see chapter 5.

84. "Deposition of Caesar (Negro) as to a Ditch Dug near the Mill of Clark and Gray's," *Suffolk Files* #48291, MSA.

85. *Boston Gazette,* 29 July 1771.

86. Boston Record Commissioners, *A Report of the Record Commissioners of the City of Boston, Containing the Boston Records from 1700 to 1728,* vol. 8 (Boston: Rockwell and Churchill, 1883), 225.

87. Josiah Quincy to James Bowdoin, 11 December 1775, and James Bowdoin to Josiah Quincy, 16 December 1775, in "The Bowdoin and Temple Papers," in *Collections of the Massachusetts Historical Society,* 6th ser., vol. 9, (Boston: Massachusetts Historical Society, 1897), 391–393.

88. *Boston Evening Post,* 22 February 1773.

89. "Case of Yaw and Caesar, Negroes, Belonging to Humphrey Scarlett," 21 August 1735, *Suffolk Files* #40201, MSA; "Estate of Humphrey Scarlett," Docket #7395, SCPR, MSA.

90. "Cunningham and Hewes," August 1747, *Suffolk Files* #63304, MSA.

91. The process of tanning in early modern England can be found in L. A. Clarkson, "The Organization of the English Leather Industry in the Late Sixteenth and Seventieth Centuries," *Economic History Review* 13, no. 2 (1960): 246–247.

92. The classic example of artisans protesting for these ends is in Robert Darnton, "Workers Revolt: The Great Cat Massacre of the Rue Saint-Séverin," in *The Great Cat Massacre and Other Episodes in French Cultural History* (New York: Basic Books, 1984), 75–106.

93. *Boston Post Boy,* 1 December 1766.

94. *Boston Evening Post,* 1 December 1766.

95. The legal records concerning Dewing and Titus can be found in *Suffolk Files* #87278, #88563, #100902, and #101112, MSA.

96. "The King v. Titus," in Superior Court of Judicature Records, 1767–1768, Microfilm Reel #13, p. 50, MSA.

97. For more on impressment and the riots, see Nash, *Urban Crucible,* 221–224; Jack Tager, *Boston Riots: Three Centuries of Social Violence* (Boston: Northeastern University Press, 2001), chap. 3; Rediker, *Between the Devil and the Deep Blue Sea,*

251–253. The newest book concerning naval impressment and the 1747 Impressment Riots in Boston is Denver Brunsman's *The Evil Necessity*, in which he argues that the 1747 riots were part of larger series of miscalculations and failed impressment attempts around the Atlantic by Knowles. Brunsman also makes an argument concerning resistance that is similar to the one made in this book. See Denver Brunsman, *The Evil Necessity: British Naval Impressment in the Eighteenth-Century Atlantic World* (Charlottesville: University of Virginia Press, 2013), esp. chap. 6.

98. Quoted in Nash, *Urban Crucible*, 223.

99. While enslaved Bostonians resisted service in the Royal Navy, it is important to note that some slaves found opportunities in naval service. The most famous case is Olaudah Equiano, who was the slave of Michael Pascal, a naval captain. Equiano so impressed his master while serving as his personal slave during the Seven Years' War and distinguished himself in battle that Pascal sent Equiano to England to learn to read and write. See Olaudah Equiano, *The Interesting Narrative of the Life of Olaudah Equiano, or Gustavus Vassa, the African* (London, 1789), chaps. 3 and 4. Brunsman paints a more benign portrait of impressment. See Brunsman, *Evil Necessity*, chaps. 4 and 5.

100. E. P. Thompson, *The Making of the English Working Class* (New York: Vintage, 1966), 81.

101. Amicus Patriae, *An Address to the Inhabitants of the Province of Massachusetts-Bay in New England, More Especially, to the Inhabitants of Boston; Occasioned by the Late and Unwarrantable Attack Upon Their Liberties, and the Unhappy Confusion and Disorders Consequent Thereon* (Boston: Rogers and Fowle, 1747). Historians have also recognized the importance of the riot as a way of understanding rights and liberties in America. See Nash, *Urban Crucible*, 223; John Law and William Pencak, "The Knowles Riot and the Crisis of the 1740s in Massachusetts," *Perspectives in American History* 10 (1976): 163–214; Jesse Lemisch, "Jack Tar in the Streets: Merchant Seamen in the Politics of Revolutionary America," *William and Mary Quarterly* 25, no. 3 (1968): 371–407.

102. *Boston Evening Post*, 8 January 1759.

103. Shine's and Lee's testimony can be found in "Deposition by John Shine and Etc.," 27 October 1701, *Suffolk Files* #162607, MSA.

104. "Inquest into the Death of London Negro," 8 October 1721, *Suffolk Files* #15551, MSA.

105. The entire case involving Titus can be found in the *Massachusetts Archives Collection*, 9:170–177, MSA.

106. "Inquisition on the Body of Bristol, a Negro Servant of Jonathan Simpson," 12 January 1745/46, *Suffolk Files* #61453, MSA.

107. "Deposition by John Haskings," February 1725/26, *Suffolk Files* #164169, MSA.

Notes to Chapter 5

1. A version of this chapter appears as Jared Ross Hardesty, "An Angry God in the Hands of Sinners: Enslaved Africans and the Uses of Protestant Christianity in Colonial Boston," *Slavery & Abolition* 35, no. 1 (2014): 66–83. It can be found online at www.tandfonline.com.

2. Phillis Wheatley, "On Being Brought from Africa to America," in *Complete Writings* (New York: Penguin, 2001), 13.

3. Russell K. Osgood, "John Clark, Esq., Justice of the Peace, 1667–1728," in Daniel R. Coquilette, ed., *Law in Colonial Massachusetts, 1630–1800* (Boston: Colonial Society of Massachusetts, 1984), 144.

4. David H. Flaherty, "Criminal Practice in Provincial Massachusetts," in Coquilette, *Law in Colonial Massachusetts*, 229.

5. For "Laborers," see Michael Dalton, *The Countrey Justice, Containing the Practice for the Justices of the Peace Out of Their Sessions . . .* (London: William Rawlins and Samuel Roycroft, 1705), 119–130. Dalton's book went through many editions in the seventeenth and eighteenth centuries, and I am using the 1705 edition, as it was commonly used in eighteenth-century Boston.

6. Ibid., 121.

7. Ibid., 122, 129.

8. Ibid., 120.

9. Flaherty, "Criminal Practice," 229n7.

10. William Nelson, *The Office and Authority of a Justice of Peace . . .* , 10th ed. (London: E. and R. Nutt and R. Gosling, 1729), 27–51. As the 1705 edition of Dalton's book covered the earlier period of my study, the 1729 edition of Nelson's book will give us a picture of the law of servitude in the middle, while Blackstone's book (see later in the chapter) provides a glimpse of it at the end of this study.

11. Ibid., 43.

12. Ibid., 44.

13. Ibid., 44–45.

14. For Blackstone's lasting influence in the United States especially, see Mary Bilder, Maeva Marcus, R. Kent Newmyer, eds., *Blackstone in America: Selected Essays of Kathryn Preyer* (New York: Cambridge University Press, 2009).

15. The professionalization of law in the late colonial period is dealt with in Kinvin Wroth and Hiller Zobel, introduction to *The Legal Papers of John Adams*, ed. Kinvin Wroth and Hiller Zobel, vol. 1 (Cambridge, MA: Harvard University Press, 1965), xxxviii–xciv.

16. William Blackstone, *Commentaries on the Laws of England*, vol. 1 (Oxford, UK: Clarendon, 1765), 410.

17. Ibid., 411.

18. Ibid., 415–416.

19. Ibid., 419–420.

20. Quoted in Josiah Quincy, Jr., ed., *Reports of Cases Argued and Adjudged in the Superior Court of Judicature of the Province of Massachusetts Bay between 1761 and 1772* (Boston: Little, Brown, 1865), 31n.

21. For more on the legal ambiguity of slavery, see Jared Ross Hardesty, "An Ambiguous Institution: Slavery, Law, and the State in Colonial Massachusetts," *Journal of Early American History* 3, nos. 2–3 (2013): 154–180.

22. See Boston Record Commissioners, *A Report of the Record Commissioners of the City of Boston, Containing Boston Records from 1700 to 1728*, vol. 8 (Boston: Rockwell and Churchill, 1883), 173–175.

23. The Boston town meeting moderator and representative Elisha Cooke attempted to pass similar legislation at the provincial level thirteen times before finally giving up. See *Journals of the House of Representatives of Massachusetts*, vol. 5 (Boston: Massachusetts Historical Society, 1924), 18, 36, 43, 48, 114, 121, 138, 145, 258, 259, 264, 274, 286.

24. Edgar J. McManus, *Black Bondage in the North* (1973; repr., Syracuse, NY: Syracuse University Press, 2001), 87.

25. Ibid., 67–68.

26. Daniel J. Boorstin, *The Americans: The Colonial Experience* (New York: Random House, 1958), 203. For a more recent study on common people, including slaves, and their relationship with the law, see Elaine Forman Crane, *Witches, Wife Beaters, and Whores: Common Law and Common Folk in Early America* (Ithaca, NY: Cornell University Press, 2011).

27. "Examination of Scipio Negro," 1 June 1727, *Suffolk Files* #20267, MSA.

28. "Scipio's Negro Sentence," Court of the General Sessions of the Peace Record Books (hereafter CGSP), 1725–1732, 89, Massachusetts State Archives, Boston, MA (hereafter MSA).

29. Richard Dana, "Justice of the Peace Records," vol. 18, April 1760–December 1767, Suffolk County, 1765 entry 17, Microfilm P-646 Reel 2, Massachusetts Historical Society, Boston, MA (MHS).

30. For more on the importance of the law in the lives of Black Bostonians, see Scott Hancock, "'The Law Will Make You Smart': Legal Consciousness, Rights Rhetoric, and African American Identity Formation in Massachusetts, 1641–1855" (PhD diss., University of New Hampshire, 1999), 2–3. Hancock has a deep understanding of the law and its effect on African Americans, but the provincial period is conspicuously missing from his study.

31. For Peter Faneuil's probate inventory, see Docket #7877, Suffolk County Probate Records (hereafter SCPR), MSA.

32. "Pompey (a Negro) and Faneuil," February 1753, *Suffolk Files* #70475, MSA; "Faneuil and Pompey," August 1753, *Suffolk Files* #71395, MSA.

33. For more about James, see Lorenzo Johnston Greene, *The Negro in Colonial New England* (1942; repr., New York: Atheneum, 1969), 295–296.

34. See, for example, Dalton, *Countrey Justice*, 128–129.

35. For the Virginia counterpoint, see Philip J. Schwarz, *Twice Condemned: Slaves and the Criminal Laws of Virginia, 1705–1865* (Baton Rouge: Louisiana State University Press, 1988).

36. "Petition of Titus, a Negro," October 1727, *Suffolk Files* #164421, MSA; "Titus Negro's Petition Dismissed," CGSP, 1725–1732, 110, MSA.

37. Osgood, "John Clark, Esq.," 129.

38. Ibid., 128–129.

39. Dana, "Justice of the Peace Records," vol. 17, March 1746–August 1748, Middlesex County, entry 19, Microfilm P-646 Reel 2, MHS.

40. Stephen's encounters with Dana can be found in ibid., vol. 18, April 1760–December 1767, 1764 entry 40 and 1765 entries 3, 10, 12.

41. Unfortunately, the British destroyed all the General Sessions records for the period Stephen was under investigation during the American Revolution, so it is impossible to know the outcomes of these cases or whether he even appeared before the court.

42. Dana, "Justice of the Peace Records," vol. 17, April 1757–April 1760, entry 42.

43. Ibid., vol. 19, January 1768–March 1772, entry 32.

44. Ibid., entry 42.

45. "Petition of Boston Negro," 28 January 1722, *Suffolk Files* #16477, MSA.

46. This petition appears in many modern editions, but I used the one contained in Robert C. Twombly, "Black Resistance to Slavery in Massachusetts," in William L. O'Neill, ed., *Insights and Parallels: Problems and Issues of American Social History* (Minneapolis, MN: Burgess, 1973), 41–42.

47. For these two cases, see Greene, *Negro in Colonial New England*, 183.

48. The summons for Lechmere to appear before the inferior court in Middlesex County can be found in the archives of the Longfellow House. The document has been digitized, along with information about the context of the case. See "1769 Court Document," in "Slavery and Abolition in the Longfellow Archives," National Park Service, n.d., http://www.nps.gov/long/historyculture/slavery-related-objects-at-longfellow-nhs.htm (accessed 6 September 2015).

49. Blackstone, *Commentaries on the Laws of England*, 412–413.

50. For more on the historiography of slave religion and its relationship to this project, see Jared Ross Hardesty, "Slavery, Freedom, and Dependence in Pre-Revolutionary Boston, 1700–1775" (PhD diss., Boston College, 2014), 233n48.

51. John Wood Sweet notes that the "choice was not so much whether to become Christian as which style of Christianity to favor." See John Wood Sweet, *Bodies Politic: Negotiating Race in the American North, 1730–1830* (Baltimore: Johns Hopkins University Press, 2003), 122.

52. "Dr. Timothy Cutler to Dr. Z. Grey," in John Nichols, ed., *Illustrations of the Literary History of the Eighteenth Century*, vol. 4 (London: John Nichols and Son, 1822), 270.

53. "Dr. Timothy Cutler to the Secretary," 11 December 1740, in William Stevens Perry, ed., *Papers Relating to the History of the Church in Massachusetts, A.D. 1676–1785* (n.p., 1873), 348. Cutler attributed the high number of baptisms to "attending the ordinance from due awakenings and a due sense of the great importance and Obligations."

54. "Dr. Cutler to the Secretary," 6 July 1739, and "Dr. Timothy Cutler to the Secretary," 11 December 1740, in ibid., 329, 349.

55. "Dr. Cutler to the Secretary," 9 October 1734, in ibid., 297.

56. "Dr. Cutler to the Secretary," 23 February 1736, in ibid., 307.

57. "Dr. Cutler to the Secretary," 9 October 1734, in ibid., 297.

58. "Mr. Plant to the Secretary," 25 October 1727, in ibid., 233.

59. "Dr. Cutler to the Secretary," 9 October 1734, in ibid., 297.

60. "Dr. Cutler to the Secretary," 6 September 1736, in ibid., 315.

61. Sweet, *Bodies Politic*, 123.

62. "Deposition of John Gyles," 13 April 1742 in *Massachusetts Archives Collection*, 9:249, MSA.

63. "Deposition of Thomas Saunders," 13 April 1742 in *Massachusetts Archives Collection*, 9:250, MSA.

64. Greene, *Negro in Colonial New England*, 211. For more about the instability of slave marriages, see chapter 3.

65. "Letters and Documents Relating to Slavery in Massachusetts," in *Collections of the Massachusetts Historical Society*, 5th ser., vol. 3 (Boston: Massachusetts Historical Society, 1877), 432–433.

66. Greene, *Negro in Colonial New England*, 210.

67. E. Jennifer Monaghan, *Learning to Read and Write in Colonial America* (Amherst: University of Massachusetts Press, 2005), 244.

68. Cotton Mather, *The Negro Christianized: An Essay to Excite and Assist That Good Work, the Instruction of Negro-Servants in Christianity* (Boston: B. Green, 1706), 29 (emphasis in original).

69. A Lady of Boston [Rebecca Warren Brown], *Memoir of Mrs. Chloe Spear, a Native of Africa, Who Was Enslaved in Childhood and Died in Boston January 3, 1815 . . . Aged 65 Years* (Boston: James Loring, 1832), 20–22. John Wood Sweet believes that the physical segregation that Spear and other blacks experienced in Boston churches actually helped "develop social networks among local servants, slaves, and free blacks." While Spear did not learn anything about Christianity, the racialized space in the churches "fostered the expansion of community networks" among blacks. Sweet, *Bodies Politic*, 123.

70. "Dr. Cutler to the Secretary," 10 October 1727, in Perry, *Papers Relating to the History of the Church*, 231.

71. On a side note, Gary Nash describes how that the Anglican Church and the SPG worked to catechize slaves and teach them how to read the Bible in Philadelphia. The Bray Associates, an Anglican charitable society, established a school in the city to instruct blacks how to read. Although the evidence is incomplete for Boston, it seems as if Timothy Cutler and other Anglican ministers established a similar school. See Gary Nash, *Forging Freedom: The Formation of Philadelphia's Black Community, 1720–1840* (Cambridge, MA: Harvard University Press, 1988), 22.

72. Edmund Gibson, *Two Letters of the Lord Bishop of London* (London, 1728), 3; quoted in Monaghan, *Learning to Read and Write*, 242.

73. Monaghan, *Learning to Read and Write*, 242.

74. For more information on the distinction between reading and writing for the enslaved, see E. Jennifer Monaghan, "Reading for the Enslaved, Writing for the Free: Reflections on Liberty and Literacy," *Proceedings of the American Antiquarian Society* 108 (1998): 309–341. David Hall explores the distinction between reading and writing education in early New England extensively. See David Hall, *Worlds of Wonder, Days of Judgment: Popular Religious Belief in Early New England* (New York: Knopf, 1989), 18, 21–70.

75. Cotton Mather, *The Diary of Cotton Mather*, vol. 2 (New York: F. Ungar, 1957), 139.

76. Ibid., 222.

77. Quoted in Kathryn S. Koo, "Strangers in the House of God: Cotton Mather, Onesimus, and an Experiment in Christian Slaveholding," *Proceedings of the American Antiquarian Society* 17, no. 1 (2007): 163.

78. Mather, *Diary*, 363.

79. For this document, see Koo, "Strangers," 166–167.

80. Ibid., 166. Most biographies of Mather also emphasize the independence the preacher granted to Onesimus. For example, see Kenneth Silverman, *The Life and Times of Cotton Mather* (New York: Columbia University Press, 1985), 265–266, 290.

81. Robert E. Desrochers Jr., Slave-for-Sale Advertisements and Slavery in Massachusetts, 1704–1781," *William and Mary Quarterly* 59, no. 3 (2002): 634–635.

82. "Dr. Cutler to the Secretary," 5 February 1738, and "Dr. Cutler to the Secretary," 6 July 1739, in Perry, *Papers Relating to the History of the Church*, 322, 329.

83. For more about Black Peter, see Carl Bridenbaugh, *Cities in Revolt: Urban Life in America, 1743-1776* (1955; repr., New York: Oxford University Press, 1971), 88. Quote from Samuel Elliot Morison's introduction to Peter's will. See "Will of a Boston Slave, 1743," in *Publications of the Colonial Society of Massachusetts*, vol. 25 (Boston: Colonial Society of Massachusetts, 1924), 253.

84. Isaiah Thomas, *The History of Printing in America, with a Biography of Printers*, vol. 1, 2nd ed. (New York: Burt Franklin, 1874), 99; Monaghan, *Learning to Read and Write*, 244-245.

85. Monaghan, *Learning to Read and Write*, 129-132. For Fowle's reply, see Daniel Fowle, *A Total Eclipse of Liberty: Being a True and Faithful Account of the Arraignment, and Examination of Daniel Fowle before the Honourable House of Representatives . . .* (Boston, 1755).

86. Thomas, *History of Printing in America*, 130n3.

87. Charles W. Brewster, *Rambles about Portsmouth, Sketches of Persons, Localities, and Incidents of Two Centuries* (Portsmouth, NH: C. W. Brewster and Son, 1859), 208.

88. Nathaniel Adams, *Annals of Portsmouth, Comprising a Period of Two Hundred Years from the First Settlement of the Town* (Portsmouth, NH: C. Norris, 1825), 289.

89. For perspectives on the difference between actual slavery and how whites remembered slavery in New England, see Joanne Pope Melish, *Disowning Slavery: Race and Gradual Emancipation in New England, 1780-1860* (Ithaca, NY: Cornell University Press, 1998); and Margot Minardi, *Making Slavery History: Abolitionism and the Politics of Memory in Massachusetts* (New York: Oxford University Press, 2010). The deskilling of black labor after emancipation is explored in Patrick Rael, *Black Identity and Black Protest in the Antebellum North* (Chapel Hill: University of North Carolina Press, 2002), chap. 1.

90. "Will of a Boston Slave, 1743," 253-254.

91. "Nathaniel Byfield, 1733 Will," Docket #6391, SCPR, 31:425, MSA. Peter Benes also discusses Byfield and Rose in his excellent article on probate records and slavery in colonial Boston. See Peter Benes, "Slavery in Boston Households, 1647-1770," in "Slavery/Antislavery in New England," *Annual Proceedings of the Dublin Seminar for New England Folklife* 28 (2003): 12.

92. Mather, *Negro Christianized*, 14, 16.

93. *Boston Gazette*, 25 August 1766. Special thanks to Janet Kay for translating the Latin.

94. "Petition of Boston, Negro Servant of Edward Bromfield of Boston, Merchant," 4 March 1742, in *Massachusetts Archives Collection*, 9:248, MSA.

95. "Lydia Sharp v. Boston (a Black Man)," 5 June 1773, *Suffolk Files* #129775, MSA.

96. Mark S. Weiner, *Black Trials: Citizenship from the Beginnings of Slavery to the End of Caste* (New York: Vintage, 2004), 36.

97. Abner Cheney Goodell Jr., *The Trial and Execution for Petit Treason of Mark and Phillis* (Cambridge, MA: Scholars Press, 1883), 13.

98. For the full text of "Deism," see Phil Lapsansky, "*Deism*—An Unpublished Poem by Phillis Wheatley," *New England Quarterly* 50, no. 3 (1977): 519.

99. Vincent Carretta, *Phillis Wheatley: Biography of a Genius in Bondage* (Athens: University of Georgia Press, 2011), 57.

100. Ibid., 61.

101. Quoted in Henry Louis Gates Jr., *The Trials of Phillis Wheatley: America's First Black Poet and Her Encounter with the Founding Fathers* (New York: Basic Civitas, 2003), 5.

Notes to the Afterword

1. Manumission, 5 September 1754, in Ezekiel Price Notarial Records, vol. 1, Boston Athenæum, Boston, MA.

2. Manumission, 12 April 1770, in ibid., vol. 5.

3. Manumission 19 October 1779, in ibid., vol. 6.

4. The standard work exploring this subject is Bernard Bailyn, *The Ideological Origins of the American Revolution* (1965; repr., Cambridge, MA: Harvard University Press, 1992).

5. For the speech, see James Otis, *The Rights of the British Colonies Asserted and Proved* (Boston: Edes and Gill, 1764).

6. *Boston Gazette*, 14 October 1765.

7. *Boston Chronicle*, 8 February 1768.

8. *Boston Post-Boy*, 11 November 1765.

9. *Massachusetts Spy*, 29 September 1770 (emphasis in original).

10. *Boston News-Letter*, 28 February 1771.

11. Wilson's indictment and trial transcripts are reprinted in the *New-York Journal*, 17 November 1768.

12. Some examples of this literature include Alan Gilbert, *Black Loyalists and Patriots: Fighting for Emancipation in the War for Independence* (Chicago: University of Chicago Press, 2012); Alexander X. Byrd, *Captives and Voyagers: Black Migrants across the Eighteenth-Century British Atlantic World* (Baton Rouge: Louisiana State University Press, 2010); Maya Jasanoff, *Liberty's Exiles: American Loyalists in the Revolutionary World* (New York: Knopf, 2011); Sylvia R. Frey, *Water from the Rock: Black Resistance in a Revolutionary Age* (Princeton, NJ: Princeton University Press, 1992); Ellen Gibson Wilson, *The Loyal Blacks* (New York: Capricorn Books, 1976); Simon Schama, *Rough Crossings: The Slaves, the British, and the American Revolution* (New York: Harper Perennial, 2007); and Cassandra Pybus, *Epic Journeys of Freedom: Runaway Slaves of the American Revolution and Their Global Quest for Liberty* (Boston: Beacon, 2007). It is also important to note that a number of formerly enslaved Bostonians appear in the *Book of Negroes*, the British army's record of all the blacks that evacuated New York City with the British. One of those Afro-Bostonians was Pompey Fleet, the son of Peter Fleet, who is discussed in chapter 5. The Nova Scotia Archives holds a copy of the book and has created a digital and searchable version. It can be found at http://novascotia.ca/archives/virtual/africanns/BN.asp (accessed 6 September 2015).

13. Sarter's essay can be found on the front page of the *Essex Journal and Merrimack Packet*, 17 August 1774.

14. Ibid.

15. The April 1773 petition can be found in Herbert Aptheker, ed., *A Documentary History of the Negro People in the United States*, vol. 1 (New York: Citadel, 1960), 7–8.

16. The 1774 petition to Gage is in ibid., 8–9.

17. Ibid., 9–10.

18. Abigail Adams to John Adams, 22 September 1774, in L. H. Butterfield, ed., *Adams Family Correspondence*, vol. 1, *December 1761–May 1776* (Cambridge, MA: Harvard University Press, 1963), 161–162.

19. Butterfield, *Adams Family Correspondence*, 162n3.

20. Abigail Adams to John Adams, 22 September 1774, 162.

21. Aptheker, *Documentary History of the Negro People*, 9.

22. *Essex Journal and Merrimack Packet*, 17 August 1774.

23. Aptheker, *Documentary History of the Negro People*, 8–9.

24. Ibid., 6–7.

25. It is also important to note that slaves were once again appropriating the language of the master class to better their condition. See chapter 5 for more on this.

26. Aptheker, *Documentary History of the Negro People*, 6; *Essex Journal and Merrimack Packet*, 17 August 1774.

27. Aptheker, *Documentary History of the Negro People*, 8–9.

28. Ibid., 6–7.

29. *Essex Journal and Merrimack Packet*, 17 August 1774.

30. Aptheker, *Documentary History of the Negro People*, 7–8.

31. Margot Minardi, *Making Slavery History: Abolitionism and the Politics of Memory in Massachusetts* (New York: Oxford University Press, 2010), 17. Richard Lechmere of Cambridge had a slave who filed suit against him, but that was the closest freedom suit to Boston.

32. Jeremy Belknap, "Queries Respecting the Slavery and Emancipation of Negroes in Massachusetts, Proposed by the Hon. Judge Tucker of Virginia, and Answered by the Rev. Dr. Belknap," *Collections of the Massachusetts Historical Society*, 1st ser., 4 (1795): 203.

33. Jeremy Belknap, "Queries Relating to Slavery in Massachusetts," *Massachusetts Historical Society Collections*, 3rd ser., 3 (1877): 386.

34. Quoted in Minardi, *Making Slavery History*, 17–18.

35. Judicial emancipation has been the long-held view of historians of slavery in Massachusetts. Lorenzo Greene contended that the decision finally "resulted in the emancipation of the slaves in Massachusetts." See Lorenzo Johnston Greene, *Negro in Colonial New England* (1942; repr., New York: Atheneum, 1969), 184. James and Lois Horton likewise see it as the end of slavery, noting that the decision "outlawed slavery in Massachusetts." James Oliver Horton and Lois E. Horton, *In Hope of Liberty: Culture, Community and Protest among Northern Free Blacks, 1700–1860* (New York: Oxford University Press, 1997), 71. Emily Blanck called the decision decisive, believing that in one fell swoop, the Cushing decision made it illegal to own "human property." See Emily Blanck, "Seventeen Eighty-Three: The Turning Point in the Law of Slavery and Freedom in Massachusetts," *New England Quarterly* 75, no. 1 (2002): 24.

36. Minardi, *Making Slavery History*, 18.

37. Quoted in Blanck, "Seventeen Eighty-Three," 29.

38. Ibid., 30. The case was *Winchendon v. Hatfield*.

39. Edgar J. McManus, *Black Bondage in the North* (1973; repr., Syracuse, NY: Syracuse University Press, 2001), 181–183; John Wood Sweet, *Bodies Politic:*

Negotiating Race in the American North, 1730–1830 (Baltimore: Johns Hopkins University Press, 2003), 260–261.

40. Bill of Sale, 11 September 1769, in Ezekiel Price Notarial Records, vol. 5, Boston Athenæum, Boston, MA.

41. Manumission, 25 February 1789, in ibid., vol. 7.

42. Minardi, *Making Slavery History*, 19.

43. Ibid.

44. For more about these creative attempts to gain freedom, see Sidney Kaplan, *The Black Presence in the Era of the American Revolution*, rev. ed. (Amherst: University of Massachusetts Press, 1989). For the experience of an enslaved soldier from New England, see Joyce Lee Malcolm, *Peter's War: A New England Slave Boy and the American Revolution* (New Haven, CT: Yale University Press, 2009).

45. For more on this process, see Joanne Pope Melish, *Disowning Slavery: Gradual Emancipation and "Race" in New England, 1780–1860* (Ithaca, NY: Cornell University Press, 1998); Patrick Rael, *Black Identity and Black Protest in the Antebellum North* (Chapel Hill: University of North Carolina Press, 2002), and Leon Litwack, *North of Slavery: The Negro in the Free States, 1790–1860* (Chicago: University of Chicago Press, 1961).

46. For more on Royall, see C. S. Manegold, *Ten Hills Farm: The Forgotten History of Slavery in the North* (Princeton, NJ: Princeton University Press, 2010).

47. Belinda's petition can be found at the website of the Royall House and Slave Quarters, the former residence of Belinda and Isaac Royall: http://www.royall-house.org/slavery/belindas-petition/ (accessed 6 September 2015).

48. For the reparations argument, see Roy E. Finkenbine, "Belinda's Petition: Reparations for Slavery in Revolutionary Massachusetts," *William and Mary Quarterly*, 3rd ser., 64, no. 1 (2007): 95–104.

49. Ibid., 101–102.

INDEX

Figures, notes, and tables are indicated by f, n, and t following the page number.

About the Author

Jared Ross Hardesty is Assistant Professor of History at Western Washington University.

Early American Places

Colonization and Its Discontents: Emancipation,
Emigration, and Antislavery in Antebellum Pennsylvania
Beverly C. Tomek

Empire at the Periphery: British Colonists, Anglo-Dutch Trade,
and the Development of the British Atlantic, 1621—1713
Christian J. Koot

Slavery before Race: Europeans, Africans, and Indians
at Long Island's Sylvester Manor Plantation, 1651–1884
Katherine Howlett Hayes

Faithful Bodies: Performing Religion and Race
in the Puritan Atlantic
Heather Miyano Kopelson

Against Wind and Tide: The African American Struggle
against the Colonization Movement
Ousmane K. Power-Greene

Four Steeples over the City Streets: The Social Worlds of
New York's Early Republic Congregations
Kyle T. Bulthuis

Caribbean Crossing: African Americans and the Haitian
Emigration Movement
Sara Fanning

Insatiable Appetites: Imperial Encounters with Cannibals in the
North Atlantic World
Kelly L. Watson

Unfreedom: Slavery and Dependence in Eighteenth-Century Boston
Jared Ross Hardesty

Printed and bound by CPI Group (UK) Ltd, Croydon, CR0 4YY

13/04/2025

14656574-0004